Praise for *Dan*

"Unflinching and historically grou
researched, this refreshing, pioneerin
rective to narrow thinking and relaxed t...
[Michael] Beckley and [Hal] Brands's ideas need to be embraced if we
are to effectively manage differences emerging in the increasingly volatile relationship between our two nations."

—General Jim Mattis, U.S. Marines (ret.) and
26th Secretary of Defense

"There is bipartisan consensus in Washington that China is the most
important long-term strategic challenge for the U.S. Hal Brands and
Michael Beckley powerfully argue that an enormously ambitious China
is peaking now and confrontation is coming sooner than we think. This
well-written, must-read book will add a sense of urgency to the national
debate about strategic competition."

—Ambassador (ret.) Eric S. Edelman,
former Undersecretary of Defense for Policy (2005–2009)

"Russian aggression notwithstanding, China constitutes the most
daunting challenge to U.S. national security and the liberal international order. In this brilliant and urgently important book, Hal Brands
and Michael Beckley explain why the threat of war with China will
likely peak in this decade—when China's global power and ambition
for primacy are swelling just as it faces severe demographic, economic,
and political strains on the horizon. Every U.S. foreign policy maker
and thinker should read this book and heed their call to rapidly mobilize
strategy, strength, and alliances to navigate through this danger zone."
—Larry Diamond, Mosbacher Senior Fellow in Global Democracy,
Freeman Spogli Institute for International Studies, Stanford University

# DANGER ZONE

The Coming Conflict with China

HAL BRANDS
*and*
MICHAEL BECKLEY

W. W. NORTON & COMPANY
*Celebrating a Century of Independent Publishing*

*For our families.*

For information about permission to reproduce selections from this book, write to Permissions, W. W. Norton & Company, Inc., 500 Fifth Avenue, New York, NY 10110

For information about special discounts for bulk purchases, please contact W. W. Norton Special Sales at specialsales@wwnorton.com or 800-233-4830

Manufacturing by Lakeside Book Company
Book design by Daniel Lagin
Production manager: Julia Druskin

ISBN 978-1-324-06610-1 pbk.

W. W. Norton & Company, Inc.
500 Fifth Avenue, New York, N.Y. 10110
www.wwnorton.com

W. W. Norton & Company Ltd.
15 Carlisle Street, London W1D 3BS

1 2 3 4 5 6 7 8 9 0

# Contents

# Introduction

It is January 18, 2025, and a war is about to start. The U.S. presidential inauguration is only two days away, but the election results remain contested. Both the Democratic and Republican candidates are claiming victory and preparing to take the oath of office while millions of their supporters clash in the streets. It is America's second straight disputed election, this time accompanied by a crisis on the other side of the world.

China is conducting massive naval exercises in the Taiwan Strait. The People's Liberation Army (PLA) has also positioned a menacing medley of forces—airborne and amphibious assault troops, strike aircraft, thousands of ballistic missiles—opposite Taiwan. Such shows of strength have become a regular occurrence over the past half-decade, as China flexes its muscles vis-à-vis an island it considers a renegade province. Xi Jinping, now in his thirteenth year atop the Chinese Communist Party (CCP), has repeatedly warned Taiwan that it must submit to Beijing's authority—and told the United States to mind its own business. Anyone who tries to slow China's progress, he likes to say, will have their "heads bashed bloody against a Great Wall of steel."[1] In the same spirit, CCP propaganda organs have taken to releasing video simulations of Taiwanese and American forces being slaughtered in a PLA attack.[2] The PLA has even threatened to vaporize Japanese cities with nuclear weapons if Tokyo gets in the way.[3]

High above the western Pacific, U.S. spy satellites watch the military preparations. America's world-class signals intelligence capabilities detect China's mobilization. But U.S. analysts assume that this is just another case of Xi's habitual saber-rattling—a feint designed to unnerve Taiwan's population and overstretch its military.

They are wrong.

At 10:01 pm EST (the next morning in Beijing and Taipei), Chinese forces unleash hell. Short- and medium-range missiles pound airfields, government buildings, and military installations all over Taiwan, as well as America's key regional air bases on Okinawa and Guam. The USS *Ronald Reagan*, the Pentagon's sole aircraft carrier in the region, suffers a direct hit from an anti-ship ballistic missile. Chinese special forces, secretly infiltrated into Taiwan beforehand, sabotage infrastructure, try to decapitate the government by killing its top leaders, and sow panic among the population. China's cyber warriors take down Taiwan's power grid, plunging the island into blackness, and spoof U.S. satellites. Meanwhile, Beijing unleashes a global disinformation campaign blaming the crisis on Taiwan and roiling a chaotic political scene in the United States.

All this is preparation for the main event. The Chinese fleet conducting "exercises" now pivots to launch an amphibious landing on Taiwan's most accessible western beach. Chinese commercial car ferries plying the strait suddenly disgorge small, amphibious landing craft. On the mainland, airborne forces prepare to seize Taiwanese airfields and ports, paving the way for the main assault of hundreds of thousands of troops. The long-feared Chinese invasion of Taiwan has begun, as has a multi-vector attack on America's ability to respond.

In Taipei, the situation soon borders on irretrievable. In Washington, the news is also grim. Aides inform an ailing President Biden that he has little time and no good options.

America cannot abandon Taiwan without betraying 25 million democratic citizens and shredding the credibility of its alliances with the Philippines and Japan. A Chinese-controlled Taiwan could be a stepping-stone to expansion throughout East Asia and beyond. But America cannot stop the assault without risking a war that could be bigger and costlier than anything since World War II.

In the White House Situation Room, the secretary of defense tells Biden that the bloodied U.S. forces in the western Pacific are unable to repel the Chinese invasion. Additional U.S. aircraft, warships, and submarines scattered everywhere from Hawaii to the Persian Gulf can try to fight their way toward the Taiwan Strait through a gauntlet of Chinese missiles, mines, and air defenses. But this will take days if not weeks and result in heavy losses with no guarantee of success. Alternatively, the U.S. Navy can blockade China's energy imports and food supplies, but that strangulation strategy will take months—time that Taiwan doesn't have.

That leaves one sure way to stop the invasion: Strike Chinese forces with low-yield nuclear weapons as they load in mainland ports and airfields. America is still the stronger power, Biden's advisers tell him; it can win a big war if it throws everything it has into the fight. But such a conflict might end up destroying Taiwan in order to save it—and prove disastrous for America and China alike.

How did the United States and China come to the brink of World War III?

At the time, most analysts assumed that Xi's decision to attack was the inevitable outcome of China's growing strength and confidence. In the years leading up to 2025, Beijing had built the world's largest navy, air defense system, and missile force. It had put new warships to sea at a rate no country had managed since World War II; it had stunned the Pentagon by leaping forward in hypersonic weapons and other advanced capabilities.[4] China was simultaneously racing for supremacy in key technologies such as artificial intelligence and quantum computing; through its Digital Silk Road initiative, it was building a twenty-first century sphere of influence. Xi Jinping had consolidated power and made himself the world's mightiest dictator since Joseph Stalin, while America's politics continued to be a tribal, polarized mess—and America's attention was diverted by other crises and conflicts around the globe. Never before had the People's Republic of China (PRC) possessed such military strength and economic influence vis-à-vis its rivals. By outward appearances, Xi's "Chinese Dream"—his ambition to make China dominant in Asia and around the globe—was on the verge of becoming a reality.

But Xi was tormented by the nightmare of Chinese decline. For years, the pressures on the CCP regime had been mounting. Once-torrid economic growth had slowed to a crawl. The legacy of the One-Child policy was demographic disaster—an impending loss of nearly 200 million working-age individuals in China by mid-century. The regime had become more repressive as it grew ever more petrified of dissent. And in response to Chinese belligerence during the COVID-19 pandemic and for years thereafter, the democratic world had gradually been closing ranks to check Beijing's rise. Taiwan was finally starting to shore up its inadequate military defenses, as its population rejected any suggestion of reunification with China. The United States—a country with a unique talent for slaying autocratic rivals—was waging a tech and tariff war against China's economy while retooling its military to take on the PLA.

On the eve of war, the world still saw China as a rising power. Yet Xi saw a future of stagnation, strategic encirclement, and decay. So he gambled, with catastrophic consequences for the region and the world, because he knew his moment of opportunity wouldn't last long.

The "rise of China" may be the most read-about news story of the twenty-first century.[5] The prevailing consensus, in Washington and abroad, is that an ascendant Beijing is threatening to overtake a slumping America.[6] "If we don't get moving," said President Biden in 2021, "they're going to eat our lunch."[7] Countries in every region, a veteran Asian diplomat reports, are "making preparations for a world" in which China will be "number one."[8]

China is certainly acting like it wants to run the show. The CCP is laying plans to create a Sino-centric Asia and reclaim what it sees as China's rightful place atop the global hierarchy. Beijing is using an impressive array of military, economic, diplomatic, technological, and ideological tools to protect the power and project the influence of a brutal authoritarian regime. The United States, for its part, is trying to defend a liberal international order it has anchored for generations and prevent Beijing from making the twenty-first century an age of autocratic ascendancy. America and China are thus locked in a fierce global struggle. It has become conventional wisdom in Washington—a rare point of agreement in a bitterly divided capital—that the two countries are running a "superpower marathon" that may last a century.[9]

Our core argument in this book is that the conventional wisdom is wrong on both points. Americans urgently need to start seeing the Sino-American rivalry less as a 100-year marathon and more as a blistering, decade-long sprint. That's because China will be a *falling* power far sooner than most people think.

★

To be sure, the contest between China and the United States won't be settled anytime soon: It is driven by clashing ideologies and strategic interests. Yet the intensity of even the longest rivalries can wax and wane over time. Both history and China's current trajectory suggest that the Sino-American competition will hit its moment of maximum danger during this decade, the 2020s.

The reason for this is China has reached the most treacherous stage in the life cycle of a rising power—the point where it is strong enough to aggressively disrupt the existing order but is losing confidence that time is on its side.

In one sense, China's economic power and military might have skyrocketed since the Cold War, fueling Xi's seemingly limitless ambitions. In crucial areas, from the Taiwan Strait to the U.S.-China tech rivalry, tantalizing opportunities have opened up as the balance of power has shifted in Beijing's favor. Until recently, the democratic nations were lethargic and unfocused in their response. Even today, Xi surveys a world that was laid low by a made-in-China pandemic and a superpower rival that often seems to be tearing itself apart. China, as Xi has put it, is now striving for a future in which it will "have the dominant position."[10]

But Beijing had better hurry, because in other ways, that future looks quite ugly. China's miraculous, multi-decade rise was aided by strong tailwinds that have now become headwinds.

For more than a decade, China has been concealing a serious economic slowdown that existentially threatens the ruling regime. Within a few years, a slow-motion demographic catastrophe will create severe economic and political strains. Through its "wolf-warrior" diplomacy and its confrontational behavior in hot spots from the Himalayas to the South China Sea, China has sprung a strategic trap on itself, scaring—and beginning to unite—potential rivals throughout Eurasia. Not least, the CCP has now violated the first rule of global politics for the past century: Don't make an enemy of the United States.

We live in an age of "peak China," not a forever rising China. Beijing is a revisionist power that wants to reorder the world, but its time to do so is already running out.

Historically, this blend of opportunity and anxiety has made a deadly cocktail. From ancient times to the present, once-rising powers have often become most aggressive when their fortunes fade, their enemies multiply, and they realize that they must reach for glory now or miss their moment forever. Fast-growing countries that slip into long economic slumps have responded with fits of expansion. Countries that fear they are being encircled by rivals make desperate bids to break the ring. Some of the bloodiest wars in history have been started not by rising, self-assured powers, but by countries—such as Germany in 1914 or Japan in 1941—that had peaked and begun to decline. Vladimir Putin's recent wars in the former Soviet Union fit this same mold. Xi's regime is tracing a fraught but familiar arc in international affairs—an exhilarating rise followed by the prospect of a hard fall.

China's predicament offers good news and bad news for America. The good news is that, over the long run, the Chinese challenge may prove more manageable than many pessimists now believe. An unhealthy, totalitarian China won't effortlessly surge past America as the world's leading power. We may one day look back on China as we now view the Soviet Union—as a formidable foe whose evident strengths obscured fatal vulnerabilities. The bad news is that getting to the long run won't be easy. During the 2020s, the pace of rivalry will be torrid, and the prospect of war will be frighteningly real.

In particular, China will do what previous peaking powers have done: It will try to rush through near-term windows of opportunity before a longer-term window of vulnerability opens wide. Beijing will push hard to create an economic empire that will allow it to squeeze concessions from countries around the world. It will try to weaken the democratic community by strengthening techno-authoritarianism at home and abroad. Most alarming, China will have strong incentives to use force against its neighbors—perhaps to teach Japan, India, or the Philippines a lesson, perhaps to bring a democratic Taiwan to heel—even at risk of war with the United States. In each of these areas, the CCP can exploit a head-start built over many years, when America and other countries were slow to meet a growing threat, and hope that bold moves can save China from its impending decline.

If the United States can successfully blunt this surge of Chinese expansion and aggression, it can win a protracted competition against Beijing. If the United States fails, then China could upend the balance of power or drag the world into conflict and tragedy. Time is on America's side in a long twilight struggle. But the defining challenge of this decade will be crossing the danger zone.

Why write a book that warns about a coming conflict with China during a year in which Russia started a major war in Europe? The simple answer is that Russian aggression in Ukraine has made the successful containment of China all the more imperative.

If China were to follow in Russia's footsteps and expand violently in its region, Eurasia would be engulfed in conflict. The United States would again face the prospect of a two-front war, only this time against nuclear-armed aggressors fighting "back to back" along their shared border. America's military would be overstretched and, likely, overwhelmed; America's alliance system might come under unbearable strain. The postwar international order could collapse as countries across Eurasia scramble to defend themselves and cope with the knock-on effects of major-power war, including economic crises and mass refugee flows. A world already shaken by Russian aggression could be shattered by a Chinese offensive.

Another reason we focus on China is that it is especially dangerous. China's economy is ten times larger than Russia's, and Beijing's military budget is quadruple the size of Moscow's. Whereas Russia is essentially a two-dimensional great power that draws influence from its military and energy resources, China possesses a wider spectrum of coercive tools and can challenge the United States and its allies in almost any domain of geopolitical competition.

Xi Jinping presides over the largest military and economy (measured by purchasing power parity) on the planet. Chinese officials occupy leadership positions in many of the world's major international institutions. More than half of the world's countries already trade more with China than with the United States; and China has recently become the world's largest overseas lender, doling out more credit than the World Bank, the IMF, or all twenty-two of the Paris Club governments (a group of the world's major lending nations) combined.[11] Beijing's economic power may be peaking, but no other country is so capable of challenging America globally.

As malevolent as an autocratic Russia is, the competition between Washington and Beijing is likely to be the defining geopolitical contest of our era. Failure to prevail in this struggle against a troubled but uniquely potent rival would have world-historical consequences.

This book offers a contrarian take on China by explaining why that country is in more trouble than most analysts think, why that trend makes the coming years so perilous, and how America can prepare for the storm that is about to strike.[12] We also challenge the received wisdom about the origins of major war and the rise and fall of great powers.

Academics have long studied these subjects, but their work commonly rests on faulty premises: Countries must either be rising or falling; those on the upswing advance while those on the downswing retreat. Massive, system-shaking wars are likeliest during a "power transition"—when a surging challenger overtakes an exhausted hegemon. These ideas date back to Thucydides, who wrote that it was the rise of Athens at the expense of Sparta that caused the Peloponnesian War; they have featured in international best sellers warning that the probability of conflict will increase dramatically as a turbo-charged China leaves a four-cylinder America in its dust.[13] Yet many of these notions are misleading or wrong.

States can rise and fall simultaneously: They may seize territory or arm themselves rapidly even as their economies wheeze and stumble. The anxiety caused by relative decline, not the confidence that comes from rising strength, can make ambitious powers erratic and violent. Finally, apocalyptic wars can occur even when power transitions do not: Once-rising challengers have gone down fighting when they realized that they had provoked rivals they *wouldn't* otherwise catch. Understanding this deadly pattern from the past—call it the "peaking power trap"—is critical to preparing for a dark future that is unfolding faster than you might think.

The stakes are hardly academic. "The history of failure in war," General Douglas MacArthur explained in 1940, "can almost be summed up in two words: too late. Too late in comprehending the deadly purpose of a potential enemy; too late in preparedness; too late in uniting all possible forces for resistance; too late in standing with one's friends." It would be "the greatest strategical mistake in all history," he added, if America failed to grasp "the vital moment."[14]

MacArthur's words were prophetic: His unprepared forces in the Philippines, and American forces throughout the Pacific, were routed in the first stage of the subsequent war with Japan.

So it was noteworthy in 2021 when the head of U.S. military intelligence for the Indo-Pacific used the same words to describe a new totalitarian threat from China. "They are on the march," he explained. "It's only a matter of time."[15]

A matter of time, indeed. The United States is entering the crucial phase of competition with China, when the risk of war is highest and decisions made or not made will shape world politics for decades. Another "vital moment" is upon us, and America must get ready before it is, once again, too late.

# DANGER ZONE

# 1

## The Chinese Dream

The greatest geopolitical catastrophes occur at the intersection of ambition and desperation. Xi Jinping's China will soon be driven by plenty of both.

We'll explain the cause of that desperation—a slowing economy and a creeping sense of encirclement and decline. But first, we need to lay out the grandness of those ambitions—what Xi's China is trying to achieve. It is difficult to grasp just how hard China's fall will be without understanding the heights to which Beijing aims to climb. And those heights are imposing, because the Chinese Communist Party is undertaking an epic project to rewrite the rules of global order in Asia and far beyond. China doesn't want to be a superpower—one pole of many in the international system. It wants to be *the* superpower—the geopolitical sun around which the system revolves.

Xi announced as much in October 2017, albeit in the opaque language that revisionist powers often use to obscure their intentions. The occasion was the Nineteenth Congress of the Chinese Communist Party, a quinquennial conclave that China's rulers use to tout their achievements and preview their plans. Xi had already made this congress memorable by enshrining "Xi Jinping Thought" in China's con-stitution, sidelining potential successors, and cementing his status as the country's most dominant leader since Mao Zedong. And as Xi consolidated power at home, he hinted—in a marathon speech lasting more than three hours—that Beijing was ready to shake up the balance of power abroad.

Under CCP leadership, Xi declared, China "has stood up, grown rich, and is becoming strong." A country that the West had once hoped would follow its democratic example was now "blazing a new trail for other developing countries" to follow. Beijing was already moving closer to "center stage" in world affairs. By the 100-year anniversary of the People's Republic in 2049, China would "become a global leader" in "composite national strength and international influence"; it would build a more "stable" world order in which China's "national rejuvena-tion" could be fully achieved.[1]

Xi's words might have seemed anodyne to the untrained observer. But his audience of Communist Party apparatchiks would have under-stood what they were hearing—a statement that China was now a great power capable of mounting a global challenge to the United States. Xi himself had put it bluntly in a less publicized speech years earlier. The road ahead would be hard, he explained, and traveling it would require "great strategic determination." Yet the destination was not in doubt: China would build "a socialism that is superior to capitalism" and ensure a "future where we will win the initiative and have the dominant position."[2]

That ambition is now hard to miss in what CCP officials are saying. It is even more obvious in what the CCP is doing, from its world-beating naval shipbuilding program to its effort to remake the strategic geography of Eurasia. China's grand strategy involves pursu-ing objectives close to home, such as cementing the CCP's hold on power and reclaiming bits of China that were ripped away when the country was weak. It also includes more expansive goals, such as carving out a regional sphere of influence and contesting American power on a global scale. The CCP's agenda blends a sense of China's historical destiny with an emphasis on modern, twenty-first century tools of power. It is rooted in the timeless geopolitical ambitions that motivate so many great powers and the insatiable insecurities that plague China's authoritarian regime.

Although China's drive to reorder the world predates Xi Jinping, it has accelerated dramatically in recent years. Today, CCP officials outwardly evince every confidence that a rising China is eclipsing a declining America. Inwardly, however, Beijing's leaders are already worrying that the Chinese dream may remain just that.

## WHAT CHINA WANTS

Discerning what China wants can be tricky, because countries that want to overturn the status quo have every reason to conceal their goals. The CCP, moreover, is a secretive authoritarian party that feels no compunction about deceiving outsiders or even its own people. As a result, China's grand strategy—the country's overarching conception of what it is trying to achieve—is typically found more in a rough consensus among elites than in detailed, step-by-step plans for the future.[3] Yet if one looks closely enough, there is ample evidence that the CCP is pursuing a determined, multilayered grand strategy with four key objectives.

That the CCP is in position to seek any of these objectives is a tribute to the greatest change in global politics during the past half-century—China's emergence as a major power. At its creation in 1949, the People's Republic was a technologically backward, poverty-ridden country—"a vast poorhouse," wrote American strategist George Kennan, "for which responsibility is to be avoided."[4] When Mao Zedong died in 1976, the country remained appallingly underdeveloped. Over time, however, the combination of good fortune and enlightened economic reforms moved China from socialist stagnation to bustling authoritarian capitalism. The resulting growth was mind-blowing: Real gross domestic product grew 37-fold between 1978 and 2018.[5] Today, China has the world's largest economy (measured by purchasing power parity), manufacturing output, trade surplus, and financial reserves. In 2018, it was the top trading partner for 128 nations.[6] All of which means that China's leaders can entertain some very big dreams.

First, the CCP has the eternal ambition of every autocratic regime—to maintain its iron grip on power. China is not what Americans would consider a normal state that hashes out its national interests through open argument and elections. China has political debates, but they occur exclusively within a one-party state in which the supremacy of the CCP is written into the constitution. Since 1949, the Chinese regime has always seen itself as being locked in struggle with domestic and foreign enemies. Its leaders are haunted by the Soviet collapse, which brought down another great socialist state. They know that the collapse of the CCP-led system would be a disaster, and probably fatal, for them personally. The resulting zero-sum ethos, one Sinologist writes, is captured in the stark formula, "You-Die, I-Live."[7]

In Chinese politics, paranoia is a virtue rather than a vice. As Wen Jiabao, then China's head of government, once said, "To think about why danger looms will ensure one's security. To think about why chaos occurs will ensure one's peace. To think about why a country falls will ensure one's survival."[8] The CCP has historically gone to enormous lengths—plunging the country into madness during the Cultural Revolution, killing hundreds or perhaps thousands of its own citizens amid the Tiananmen Square protests in 1989—to protect its power. And the goal of perpetuating the CCP's authority is at the core of every key decision. Xi's fundamental purpose, one official explained in 2017, was "ensuring the leading role of the Communist Party in all aspects of life."[9]

Second, the CCP wants to make China whole again by regaining territories lost in earlier eras of internal upheaval and foreign aggression. This goal, too, dates back decades: The CCP seized and annexed Tibet just after it took power in China. Today, Xi's map of China includes a Hong Kong that is completely reincorporated into the CCP-led state (a process that is virtually complete) and a Taiwan that has been brought back into the PRC's grasp. That self-governing island's anomalous status cannot "be passed on from generation to generation," Xi has said: Beijing cannot wait forever for its renegade province to return.[10]

Elsewhere along its periphery, the CCP has outstanding border disputes with countries from India to Japan. Beijing also claims some 90 percent of the South China Sea—one of the world's most commercially vital waterways—as its sovereign possession. Chinese officials say that there is no room for compromise on these issues. "We cannot lose even one inch of the territory left behind by our ancestors," Xi told U.S. secretary of defense James Mattis in 2018, generously adding, "What is other people's we do not want at all."[11]

Because China's claims in the East and South China Seas reach hundreds of miles from its borders, it can be hard to differentiate these "sovereignty issues" from a larger campaign to achieve mastery in East Asia. The CCP's third objective is to create "Asia for Asians," a regional sphere of influence in which China is supreme because outside actors, especially America, are pushed to the margins.

Beijing probably doesn't envision the sort of outright physical dominance that the Soviet Union exercised in Eastern Europe during the

Cold War. It may not go rampaging militarily across Asia. The CCP envisions, rather, using a mix of attraction and coercion to ensure that the economies of maritime Asia are oriented toward Beijing rather than Washington, that smaller powers are properly deferential to the CCP, and that America no longer has the alliances, regional military presence, or influence necessary to create problems for China in its own front yard. As Zbigniew Brzezinski once wrote, "a Chinese sphere of influence can be defined as one in which the first question in the various capitals is, 'What is Beijing's view on this?'"[12]

The closest Xi Jinping has come to publicly declaring this ambition was when he said, in 2014, that "it is for the people of Asia to run the affairs of Asia, solve the problems of Asia and uphold the security of Asia"—a euphemism for a situation in which America has been kicked out of a region that then has no way of resisting China's power.[13] Other officials have been more explicit. In 2010, PRC foreign minister Yang Jiechi told ten Southeast Asian countries that they must defer to Beijing's wishes because "China is a big country and you are small countries, and that is a fact."[14]

Beijing wants more than regional hegemony, however, and the fourth objective of its strategy focuses on achieving global power and, eventually, global primacy. State media and party officials have explained that an increasingly powerful China cannot comfortably reside in a system led by the United States. That system is a "suit that no longer fits," wrote Fu Ying, a leading foreign policy official, in 2016.[15] Xi has talked of creating a global "community of common destiny" that would involve "all under Heaven being one family" and presumably obeying the fatherly guidance of the CCP.[16] Xinhua, the PRC's state-run news agency, makes no bones about who will shape global affairs once China's national rejuvenation is achieved: "By 2050, two centuries after the Opium Wars, which plunged the 'Middle Kingdom' into a period of hurt and shame, China is set to regain its might and re-ascend to the top of the world."[17] The struggle to "become the world's No. 1 . . . is a 'people's war,'" the nationalist newspaper *Global Times*, declares. "It will be as vast and mighty as a big river. It will be an unstoppable tide."[18]

The regime has not, understandably, offered up any detailed plan for world order with Chinese characteristics. Until a few years ago, CCP officials scrupulously avoided suggesting that China might challenge, let alone surpass, the United States. But Xi's speeches, government white papers, and other sources leave little doubt that Beijing is striving for a world-class military that can project power globally and for Chinese dominance of the high-tech industries that generate economic and military power.[19] In a Sino-centric world, America's global network of alliances would be weakened and neutralized; Beijing would exercise global leadership through its own strategic relationships and international institutions that it can bend to its will. Not least, authoritarian forms of government would be protected and even privileged in the age of Chinese ascendancy, as the period of democratic dominance ends.[20]

Beijing may not intend to fully "rule the world," the scholar Nadège Rolland writes. "Asserting its dominant position over a world where the influence of Western liberal democracies has been reduced to a minimum, and where a large portion of the globe resembles a Chinese sphere of influence, will suffice."[21] Another Sinologist, Liza Tobin, offers a stark appraisal of Xi's "community of common destiny": "A global network of partnerships centered on China would replace the U.S. system of treaty alliances, the international community would regard Beijing's authoritarian governance model as a superior alternative to Western electoral democracy, and the world would credit the Communist Party of China for developing a new path to peace, prosperity, and modernity that other countries can follow."[22]

As these assessments indicate, the four layers of Chinese grand strategy all go together. The CCP argues that only under its leadership can China achieve its long-awaited "national rejuvenation." The quest for regional and global power, in turn, should reinforce the CCP's authority at home. This quest can provide legitimacy by stoking Chinese nationalism at a time when the regime's original ideology—socialism—has been abandoned. It can deliver prestige, domestic as well as global, for China's rulers. And it can give China the ability, which it is using aggressively, to silence its international critics and create global rules that protect an autocratic state.[23]

Chinese grand strategy thus encompasses far more than the narrowly conceived defense of the country and its ruling regime. Those goals are tightly linked to the pursuit of an epochal change in the regional and global rules of the road—the sort that occurs when one hegemon falls and another arises. "Empires have no interest in operating within an international system," writes Henry Kissinger. "They aspire to *be* the international system."[24] That's the ultimate ambition of Chinese statecraft today.

## THE PROOF IS IN THE POLICIES

Not so long ago, many U.S. officials would have found this assessment unduly alarmist. As late as 2016, President Obama argued that America should root for a "successful, rising China" that could constructively share the burdens of leadership in a complex world.[25] More recently, American views have darkened, but the idea that Beijing is trying to create a totally different reality in Asia and the world still invites skepticism in some quarters.[26] The proof, alas, is in what China is doing.

There is, for starters, the unrelenting military buildup. China's inflation-adjusted military spending spending grew *10-fold* between

1990 and 2020, a rate of sustained expansion unparalleled in modern history.[27] The PLA has used that money to build the weapons, from anti-ship ballistic missiles to quiet attack submarines, needed to keep American ships and planes out of the western Pacific—and give Beijing a free hand against Taiwan or another nearby foe. Beijing now accounts for more than half of Asia's military spending; it wields the world's largest ballistic missile force, navy by number of ships, and integrated air defense system.[28] Chinese forces are preparing for "short, sharp wars" against America and its regional allies; they are racing to complete reforms that would allow the CCP to conquer Taiwan. The PLA, meanwhile, has also begun rapidly expanding its nuclear arsenal and developing more sophisticated means of delivering it; Beijing is on pace to become a full-fledged nuclear peer of the United States by the 2030s. And China is building aircraft carriers, acquiring overseas bases, and developing the ability to project power into the Indian Ocean and, eventually, around the world. One telling statistic: between 2014 and 2018, Beijing launched more ships than are in the entire British, Indian, Spanish, Taiwanese, and German fleets combined.[29]

The military buildup is just one way in which Beijing's ambitions are being translated into action. Over more than a decade, Beijing has used multifaceted coercion to strengthen its control of the South China Sea; most notably, by building artificial islands and then piling air bases, missiles, and other military capabilities on top of them. It has grabbed control of disputed features from the Philippines and sent oil rigs, fishing fleets, and a quasi-official maritime militia into the exclusive economic zones of its neighbors. (Chinese ships have also dumped piles of human excrement near contested reefs and features, causing one environmental expert to exclaim, "China, stop shitting in the Spratlys."[30]) "We don't want to quarrel with you," Xi told the president of the Philippines in 2017. "But if you force the issue, we'll go to war."[31] Looking further afield, the PLA has tested Japan's air and naval defenses around the disputed Senkaku Islands in the East China Sea, harassed India militarily in the Himalayas, and made menacing threats toward Taiwan. That island "won't stand a chance" if China invades, PLA officials have taunted.[32]

Even more audacious is the Belt and Road Initiative (BRI), a globe-spanning trade, infrastructure, and investment gambit that Xi calls "project of the century."[33] BRI has many facets and motives, some of which are relatively mundane. But at its strategic core, BRI is a $1 trillion effort to turn the historic heartland of Eurasia into a geopolitical space oriented toward Beijing.[34]

China is using infrastructure projects, loans, and trade to secure resources, markets, and influence from Southeast Asia to southern Europe. It is building overland supply routes to keep the U.S. Navy from interfering with critical shipments of oil and food in time of war. It is using development projects to create greater influence along China's long land borders in Central Asia. And it is gaining access to ports and other facilities that will give China improved access to the Indian Ocean and extend the PLA's strategic reach. The tools of BRI thus include everything from state-owned enterprises to China's growing navy. The fundamental ambition appears to be making the world's largest landmass a platform for the projection of Chinese power. "Access to Eurasia's resources, markets, and ports could transform China from an East Asian power to a global superpower," scholar Daniel Markey writes.[35]

Critical to BRI—and everything else China is doing—is the pursuit of technological supremacy. The CCP has long sought to hasten China's rise with a world-class program of intellectual property theft, forced technology transfer, and commercial espionage. Through its Digital Silk Road project, Beijing is now trying to position companies such as Huawei and ZTE as the world's chief providers of telecommunications infrastructure and advanced surveillance equipment. In 2018, Huawei alone claimed to be running upwards of 700 high-tech "safe city" projects in more than 100 countries.[36] Through some of the same firms, China is seeking to build or buy the fiber-optic cables and data centers that make up the physical wiring of the Internet—a modern version of the power Great Britain once wielded through its network of undersea telegraph cables—and to vacuum up the world's data for exploitation by Beijing.[37] Underlying all this is the "Made in China 2025" program, which involves generational investments in key technologies—artificial intelligence, quantum computing, and others—that will shape the future balance of economic and military power. "Under a situation of increasingly fierce international military competition," Xi has announced, "only the innovators win."[38]

The CCP is positioning China as an institutional superpower, too. America has long punched *above* its considerable weight by wielding power through a vast network of international bodies, such as the International Monetary Fund or the World Bank. Beijing has learned the lesson, pursuing a calculated, long-term strategy to build influence in the World Health Organization, UN Human Rights Council, and other organizations by using its economic leverage and putting its nationals in positions of authority. Likewise, China has taken a leading role in bodies dealing with arcane but crucial matters such as regulating new technologies and managing the Internet. In other cases, China has built its own institutions, such as the Asian Infrastructure Investment Bank, to make itself central to global governance. Fighting for influence in the world's institutions, the CCP's state press agency explains, is how China will "create a favorable environment" for the rise of a "great modern socialist country."[39]

Then there is the ideological offensive. Beijing may not be a messianic Marxist regime, fanatically spreading its political model to the ends of the earth. But its policies—selling advanced surveillance systems, training foreign officials in the art of repression, bolstering embattled tyrants in places as far away as Africa and South America— unquestionably make the world a more autocratic place. On the global stage, China twists concepts of human rights to emphasize economic development rather than political freedom; it champions notions of sovereignty meant to protect dictators from nosy democrats.[40] And Beijing has cast off whatever modesty it once had about selling its own blend of authoritarian capitalism abroad. It is "inevitable that the superiority of our socialist system will be increasingly apparent," Xi predicted in 2013. "Inevitably, our road will become wider; inevitably, our country's road of development will have increasingly greater influence on the world."[41]

Finally, China has given its policies sting by developing a global capacity to coerce. "We treat our friends with fine wine, but for our enemies we got shotguns," bragged one Chinese diplomat.[42] When South Korea agreed to host a U.S. missile defense radar in 2016, China responded with a campaign of sustained economic punishment. When the Nobel Peace Prize went to a Chinese dissident in 2010, Beijing hit Norway with furious criticism and trade penalties. Countries from Australia to Lithuania have suffered similar fates. This coercion in plain sight is merely the public face of a deeper, more sinister offensive— one that uses bribes, hidden political donations, disinformation, and even members of the Chinese diaspora to deform public debates within democratic societies. These techniques, Xi has said, are China's "magic weapons," used to sow dissension in rival states and ease Beijing's path to primacy.[43] At the same time, China is increasingly trying to apply its own laws—and kidnap or otherwise forcibly repatriate dissidents—in countries far beyond its borders.[44]

We could go on and on about the things China is doing to rewire the world. But the basic point would remain the same: Chinese strategy is "grand" in every sense of the word. It marries the geopolitical insights of Alfred Thayer Mahan, who argued that great powers must build ocean-going navies and rule the waves, with those of Halford Mackinder, who popularized the idea that the Eurasian "heartland" could become an unassailable geopolitical fortress if controlled by a single actor.[45] That strategy envisions preeminence within China's regional surroundings as a springboard to global influence; it wields a vast array of tools to achieve a vast array of military, economic, diplomatic, and ideological ends. China's strategy is also grand in one final way: It requires severe competition, perhaps confrontation, with the United States.

## CHINA'S AMERICA PROBLEM

Americans might be surprised to find that Chinese leaders view the United States as a dangerous, hostile nation determined to hold other countries down. In 2010, then–secretary of state Hillary Clinton scoffed at the idea that America was "bent on containing China," pointing out that "China has experienced breathtaking growth and development" in the American world order.[46] Yet even as China has, in many ways, flourished in the *Pax Americana*, its leaders have long worried that Washington threatens nearly everything the CCP desires.[47]

History casts an imposing shadow. It cannot escape the attention of Chinese policy makers that the United States has a distinguished record of destroying its most serious global challengers—imperial Germany, imperial Japan, Nazi Germany, the Soviet Union—as well as a host of lesser rivals. "The mortuary of global politics is piled high with the corpses of socialist countries," one PLA official remarked in 2014, and America put many of them there.[48] Nor can Chinese officials forget that the United States is poised to frustrate all of the CCP's designs.

From Mao to Xi, Chinese leaders have seen the United States as a menace to the CCP's political primacy. When America and China were avowed enemies during the early Cold War, Washington both sponsored Tibetan rebels who fought against that regime and supported Taiwan's Chiang Kai-shek and his claim to be China's rightful ruler. In recent decades, American leaders have insisted they wish China well. But they have also proclaimed, as President Bill Clinton said, that the country's authoritarian political model puts it "on the wrong side of history."[49] After the Tiananmen Square massacre, and in response to CCP atrocities against the Uighur population more recently, the United States even led coalitions of countries that slapped economic sanctions on China. The CCP sees through the subterfuge, one Chinese leader explained: "The U.S. has never given up its intent to overthrow the socialist system."[50]

Even when the United States has no conscious design to undermine dictators, it cannot help but threaten them. America's very existence serves as a beacon of hope to dissidents. CCP members surely noticed that protestors in Hong Kong prominently displayed American flags when resisting the imposition of authoritarian rule in 2019–2020, just as the protestors in Tiananmen Square erected a giant replica of the Statue of Liberty thirty years earlier. They howl in anger when American news organizations publish detailed exposés of official crimes and corruption in Beijing.[51] Things that Americans view as innocuous— for instance, the operation of nongovernmental organizations focused on human rights and government accountability—look like subversive menaces to a CCP that recognizes *no* limits on its own power. America simply cannot cease threatening the CCP unless it somehow ceases to be what it is—a liberal democracy concerned with the fate of freedom in the world. It is little wonder, as the influential Chinese scholar Wang Jisi wrote in 2012, that the regime harbors "a constant and strong belief that the U.S. has sinister designs to sabotage the Communist leadership and turn China into its vassal state."[52]

The United States stands athwart China's road to greatness in other ways. The CCP cannot make China whole again without reclaiming Taiwan, but America shields that island—through arms sales, diplomatic support, and the implicit promise of military aid—from Beijing's pressure. Similarly, America's navy and its calls for freedom of navigation obstruct China's drive for dominance in the South China Sea; U.S. military alliances and security partnerships in Asia give smaller countries the temerity to resist Chinese power. Vietnam, the Philippines, and Japan, remarks one Chinese military official, are "the three running dogs of the United States in Asia."[53] Washington maintains a globally capable military and bristles when China tries to develop something similar, while using its heft to shape international views of how countries should behave and what sort of political systems are most legitimate. Beijing must "break the Western moral advantage," notes one Chinese analyst, that comes from determining which governments are "good and bad."[54] Almost everywhere CCP elites look, American power is a barrier to Chinese power.

To be clear, China doesn't reject all aspects of the American-led order: The CCP has brilliantly exploited access to an open global economy and its military forces have participated in UN peacekeeping missions. But Chinese leaders nonetheless appreciate, better than many Americans do, that there is something fundamentally antagonistic about the relationship: The CCP cannot succeed in creating arrangements that reflect its own interests and values without weakening, fragmenting, and ultimately replacing the order that currently exists. As Wang Jisi writes, "Many of China's political elites . . . suspect that it is the United States, rather than China, that is 'on the wrong side of history.'" They understand that "the rise of China . . . must be regarded in the United States as the major challenge to its superpower status."[55]

Even at moments when Beijing and Washington have seemed friendly, Chinese leaders have harbored extremely jaded views of U.S. power. Deng Xiaoping, whose economic reforms relied on American markets and technology, argued that Washington was waging a "smokeless World War III" to overthrow the CCP.[56] In 2014, two distinguished Western statesmen reported a prevailing belief in Beijing that America's China policy revolves around "Five to's": "to isolate China, to contain China, to diminish China, to internally divide China, and to sabotage China's leadership."[57] These perceptions lead to a belief that realizing China's dreams will ultimately require a test of strength. The CCP faces a "new long march" in its relations with America, said Xi in 2019—a dangerous struggle for supremacy and survival.[58]

Xi is right that the countries are on a collision course. The CCP's grand strategy imperils America's long-declared interest in preventing any hostile power from controlling East Asia and the western Pacific. That strategy is activating America's equally long-standing fear that a rival that gains preeminence on the Eurasian landmass could challenge the United States worldwide. As early as 2002, Andrew Marshall, the legendary director of the Pentagon's Office of Net Assessment, argued that America must gear up "for a long-term competition . . . for influence and position within the Eurasian continent and the Pacific Rimland."[59] China's drive for technological supremacy is no less ominous: A world in which techno-autocracy is ascendant may not be one in which democracy is secure.

The basic reason why U.S.-China relations are so tense today is that the CCP is trying to shape the next century in ways that threaten to overturn what America has achieved over the past century. Which raises a deeper question: *Why* is Beijing so set on fundamentally revising the system, even if doing so leads to a dangerous rivalry with the United States?

## SOURCES OF CHINESE CONDUCT

The answer involves geopolitics, history, and ideology. In some ways, China's bid for primacy is a new chapter in the world's oldest story. Rising states typically seek greater influence, respect, and power. Humiliations that were once tolerable when a country was weak become intolerable once it grows strong; states discover vital interests in places that were simply beyond their reach before. During the late nineteenth and early twentieth centuries, a rising Germany demanded its due; after the Civil War, an economically ascendant America tossed its rivals out of the Western Hemisphere and began throwing its weight around globally. As the great realist scholar Nicholas Spykman wrote, "The number of cases in which a strong dynamic state has stopped expanding . . . or has set modest limits to its power aims has been very few indeed."[60]

From this perspective, the only thing unusual about China is just how dynamic it has been. No country in the modern era has grown so fast for so long. No country in the modern era has seen its *ability* to change the world expand so dramatically. This being the case, it was always improbable that China would happily settle into America's world, because doing so would have required accepting arrangements—such as U.S. protection of Taiwan and U.S. military alliances arrayed along China's maritime periphery—that no great power would tolerate forever. It was inevitable that Beijing would want to subdue its geopolitical periphery, as America did during its own rise to global power; spread its influence into faraway regions; and make the world conform to Chinese desires. "Of course" a surging China would contest American supremacy, the great Singaporean prime minister Lee Kwan Yew remarked. "How could they not aspire to be number one in Asia and in time the world?"[61]

Yet China isn't simply moved by the cold logic of geopolitics. It is also reaching for glory as a matter of historical destiny. China's leaders view themselves as heirs to a Chinese state that was a superpower for most of recorded history. A series of Chinese empires claimed "all under heaven" as their mandate; they commanded deference from smaller states along the imperial periphery. "This history," writes veteran Asia-watcher Michael Schuman, "has fostered in the Chinese a firm belief in what role they and their country *should* play in the world today, and for that matter, into the distant forever."[62]

In Beijing's view, an American-led world in which China is a second-tier power is not the historical norm but a profoundly galling exception. That order was created after World War II, at the tail end of a "century of humiliation" in which a divided China was plundered by rapacious foreign powers. The CCP's mandate is to set history aright by returning China to the top of the heap. "Since the Opium War of the 1840s the Chinese people have long cherished a dream of realizing a great national rejuvenation," said Xi in 2014. Under CCP rule, China "will never again tolerate being bullied by any nation."[63] When Xi invokes the idea of a CCP-led "community of common destiny," when he speaks of re-creating a world in which Beijing receives its proper deference, he is channeling this deeply rooted belief that Chinese primacy is the natural order of things.

Not least, there is the ideological imperative. A strong, proud China might still pose problems for Washington even if it were a liberal democracy. But the fact that the country is ruled by autocrats committed to the ruthless suppression of liberalism domestically turbocharges

Chinese revisionism globally. A deeply authoritarian state can never feel secure in its own rule because it does not enjoy the freely given consent of the governed; it can never feel safe in a world dominated by democracies because liberal international norms challenge illiberal domestic practices. "Autocracies," writes the China scholar Minxin Pei, "simply are incapable of practicing liberalism abroad while maintaining authoritarianism at home."[64]

This is no exaggeration. The infamous Document No. 9, a political directive issued at the outset of Xi's presidency, shows that the CCP perceives a liberal world order as inherently threatening: "Western forces hostile to China and dissidents within the country are still constantly infiltrating the ideological sphere."[65] The perpetual, piercing insecurity of an autocratic regime has powerful implications for Chinese statecraft. Chinese leaders feel a compulsion to make international norms and institutions friendlier to illiberal rule. They seek to push dangerous liberal influences away from Chinese borders. They must wrest international authority from a democratic superpower with a long history of bringing autocracies to ruin. And as an authoritarian China becomes powerful, it inevitably looks to strengthen the forces of illiberalism overseas as a way of enhancing its influence and affirming its own model.[66]

There is nothing extraordinary about this. When America became a world power, it forged a world that was hospitable to democratic values. When the Soviet Union controlled Eastern Europe, it imposed Communist regimes. In great-power rivalries since antiquity, ideological cleavages have exacerbated geopolitical cleavages: Differences in how governments see their citizens produce profound differences in how those governments see the world.

China is a typical revisionist state, an empire trying to reclaim its cherished place in the world, and an autocracy whose assertiveness flows from its unending insecurity. That's a powerful—and volatile—combination.

## NO TIME LIKE THE PRESENT

All this means the sources of Chinese conduct are not tied to any one leader. America has a China problem, not a Xi Jinping problem. The CCP's revisionist project began before Xi took office; it has deep roots in the nature of international politics and the nature of the Chinese regime. Yet the Chinese challenge has undoubtedly become sharper over time.

As early as the late 1980s and early 1990s, CCP leaders understood that their plans for China would eventually come into conflict with America's premier status in the world. Yet Deng saw that it was foolish, if not suicidal, to alienate the world's sole superpower when China desperately needed a calm international environment and access to the global economy. "We won't close any doors," Deng commented; "our biggest lesson from the past has been not to isolate ourself from the world."[67] This was the genesis of Deng's aphorism that China must "hide its capabilities and bide its time"—it must avoid confrontation and find subtle ways of blunting American power until it grew strong enough to begin asserting itself more openly. Once China reached "the level of the developed countries," Deng had explained, "the strength of China and its role in the world will be quite different."[68]

During the 1990s, China practiced the politics of reassurance with Washington, pledging that it would never seek "expansion or hegemony." Beijing built deep commercial and financial ties with the United States, as a way of powering its own development and making it more painful for America to isolate China. It pursued a diplomatic charm offensive with its Asian neighbors, in hopes of wooing them away from any coalition America might try to rally.[69] At the same time, the

PLA quietly began preparing for trouble by developing the capabilities necessary to hold the high-tech U.S. military at bay. Beijing even strengthened ties with regional organizations, such as the Association of Southeast Asian Nations (ASEAN), to hollow them out from the inside and ensure that they could not be turned to anti-China purposes. The overall goal, Chinese academic Yan Xuetong concedes, was to "prevent the United States from focusing on containing the rise of China as a global superpower."[70] China would rise by stealth.

Chinese statecraft gradually became less subtle over time. America's post-9/11 wars in the Middle East created what Chinese leaders called a "period of strategic opportunity" by embroiling Washington in draining conflicts far from the Pacific. The global financial crisis of 2008–2009 then persuaded many Chinese analysts—as one American official noted—"that the United States was in decline or distracted or both."[71] In response, Hu Jintao and then Xi Jinping began more openly projecting Chinese influence. The quest for control of the South China Sea and calls for Washington to embrace a "new model of great-power relations" that would imply acceptance of Chinese predominance in Asia all occurred during this period. Beijing even cast off the "hide and bide" strategy in favor of Xi's motto of "striving for achievement." "In the past we had to keep a low profile because we were weak while other states were strong," Yan remarked. "Now . . . we are indicating to neighboring countries that we are strong and you are weak."[72]

The change accelerated again after 2016. The election of Donald Trump, the crisis of the European Union after Britain's decision to bolt the bloc in 2016, and other disruptions created great chaos within the existing order. Chinese officials began to talk openly about the possibility of a historic transition away from American leadership. Beijing took the offensive in international organizations, in promoting BRI and the Digital Silk Road, in trying to drive wedges between America and its allies, and in punishing countries that displeased it. China also issued progressively less disguised declarations of intent to push past the United States. "No force can shake the status of our great motherland," Xi said in 2019. "No force can stop the advance of the Chinese people and the Chinese nation."[73]

All this was prelude to COVID-19. A global crisis that initially seemed to knock America on its back, while China regained its footing relatively quickly, gave Beijing the chance to advance on multiple fronts. It did so by increasing military pressure on Taiwan, destroying the last vestiges of Hong Kong's political autonomy, escalating—sometimes violently—disputes with several neighbors at once, and engaging in hyperaggressive "wolf-warrior" diplomacy against countries that questioned the CCP's behavior.[74] And as the disorder in America deepened in late 2020 and early 2021, with a disputed presidential election and an insurrectionist assault on Congress, the abrasiveness of Chinese policy became almost tangible. When U.S. and Chinese officials met in March 2021, Yang Jiechi openly mocked the idea that Washington could speak to Beijing from a "position of strength."[75] China's leaders, the U.S. intelligence community assessed, were convinced that an "epochal geopolitical shift" was under way.[76]

That was certainly the view expressed at the top. "The East is rising and the West is declining," Xi announced in January: The era of American hegemony was ending, and the age of Chinese power had arrived.[77]

This is the China that America, and the world, are now familiar with— one that appears ascendant, supremely confident, and determined to claim an outsized share of influence almost everywhere. A country that strides forward as a confused, divided America falters. But it is sometimes hard not to wonder whether Xi and his lieutenants are as buoyant as they seem.

Careful analysts of Chinese politics detect subtle anxiety in government reports and statements. Themes of bounding optimism are mixed with "words of caution and deep insecurity."[78] Xi acknowledges, even as he touts Beijing's power, that there are many ways in which "the West is strong and the East is weak." He warned, even in the wake of COVID-19, of "looming risks and tests." He declared that China must make itself "invincible" to ensure that "nobody can beat us or choke us to death." And he advised his cadres to prepare for a brutal struggle ahead.[79]

Xi's not wrong to worry. On closer inspection, it turns out that there is also another China, one beset by multiplying problems at home and multiplying enemies abroad. Whatever its propagandists may say, this China will struggle mightily to surpass America over the long term. For that very reason, it may actually be *more* dangerous in the near future.

# 2

---

# Peak China

America isn't the only menace the CCP worries about. In 2021, the party took aim at another lethal enemy of China's rejuvenation: divorce.

Beijing mandated a thirty-day cooling-off period for married couples seeking a divorce, during which either party could call off the split. Women's rights advocates warned that the new policy would make it harder for battered wives to leave abusive husbands and pointed out that the measure was part of a larger trend. In 2018, Chinese judges granted divorces in just 38 percent of cases brought before the courts, the lowest percentage on record. During the COVID-19 pandemic, Chinese officials openly hoped that prolonged lockdowns would lead to vigorous patriotic baby-making and proposed special taxes on childless couples. The CCP has even cracked down on vasectomies.

Beijing explains these measures as efforts to promote family values. But what's really at issue is an acute fear of demographic decline. For decades, China's birthrate has been far below the level required to maintain current population size. A shrinking, aging population cannot deliver robust economic growth. Without robust economic growth, the Chinese dream is an illusion. Which means that divorces, childless women, and sterilized men are, from the CCP's perspective, a threat to the country's geopolitical future.

If American politicians often say that foreign policy begins at home, the CCP is taking that aphorism literally. It is also, characteristically, stifling any suggestion of trouble on the horizon. After the *Financial Times* reported in April 2021 that China was on the verge of registering its first population decline since the 1960s—when Mao's Great Leap Forward was killing more than 30 million people—Beijing's National Bureau of Statistics hastily issued a one-sentence statement insisting that the country's population "continued to grow."[1]

Today, the U.S. debate on China focuses on the problems posed by a rising and confident power—the Athens to America's Sparta, as the tired formula goes. But the United States actually faces a more complex and volatile threat: An already strong but insecure China that views the future with as much anxiety as optimism. Thanks to decades of rapid growth, China has the economic and military muscle to fundamentally challenge America and the international order. But the country isn't doing as well as it might seem.

For years, China has been experiencing, and concealing, a sharp economic slowdown. It confronts growing political pathologies, worsening resource shortfalls, and an epic demographic catastrophe. Not least, the CCP is losing access to the open, welcoming world that assisted its ascent. China rose so high and so fast from the 1970s onward because it enjoyed blessings unprecedented in the country's modern history. But now those blessings are vanishing, and China is looking at a hard future of stagnation and repression. Welcome to the age of "peak China." Beijing is rapidly becoming that most menacing type of revisionist power—one whose window of opportunity has begun to open but won't stay open for long.

## MAKING A MIRACLE

China's rise has been so phenomenal and sustained that many observers think the country's ascendance is inevitable. More than half of the world's people alive today were born after 1980 and have only known a China that was growing relentlessly. But there is nothing foreordained about China's rise, and CCP officials know it. Beginning in the 1970s, China benefited from a serendipitous combination of five factors: an unusually welcoming geopolitical environment; a leadership committed to economic reform; institutional changes that diluted one-man rule and empowered a professional bureaucracy; the greatest demographic dividend in history; and an abundance of natural resources. Understanding what enabled China's rise will help us see why its future will be so rocky.

### A Welcoming World

In 1969, Mao Zedong ordered four retired PLA marshals to analyze China's geopolitical situation. It wasn't good.

China had been locked in hostility with the United States since Mao's Communists took power in 1949. It had fought two undeclared but bloody wars against America, in Korea and Vietnam. But now a new threat loomed in the north. The Soviet Union, China's nominal ally, was menacing Beijing as a rancorous split between the Communist powers led to border clashes and the specter of nuclear war. "The Soviet revisionists," the marshals concluded, had become more hostile than "the U.S. imperialists."[2] Over the next three years, Mao quietly explored a marriage of convenience with Washington to contain the common Soviet foe. When Richard Nixon made his dramatic visit to China in 1972, he declared, "This was the week that changed the world."[3] The trip certainly revolutionized China's strategic position.

China has historically lived in a rough neighborhood.[4] It occupies a uniquely vulnerable chunk of territory at the nexus of Eurasia and the Pacific that enmeshes it in five complex subregions: Northeast Asia, Southeast Asia, South Asia, Central Asia, and Oceania. The upside of this central location is influence; China is, almost by default, a major player in world politics. The downside is omnidirectional exposure to foreign instability and pressure.

To make matters worse, China's territory does not naturally hold together. The political core and most of the country's farmland are concentrated on the North China Plain, a flood- and drought-prone area that suffered several millennia of brutal warfare among dozens, and sometimes hundreds, of warlords. Most of China's freshwater and harbors are located in the south, where they are separated from the rest of the country by thick jungles and rolling highlands. Many major southern coastal cities have had extended periods where they did more business with foreign merchants than with their ostensible compatriots in the north. Finally, the bulk of China's minerals and the headlands of its major rivers are located in the west, an area that comprises 75 percent of China's landmass and consists mostly of desert, tundra, or the tallest mountains on earth. In the past, these regions were vectors for invasion and upheaval. To this day, they are full of minorities that do not consider themselves Chinese and resist Beijing's rule.

For much of modern history, China's punishing environment condemned it to conflict and hardship. From the first Opium War in 1839 until the end of the Chinese Civil War in 1949, the country was torn apart by foreign powers, wracked by internal rebellion, and plagued by poverty and famine. China was forced to fight more than a dozen wars on its home soil during this "Century of Humiliation," resulting in devastation and territorial dismemberment. China also suffered two of the deadliest civil wars in history: the Taiping Rebellion (1850–1864, 20–30 million dead) and the Chinese Civil War (1927–1949, 7–8 million dead).

Even after China unified in 1949, its security situation remained terrible. U.S. intervention against Japan had allowed China to escape World War II with its territory mostly intact. But after Mao's Communists won the civil war and leaned toward the Soviet Union, Washington responded with a "policy of pressure" designed to subvert the CCP, surround it with military bases, and rupture its relationship with Moscow.[5] The United States armed and allied with Chiang Kai-shek's Nationalist government on Taiwan. It imposed harsh sanctions on China, effectively cutting it off from the global economy. During crises in the Taiwan Strait in the 1950s, the United States threatened nuclear strikes against the PRC. Matters worsened when the Sino-Soviet alliance fell apart over ideological disputes and the inevitable frictions between giant authoritarian neighbors. By the late 1960s, the Sino-Soviet border was the most militarized boundary on the planet, and China was surrounded by hostile forces on all sides.

Yet Soviet hostility proved to be a valuable asset for China, because it made possible Mao's opening to America. That strategic masterstroke did three things that enabled the rise of the China we know today.

First, it turned the United States from a mortal enemy into a quasi-ally. The United States began withdrawing its forces from Vietnam and Taiwan; it started backing China as a Cold War counterweight to the Soviet Union. Henry Kissinger shared sensitive intelligence on Soviet troop movements and warned Moscow that an attack on China would be an attack on America's vital interests.[6] When China invaded Soviet ally Vietnam in 1979, the United States again warned Moscow not to interfere.[7] Thanks to the quirks of Cold War geopolitics, Beijing now had a superpower on its side.

Second, the opening to America fast-tracked China's integration with the wider world. The United Nations made Beijing, not Taipei, the holder of China's seats in the General Assembly and Security Council. The PRC began its entry into institutions such as the World Bank and International Monetary Fund (IMF). Country after country switched diplomatic recognition from Taipei to Beijing; Japan, China's historical enemy, became its largest aid donor. With these new diplomatic connections, China was able to counter-encircle the Soviet Union, forging partnerships with Soviet neighbors stretching from Japan through Iran to West Germany.

Third, rapprochement allowed a breakout from economic purgatory. For the first time, the PRC was able to reduce military spending and focus on economic development. The end of hostility with the West meant access to global commerce and safety for Chinese shipping. China had the best of all worlds—a secure homeland and easy access to foreign capital, technology, and consumers. The greatest oddity of the current Sino-American antagonism is that it was reconciliation with Washington that freed China from perpetual insecurity and immiseration. And the timing could not have been better, because China also had, at last, a government that could exploit this opportunity.

## Reform and Opening

Even after the rapprochement with America, Mao remained an immovable obstacle to China's development. The author of the Great Leap Forward, a man-made economic disaster of the highest order, Mao refused to allow any criticism of his policies. He encouraged a group of CCP radicals (the "Gang of Four") led by his fourth wife to obstruct any economic or political reforms.

The deadlock broke only when Mao died in 1976 and, two years later, Deng Xiaoping became paramount leader. Deng and a few key advisers understood that the Maoist model of economic autarky and self-induced political chaos was taking China backward. They grasped that saving Chinese "socialism" required embracing capitalism.[8] The CCP allowed rural communities to run localized experiments by creating loosely regulated village enterprises. Foreign businesses were allowed to operate freely in Special Economic Zones (SEZs) because they would bring money and technology to China.

The reform movement almost disintegrated after the Tiananmen Square massacre, when CCP hardliners sought to roll back reforms across the board. But they lacked a viable economic program to propel China forward. In early 1992, Deng emerged from semi-retirement to conduct a high-profile "Southern Tour" in which he visited and endorsed the SEZs created a decade earlier. Later that year, reformers prevailed at the Communist Party Congress, which endorsed the oxymoronic concept of a "socialist market economy." In 1993, the CCP approved a broad economic reform program that gave China a more modern legal and regulatory framework and a robust tax collection system.

Foreign investment flooded into China, while a bloated state sector shrank dramatically—from 76 million employees in 1992 to 43 million in 2005—thanks to increased competition and reduced state support.[9] China's turn to the market culminated in 2001 with its entry into the World Trade Organization (WTO). Collectively, these measures ignited a period of ultrarapid economic growth, and they were possible only because the Chinese regime was committed to a profound process of reform and opening.

Indeed, China was perfectly positioned for success in a world economy that was changing rapidly. Between 1970 and 2007, world trade surged sixfold. China, with its low production costs, rode the wave of hyperglobalization.[10] China's trade grew 30-fold between 1984 and 2005. Trade as a share of GDP reached 65 percent, an astoundingly high ratio for a large economy.[11] The influx of foreign technology, capital, and know-how turned China into the workshop of the world and lifted hundreds of millions of Chinese citizens out of abject poverty. What sustained this reformist moment, in turn, was the CCP's willingness to embrace a slightly milder form of tyranny.

## A Smarter Autocracy

The CCP has never been anything but authoritarian. It has rarely hesitated to use the most lethal forms of repression when threatened. But not all autocracies are the same, and the CCP's approach to tyranny has varied over time.

Mao's tenure represented the apotheosis of one-man rule, complete with the obscene personality cult and wild policy gyrations that accompany an extreme centralization of power. Mao's successors understood that his model was incompatible with the stability, growth, and innovation the country needed to become a first-tier power. For roughly thirty-five years after Mao's death, China evolved—haltingly and partially—toward a smarter form of autocracy.

The CCP diluted the power of its paramount leader, who now ruled as something closer to first among equals. The introduction of term limits at the top made it less likely that a "bad emperor" could reign for a generation or longer. In the same vein, political elites emphasized the search for consensus within the party, particularly after Tiananmen Square. The CCP began to reward technocratic competence in the bureaucracy and good economic performance at the local and pro-vincial levels. Politics remained the exclusive preserve of the CCP. But within the one-party system, China's government became more accountable and less self-destructive.[12]

This change was crucial. It encouraged the inflow of capital and technology by giving outsiders greater confidence in China's trajectory. It eased the moral qualms that might otherwise have complicated doing business with a dictatorial regime. It helped reassure the outside world that China was changing in ways that would make it less threaten-ing over time. And it produced a degree of relative internal stability that China had not known in generations, laying a strong political foundation for the country's economic success. All great powers need effective institutions that allow them to exploit their other attributes. After 1976, China's institutions were effective enough not to thwart the country's advance.

### The Demographic Dividend

It helped that China was enjoying the greatest demographic dividend in history. Growth requires people as well as sound policies: A large, healthy working-age population is the lifeblood of economic success.[13] And for forty years, Chinese demographics were an economist's dream.

In the 2000s, China had a remarkable *ten* working-age adults for every senior citizen aged 65 or older.[14] For most major economies, the average is closer to five. China's extreme demographic advantage was the happy upshot of wild policy fluctuations.

In the 1950s and 1960s, the CCP encouraged Chinese women to bear many children as a way of boosting the working-age population, which had been decimated by years of warfare and famine. Chinese families dutifully obliged, and the population exploded 80 percent in thirty years.[15] In the late 1970s, the Chinese government, now worried about runaway population growth, instituted its policy limiting each family to one child.

As a result, by the 1990s, China had a huge baby-boom generation entering the prime of their working lives with relatively few elderly parents or young children to care for. No population has ever been more primed for productivity. Demographers think this imbalance alone explains a quarter of China's rapid growth during the 1990s and 2000s.[16]

*Resources Galore*

Finally, great powers need resources. In the early nineteenth century, Britain surged ahead of other countries in part because it had massive coal deposits that fueled its railroads, steamships, and industries.[17] America rose rapidly in the late nineteenth century in part because it had more arable land and internal waterways than any other nation, while its vast oil reserves ignited a transformative manufacturing boom.[18]

Today, many natural resources are sold on global markets, but studies still find a strong relationship between resource abundance and wealth.[19] Countries that are packed with arable land, energy, and water reserves are generally rich; countries that lack these endowments are mostly poor. Resource scarcity also leads to conflict: Most wars have been motivated in part by desperate (or greedy) resource grabs.

For much of the past forty years, China was lucky: It was nearly self-sufficient in food, water, and most raw materials. Cheap access to these inputs, plus low labor costs and lax environmental standards, helped make China an industrial powerhouse. Its firms could outcompete foreign manufacturers and dominate industries such as cement and steel. And the fact that China had a relatively pristine environment and untapped resources at just the right moment—the start of the reform and opening period—made the vital difference.

## REVERSAL OF FORTUNES

China had it all—just the mix of endowments and environment, people and policies to take off as a great power. But once-in-an-epoch windfalls don't last forever. During the past decade, the conditions that enabled China's ascent have deteriorated. Many of the assets that once lifted the country up are fast becoming liabilities weighing it down.

### Demographic Disaster

For one thing, China is running out of people—especially the healthy, working-age people that fuel economic growth. Having just recently benefited from an unprecedented demographic dividend, China is now about to suffer one of history's worst peacetime demographic crises.

Blame the One-Child policy. When China first implemented that policy, it provided powerful economic stimulus by creating a generation of upwardly mobile, relatively unencumbered parents. But the bill is coming due because now there are no children to take the places of those parents. By 2050, the country will only have two workers available to support every retiree (compared to ten workers for every retiree in the early 2000s), and nearly one-third of the country will be over the age of sixty.[20] China's population will be just *half* its current size by the end of the century and perhaps as soon as the 2060s.[21] The economic consequences will be dire.

Current projections suggest China's age-related spending will need to triple as a share of GDP, from 10 percent to 30 percent, over the next thirty years to provide a basic level of elder care—to prevent senior citizens from dying in the streets.[22] To put that in perspective, consider that *all* of China's government spending currently totals about 30 percent of GDP. China will somehow have to raise this astronomical amount of revenue from a collapsing tax base and a less productive workforce, as it loses nearly 200 million working-age adults while gaining nearly 200 million senior citizens. Not least, China will have to care for its ballooning elderly population without its traditional source of social security: family. The average Chinese thirty-something currently has fifty living cousins—plenty of breadwinners to support grandma. By the 2050s, however, that number will have dropped fivefold. At that point, 40 percent of Chinese under the age of fifty will be only children with few if any close blood relatives, except aging parents that they have to support alone.[23]

The Chinese government recognizes the gravity of the situation but is powerless to change it. China's huge population of soon-to-be senior citizens, and the tiny one-child generation that will have to support them, have already been born. In 2016, China started allowing parents to have two children; the limit was later raised to three. Yet birthrates fell by nearly 50 percent from 2016 to 2020.[24] Fewer Chinese babies were born in 2020 than in any year since 1961, when China suffered the largest famine in history and its population was less than half its current size, and the Chinese government expects the birthrate to decline for the foreseeable future.[25] (By 2025, according to some projections, sales of adult diapers may outpace sales of baby diapers in China.[26]) One reason for this slump is an acute shortage of women of childbearing age. The One-Child policy incentivized parents to abort daughters in hopes of having sons.[27] Now China is paying the price: China's population of women in their twenties dropped by 35 million from 2010 to 2021.[28] There are roughly 40 million more bachelors than

single women of similar age.[29] To make matters worse, fewer women
are choosing to get married or raise families. Marriage rates fell nearly
a third and divorce rates rose by a quarter between 2014 and 2019.[30]
The brutal fact is that China's population is about to implode, and that
will make sustained economic growth almost impossible.

It will also lead to other problems. Political tensions within China
will rise, as an aging population places more demands on a government that is ill-equipped to meet them. Internal violence may
surge—a common outcome in societies where there are too many
men competing for too few women. The Chinese government might
even become more willing to start wars, if for no other reason than
to throw surplus men into a meatgrinder. A demographically barren
China won't be nearly as dynamic as it once was—but it may well be
more reckless.[31]

### Dwindling Resources

China isn't just running out of people. It is running out of resources,
too. China's impressive economic performance was the very definition
of unsustainable growth because the country trashed its environment
in the process. As a result, Beijing now has to pay premiums for basic
resources, and economic growth is becoming very expensive.

To see what we mean, look at China's capital-output ratio, which
measures the amount of spending required to produce every dollar
of output. Countries where raw materials are cheap tend to have low
ratios; countries where inputs are pricey have higher ones. China's
capital-output ratio has *tripled* since 2007, meaning that it now takes
three times as much economic investment to generate the same amount
of economic output.[32] China's ratio recently surpassed the average ratio
in rich countries such as America, a remarkable development given

that untapped investment opportunities are usually more abundant in developing than developed countries.[33]

China's environmental crisis can be captured by many statistics. But it is only when one breathes its air and drinks its water that the sheer volume of destruction becomes apparent. Half of China's river water and nearly 90 percent of its groundwater is unfit to drink.[34] A quarter of China's river water and 60 percent of its groundwater is so contaminated that the government has declared it "unfit for human contact" and unusable even for agriculture or industry.[35] China's availability of water per person is roughly half that of the world median, and more than half of China's major cities suffer from extreme water scarcity.[36] Beijing has roughly the same amount of water per person as Saudi Arabia. This crisis is exacerbated because China remains one of the least efficient users of water on the planet—and because its geography forces it to divert water from the Yangtze in the south to parched cities and fields in the north. Dealing with water scarcity costs China at least $140 billion per year in government expenditures and reduced productivity, a price that will rise with time.[37]

China's food security is also deteriorating, the consequence of increasing consumption (a good thing) and the resulting devastation of arable land (a bad thing).[38] In 2008, China became a net importer of grain, breaking its traditional policy of self-sufficiency.[39] In 2011, China became the world's largest importer of agricultural products. The government is trying to regain self-sufficiency by heavily subsidizing farmers, but doing so is simply accelerating the depletion of agricultural land. In 2014, Xinhua reported that more than 40 percent of China's arable land was suffering "degradation" from overuse.[40] According to official studies, pollution has destroyed nearly 20 percent of China's arable land, an area the size of Belgium.[41] An additional 1 million square miles of farmland have become desert, forcing the reset-

tlement of 24,000 villages and pushing the edge of the Gobi Desert
to within fifty miles of Beijing.[42] With few options for increasing the
food supply, Beijing has turned to belt tightening. In 2021, the government banned binge eating and lavish feasts and started requiring
caterers to encourage customers to order smaller servings. Rationing
is on the rise.[43]

Finally, breakneck development has made China the world's largest net energy importer. Just a decade ago, Americans fretted about
their own dependence on foreign oil. Today, Beijing imports nearly
75 percent of its oil and 45 percent of its natural gas, while the United
States—thanks to the fracking revolution—has become a net energy
exporter.[44] China's energy imports cost the country half a trillion dollars each year.[45] They are also forcing China to take expensive energy
security measures such as building overland pipelines through Central
Asia and an ocean-going navy that can patrol the Indian Ocean and
Persian Gulf. Any interruption in Persian Gulf oil flows would plunge
China into an energy crisis far worse than what hit the United States
in the late 1970s.

### Institutional Decay

A country needs capable and accountable institutions in the same way
a computer needs a powerful and efficient operating system.[46] A good
government strikes a balance between authority and accountability; it
is powerful enough to enforce laws and get things done, yet it is also
accountable to society and treats people equally on the basis of citizen-
ship rather than their political connections.

China could not have thrived since the 1970s without the institutional reforms that gave it better, if perhaps not *good*, governance. Yet it
is hard to preserve indefinitely a system that is simultaneously orderly,

accountable, *and* autocratic.[47] Under Xi Jinping, China is now sliding back toward neo-totalitarianism, and this deterioration is undermining its economic growth.

China clearly has become more patrimonial and repressive during the past decade. Since taking power in 2012, Xi has appointed himself "chairman of everything," helming all important committees and doing away with any semblance of collective rule. At the 2017 Party Congress, Xi Jinping Thought—a conscious echo of Mao Zedong Thought—was made part of the country's guiding ideology. Indoctrination has become more pervasive at all levels of education and in nearly all facets of everyday life; individuals—even business titans and movie stars—who get crosswise with the great leader are simply disappeared from public view. Taking no chances, Xi has packed the highest levels of government with lackeys and has abolished presidential term limits.[48] In effect, he has systematically stripped away the post-Mao safeguards against one-man rule. Now China is a rigid oligarchy ruled by a dictator for life.

This might not be so bad if Xi was an enlightened economic reformer. But he consistently prioritizes political control over economic efficiency. For example, private firms generate most of China's wealth, yet under Xi, politically connected state-owned enterprises have received 80 percent of the loans and subsidies doled out by Chinese banks.[49] State zombie firms have been propped up while private firms have been starved of capital and forced to bribe party members for protection.

To take another example, innovation by local governments spearheaded China's economic development.[50] But Xi, in what one insider-turned-dissident calls a "great leap backward," has accelerated a return to Maoist centralization.[51] His brutal and far-reaching anti-corruption campaign has scared local leaders from engaging in economic experimentation, lest they disrupt the wrong patronage networks and end up accused of malfeasance.[52] Meanwhile, censorship has silenced independent economists and journalists, making sensible reform and adjustment almost impossible. And Xi's political work campaign has stifled entrepreneurship. Every company with more than fifty employees is required to have a Communist Party political commissar on staff.

Under Xi, the CCP is crushing dissent and strengthening its grip on nearly all aspects of society. In 2021, his government released a five-year plan imposing severe regulations on every Internet and technology-related sector of the economy, including seemingly nonstrategic industries such as health care, education, transportation, meal delivery, video gaming, and insurance. Companies must hand over their data to the state and can't get a loan, list overseas, merge, or make any moves related to data security or consumer privacy without Beijing's blessing and guidance. By the fall of 2021, the country's largest tech firms had already lost more than $1 trillion in market capitalization as a result of these regulations.[53] This is a formula for tight political control—and economic stagnation.[54]

### A More Hostile Geopolitical Environment

Finally, the world beyond China is no longer conducive to easy growth. Cold War politics made the Chinese economic miracle possible by giving that country a respite from incessant militarization. But Beijing now faces a different situation.

The turning point, in retrospect, was the 2008–2009 financial crisis. By knocking the United States and many Western democracies on their heels, the crisis also made those countries more anxious about China's rise. Books with titles such as *When China Rules the World*, *Becoming China's Bitch*, and *Death by China* became best sellers;

Western intelligence agencies predicted that China would overtake the United States as the world's leading economy. These fears exacerbated growing concerns about China's rise as a trade juggernaut: According to one study, China's entry into the WTO cost the United States 2.4 million jobs as multinational corporations shifted labor-intensive manufacturing activities to China.[55] Beijing was now a potent economic rival, which made it a target of anger as America and other countries entered harder times.

China, meanwhile, emerged from the crisis cocky abroad but insecure at home—a toxic combination. Chinese leaders worried about the sustainability of their growth model, which relied heavily on exports to foreign markets that were now closing up.[56] This gloomy economic picture put China's Communist Party in a bind. The party could not allow a sustained downturn without risking political upheaval. Yet it could not implement Western-style economic reforms without disrupting the crony capitalist networks that sustained the party's grip on power.

To boost growth while maintaining domestic order, the Chinese government decided to crack down on internal dissent and erect protectionist barriers. It engaged in mercantilist expansion abroad, trying to lock up resources, markets, and economic influence through initiatives such as BRI. Powerful interests in the United States and other countries took notice. China's economic protectionism and mercantilist expansionism alarmed Western business communities. Organized labor, which had never liked the flood of low-cost Chinese imports, clamored for retaliation. In 2012, Republican presidential candidate Mitt Romney promised to punish China for its trade practices "on day one." Four years later, Donald Trump declared, more graphically, that "we can't continue to allow China to rape our country."[57]

Trade wasn't the only area in which Chinese policies were provoking a tougher response. But for now, suffice it to say that the eventual result was a wave of trade barriers, investment and technology restrictions, and supply-chain movement. The countries making up the Group of 20—the world's largest economies—hit Chinese companies with more than 2,000 trade restrictions between 2008 and 2019.[58] Overall, China faced nearly 11,000 new trade barriers from foreign countries between 2008 and 2021.[59] By late 2020, nearly a dozen countries had dropped out of BRI and another sixteen—mostly Western economic powerhouses—were walling off their telecommunications networks from Chinese influence. The United States and many of its allies imposed severe technology bans on major Chinese companies, denying them critical inputs (for example, semiconductors) and threatening their long-term survival. Today, many countries are actively looking to cut China out of their supply chains. Some, such as Japan, are paying their companies to exit China.

China is losing the easy access it used to enjoy to foreign markets, technology, and capital. The era of hyperglobalization that facilitated China's rise is coming to an end. And it couldn't be happening at a worse time.

### China's Economic Quagmire

China's astonishing economic performance was never going to continue in perpetuity: Growth slows once countries pick the low-hanging fruit of development. The economic formula that allows a country with low wages and vast labor resources to become an industrial superstar is not the same formula that will allow it to make the transition to a mature information-age economy. Yet if headwinds were always inevitable, you might be surprised to learn just how ferocious those headwinds really are. Because of its accumulating problems, the Chinese economy has entered the most sustained slowdown of the post-Mao era—with no end in sight.

Consider one telling statistic: China's official gross domestic product (GDP) growth rate dropped from 15 percent in 2007 to 6 percent in 2019. That was already the slowest rate in thirty years, and then the COVID-19 pandemic pushed China's economy into the red.

A growth rate of 6 percent would still be spectacular, but only if it were true. Rigorous studies based on objectively observable data—such as electricity use, construction, tax revenues, and railway freight—show that China's true growth rate is roughly half the official figure and China's economy is 20 percent smaller than reported.[60] Senior officials, including the former head of the National Bureau of Statistics of China and the current Chinese premier, have confirmed that the government cooks its economic books.

To make matters worse, practically all of China's GDP growth since 2008 has resulted from the government pumping capital through the economy. Take away government stimulus spending, some economists argue, and China's economy may not have grown at all.[61] Total factor productivity, the vital ingredient for wealth creation, declined 1.3 percent every year on average between 2008 and 2019, meaning that China is spending more to produce less each year.[62]

The signs of this extended era of unproductive growth are easy to spot. China has built more than fifty ghost cities—sprawling metropolises of empty offices, apartments, malls, and airports.[63] Nationwide, more than 20 percent of homes stand vacant, and there are enough empty properties for some 90 million people—a number greater than the entire population of Germany.[64] Excess capacity in major industries tops 30 percent, with factories sitting idle and goods rotting in warehouses.[65] Nearly two-thirds of China's infrastructure projects cost more to build than they will ever generate in economic returns. Total losses from all this waste are difficult to calculate, but China's government estimates that it blew at least $6 trillion on "ineffective investment" between 2009 and 2014 alone.[66]

The world hasn't seen such a plunge in productivity from a great power since the Soviet Union in the 1980s.[67] No doubt, the Soviets had other problems, including sinking oil revenues and sky-high defense spending; and China has additional advantages, including a market-oriented private sector and a growing middle class. But China's productivity problem is strikingly similar to what afflicted the Soviet Union: state-directed investment piling up in stagnant parts of the economy. China's private sector is dynamic, but it is shackled to a bloated state sector that destroys more value than it creates.[68]

The unsurprising result of this inefficient system is massive debt. China's total debt jumped eightfold between 2008 and 2019 and exceeded 335 percent of GDP on the eve of the COVID-19 pandemic.[69] No country has racked up so much debt so fast in the past 100 years outside of wartime or the mega-shock of the pandemic.[70] The problem has become so bad that roughly a quarter of China's thousand biggest firms owe more money in interest than they earn in gross profits. Half of all new loans in China are being used to pay interest on old loans, a phenomenon known as "Ponzi finance."[71]

Many bankers—93 percent, according to one survey—believe that China's debt is even worse than the above data indicate, because many Chinese companies take loans from shadow banks, whose transactions are not included in official statistics.[72] In addition, Chinese citizens made rampant use of peer-to-peer lending services on their phones, from roughly 2010 until the government cracked down in 2020, to obtain loans they never could get through regular channels. Such "back-alley banking" severely exacerbated China's debt problem.[73] From 2010 to 2012, Chinese shadow lenders doubled their outstanding loans to $5.8 trillion—a sum equivalent to 69 percent of China's GDP. From 2012 to 2016, Chinese shadow loans increased by an additional 30 percent each year. China may be sitting on an impressive $3 trillion in foreign exchange reserves, but this amounts to less than one-tenth of Beijing's total debt.[74]

We know how this story ends: with investment-led bubbles that collapse into prolonged economic slumps. As every country that has followed a similar growth-over-productivity model has discovered, throwing more money into an inefficient system yields diminishing returns. In Japan, it resulted in three lost decades of deflation and near-zero growth. In the United States, excessive lending created the Great Recession. The heavily indebted Indonesian economy crashed in the 1997–1998 Asian financial crisis. China's bust could be even worse. Beijing's debt mountain is easily an order of magnitude larger than Indonesia's was, and it has been relying on an expansion-at-all-cost development model longer than anyone since the Soviet Union. The cascading financial crisis that struck the Chinese real estate development giant Evergrande in late 2021 may merely be a sign of things to come.

This gathering economic storm poses an existential threat to the CCP, which is one reason why the party finds it so hard to kick its potentially fatal addiction to debt. Since the 1970s, the party's primary source of legitimacy has been the delivery of rising wages and improving living standards. Stellar economic performance has allowed the CCP to present Chinese citizens with a simple and strict social contract: The party retains absolute power while the people receive more wealth—and that's it. No elections. No independent media. No unsanctioned protests and absolutely no organized political opposition. This basic bargain has made China's political system strong but extremely brittle, because it only works if the country's economic engine keeps humming.

Without economic performance, the CCP will have to fall back on its pre-1970 sources of legitimacy: militant nationalism and the regular delivery of beatdowns, imprisonment, and even execution. That system

condemned China to chronic poverty, strife, and conflict, so it is little
wonder that CCP leaders are determined to rekindle rapid growth.

Unfortunately for them, their options are limited. One route would
be to fully liberalize the economy by establishing secure private property rights, allowing free flows of capital and labor, and encouraging
greater competition. But history shows that authoritarian regimes are
loath to implement liberal reforms. To follow such a path, subsidies
to state-favored firms would need to be cut. Access to credit would
have to be granted on economic merits rather than political connections. Inefficient state-favored firms would have to be allowed to fail.
Free exchanges of information would have to be permitted. Needless
to say, such policies encounter fierce resistance from entrenched interests. Case in point: In November 2013, the CCP floated sixty reform
proposals designed to transform China's growth model by allowing
markets to "play a decisive role in allocating national resources." Less
than 10 percent of these reforms were ever implemented.[75]

A second route would involve China innovating its way out of
its economic problems.[76] Since 2006, Beijing has tripled spending on
research and development (R&D), employed more scientists and engineers than any other country, and mounted the most extensive corporate espionage campaign the world has ever seen. So far, however,
these measures have failed to boost flagging productivity. China *has*
developed pockets of economic excellence. It leads the world in some
manufacturing industries—especially in the production of household
appliances, textiles, steel, solar panels, and simple drones—because low
wages and generous government subsidies enable its companies to churn
out inexpensive goods. China also has the world's largest e-commerce
market and mobile payments system; it has been developing and rolling
out a digital currency. And it holds solid shares of global markets for
Internet software and communications equipment—primarily because

the Chinese government prevents foreign Internet and telecommunications firms from operating in China, giving Chinese firms, such as Alibaba, Baidu, and Tencent, a captive market of 1.4 billion people.

Yet in high-technology industries, meaning those that involve the commercial application of advanced scientific research (for example, pharmaceuticals, biotechnology, and semiconductors) or the engineering and integration of complex parts (for example, aviation, medical devices, and system software), the story is different. Here, China generally accounts for small shares of global markets compared to the United States, Japan, or major European powers.[77] The main reason is that China's top-down R&D system, though excellent at mobilizing resources, stifles the open flows of information and willingness to challenge conventional wisdom necessary for sustained cutting-edge innovation.

Take semiconductors, which are arguably the linchpins of computers and therefore of the modern economy. China has spent tens of billions of dollars trying to become a leader in this area. Yet it still depends on imports of high-end semiconductors and semiconductor manufacturing equipment from America and its allies, a vulnerability that the U.S. government is now using to squeeze Chinese firms such as Huawei and ZTE.[78] China's national champion, Semiconductor Manufacturing International Corporation, still relies on subsidies for 40 percent of its revenue (versus 3 percent for U.S. firms) and produces chips that lag those of foreign competitors by half a decade, which might as well be a century in the battle for computer shoppers.[79]

## RED ALERT

China's leaders see the writing on the wall. They know their investment-driven growth model is running out of steam, their people are about to age and die off in huge numbers, their country is becoming a barren wasteland, and their efforts to engineer innovation from the top down may not pan out. They also recognize that a prolonged economic slump spells the end of their country's rise and, perhaps, of the CCP.

Without sustained economic growth, the gravy train of subsidies and bribes that China's leaders use to keep powerful interests (state-owned enterprise bosses, local governments, and, above all, the military and security services) in line will grind to a halt. The same goes for China's ability to buy loyalty abroad. What would remain of Chinese soft power without piles of cash to dole out to foreign partners? Slowing growth also will force the CCP to make excruciating choices between buying guns for the military or social services for an aging population. If China's leaders prioritize the military over the people, they risk revolt. But if they slash defense spending to make way for social security, they can kiss their dreams of reconquering lost territory goodbye.

As if these dilemmas weren't vexing enough, China's leaders also have to worry about their personal fortunes, which are invested in the heart of China's economy. The party owns almost all of China's land and roughly two-thirds of its assets, including all of the largest banks and industrial firms. In addition, party members hold executive positions in 95 percent of China's largest private companies.[80] A slowing economy threatens not only the CCP's domestic legitimacy and international clout but also the livelihoods of its 80 million members.

In public, China's leaders maintain an air of serenity about the economy. Behind the scenes, their anxiety is palpable. Internal Chinese government reports paint pessimistic economic pictures and vividly describe these debt, diminishing returns, and demographic and environmental crises.[81] In 2007, at the height of a years-long economic boom, Premier Wen Jiabao warned that China's growth model had become "unsteady, unbalanced, uncoordinated, and unsustainable."[82] His successor, Li Keqiang, echoed that assessment in 2021.[83] And Xi

Jinping, the ultimate Chinese triumphalist, has given multiple internal speeches warning of the potential for a Soviet-style collapse triggered by "black swans" and "gray rhinos"—investor jargon for system-crippling economic crises.[84]

The party's economic apprehension is also evident in what is not said in China, or rather, what is not allowed to be said. Under Xi's rule, the government has essentially outlawed negative economic news, including unofficial data showing slowing growth, rising local government debt, or signs of declining consumer confidence.[85] Objective economic analysis is being replaced by government propaganda. And technocrats are being replaced by political hacks: Xi's government has whittled away the relative autonomy that the country's central bank once enjoyed.[86]

Many Chinese citizens know that their government's economic story doesn't add up, and they are voting with their feet. The rich are moving their money and children out of the country en masse. In any given year, 30–60 percent of Chinese millionaires and billionaires say they are leaving China or have plans to do so.[87] In the decade after 2008, Chinese nationals received at least 68 percent of all of the "golden visas" in the world, which refer to residence permits obtained by investing large sums in a host nation."[88] Chinese laborers have been staging thousands of protests every year demanding compensation for their "blood and sweat."[89] It is never a good sign when a country's elite flee and its workers rise up. As one Chinese tycoon explained after emigrating to Malta, "China's economy is like a giant ship heading to the precipice . . . without fundamental changes, it's inevitable that the ship will be wrecked and the passengers will die."[90]

The worst sign, however, is the exponential increase in Chinese government repression. China's internal security budget doubled between 2008 and 2014—surpassing military spending in 2010—and has grown a third faster than overall government spending ever since.[91] Half of China's major cities have been put under grid-style management, a system in which every block is patrolled by a team of security officers and surveilled 24 hours a day by cameras.[92] Now the government is rolling out a social credit registry that uses speech- and facial-recognition technologies to monitor each of China's citizens constantly and punish them instantly. That system, the CCP says, will "allow the trustworthy to roam everywhere under heaven while making it hard for the discredited to take a single step."[93]

Building an Orwellian police state is hardly the hallmark of a vibrant economic superpower. Neither is the fact that Xi's top priority since assuming power has been to imprison, execute, or disappear anyone that could conceivably become a political rival. Since late 2012, the authorities have investigated nearly 3 million officials and punished more than 1.5 million others, including a dozen Politburo-level leaders and two dozen military generals.[94] That amounts to a generational clean-out of the CCP's upper echelons—and speaks to the paranoia of a regime that knows its economic bedrock is starting to crumble.

Don't get us wrong: We're not saying that China is on the brink of economic collapse or that it lacks the money or muscle to pose major problems for the world. But we are saying that the conventional wisdom about China's ascendance is flawed. Where others see rapid Chinese growth, we see massive debt and Soviet-level inefficiency. Where others see gleaming infrastructure, we see ghost cities and bridges to nowhere. Where others see the world's largest population, we see a looming demographic catastrophe. Where others see an ocean of Chinese exports, we see vulnerable supply lines and a dearth of domestic consumption. And where others see an enlightened leadership confidently carrying out a master plan for economic supremacy, we see a decadent elite that views China a lot like we do, which is why it is building the most advanced internal security machine the world has ever seen.

Any one of the trends we highlighted in this chapter—surging debt, declining productivity, rapid aging, foreign protectionism, environmental degradation—could derail China's economy. Collectively, they all but guarantee that China will suffer a severe and sustained economic slowdown. And that slump will shake China's system to the core just as another threat—strategic encirclement—starts to bite.

# 3

## The Closing Ring

On the night of June 15–16, 2020, the Galwan River valley, an isolated area along the disputed Himalayan border between India and China, became a high-altitude field of horrors. A hand-to-hand battle in near-blackout conditions took the lives of dozens of Indian and Chinese soldiers. For Beijing, the bloodbath represented a minor tactical victory and a larger strategic defeat.

The causes of the Galwan clash go back decades. Since the 1950s, the two Asian giants have wrestled over the location of their shared frontier in some of the most forbidding, mountainous terrain on the globe. In late 1962, while the world was preoccupied with the Cuban Missile Crisis, China and India fought a major war resulting in a resounding Indian defeat. Since then, New Delhi and Beijing have continued to jockey for advantage, both in the eastern section of the border region, between Burma and Nepal, and in the western section between Nepal and Pakistan. In the years before 2020, the intensity of the dispute gradually ratcheted upward.

In 2017, there was a prolonged military standoff after the PLA began building a strategically located road in territory claimed by Bhutan, which India views as a friendly buffer state. Even more brazenly, China surreptitiously constructed, on land globally recognized as Bhutanese, entire villages with an accompanying PLA presence. In 2019, there was a marked increase in Chinese violations of the de facto border with India.[1] Throughout this period, there were also periodic clashes between Indian and Chinese patrols, governed by a long-standing set of implicit rules—no guns, no killing—that kept simmering tensions below a boil. It was that code of conduct that gave way in 2020, with ramifications reaching far beyond the Himalayan frontier.

The fireworks began in May, with Chinese forces briefly occupying swaths of Indian-claimed territory. When Indian forces pushed back, the resulting scrapes were initially conducted according to the familiar rituals. But after dark on June 15, the skirmishing turned deadly. Chinese soldiers attacked an Indian patrol using primitive but brutal weapons, such as sticks studded with rusty nails. According to reports, PLA personnel even tried to crush Indian soldiers by pushing boulders down on top of them.[2] A pitched battle ensued, lasting six hours and involving up to 600 troops. What exactly happened in the darkness remains unclear; the governments told sharply contrasting stories in the aftermath. Yet some twenty Indian soldiers and an unknown number of Chinese troops ended up dead, many of them killed when they fell or were pushed off a mountain ridge into the river valley below.

Viewed narrowly, the episode was a victory for China. It showed how easily the PLA could grab chunks of territory claimed by India and how hard it was for New Delhi to respond without touching off a larger war against a stronger power. Nonetheless, China lost more than it gained.

Indian officials had long been concerned about China's ambitions. Narendra Modi's nationalist government had more recently worried that Beijing was using BRI projects in Sri Lanka and Pakistan to pressure India from all sides. After Galwan, the backlash was sharp. Indian crowds destroyed Chinese smartphones and burned effigies of Xi Jinping. The nationalist press called for revenge. Modi warned that "the entire country is hurt and angry. . . . No one can even dare look towards an inch of our land."[3]

It wasn't just rhetoric. To shore up its defenses, India sought emergency purchases of Russian fighter jets and other military assets. To limit digital dependence on a rival, the Indian government banned dozens of Chinese mobile applications, including TikTok and WeChat, and barred Huawei and ZTE from its 5G network trials. Most important, India's long, slow move toward America accelerated.

The year after June 2020 saw a flurry of diplomacy around the Quad, a U.S.-Australia-India-Japan partnership that looks a lot like an anti-China alliance of Indo-Pacific democracies. In March 2021, New Delhi agreed to be the manufacturing hub for a COVID-19 vaccine initiative aimed at rolling back Chinese influence in Southeast Asia by distributing 1 billion jabs there. At a virtual Quad summit, Modi and his counterparts effectively announced that they would frustrate China's geopolitical ambitions—by cooperating to preserve a free and open Indo-Pacific—even as they never publicly mentioned China by name.[4] In the summer of 2021, India moved tens of thousands of additional troops to the border, while also studying how it might help Washington choke off China's maritime supply lines in a war.[5] U.S. officials began publicly referring to India as a keystone of their counter-China strategy.[6]

Experts on Sino-Indian relations speculated that Beijing's motive in escalating the border dispute a year earlier may have been to punish New Delhi for working with America.[7] If so, Xi miscalculated—and it wasn't the first time. The deadly struggle at Galwan was just one example of how China's aggressive behavior has begun to backfire.

For a generation after the Cold War, China escaped the fate that has befallen so many aspiring Eurasian hegemons—the emergence of a countervailing coalition committed to checking its power. That achievement is now in the past. Thanks to its own overreach, Beijing has made an enemy of the superpower that did so much to assist its rise. It has provoked fear and resistance from countries near and far. The strategic holiday that China enjoyed for decades is over. A strategic vise is tightening as the CCP's rivals close in on all sides.

## THE EURASIAN CAULDRON

Strategic encirclement is a rude awakening for Xi's China, but it has a familiar feel for those steeped in history. If the past few centuries teach us anything, it is that nations with fish and friends as neighbors have the best chance of claiming global power without provoking global resistance. Those ringed by rivals must constantly fear that expansion will result in their own isolation and defeat. In world politics as in real estate, location matters: Countries that sit comfortably outside the geopolitical cauldron of Eurasia are far better positioned for primacy than those trapped within it.

To see why, look at the difference between America and China. The United States didn't always enjoy "free security" thanks to its geographic isolation: It spent its first century battling European empires and Native Americans for control of the North American continent.[8] Yet the fact that this contest was an away game for America's great-power rivals, which had to defend holdings thousands of miles from their capitals, gave Washington the decisive advantage. By the late nineteenth century, no combination of countries in the Western Hemisphere could meaningfully threaten America's security. The one European power—Britain—that might have challenged the United States in its own backyard was menaced by Germany and chose to appease the Americans instead.[9] The United States was the sole great power in its hemisphere, which allowed it to project that power around the world.

America could build an ocean-going navy rather than heavily fortifying its frontiers. It could enter the world wars of the twentieth century late and allow countries in Europe and Asia to bear the brunt of the fighting and dying. And because the United States was so far away from Europe and Asia, the countries of those regions were less likely to fear being conquered by America than to try to enlist it as an ally against predators closer to home. This was what the countries of Western Europe did in dragging the United States into NATO in the 1940s. It was what China itself did in the 1970s: Mao explained his pivot to America as a way of using the "far barbarians" to keep the "near barbarians" in check.[10] By dint of *not* being located in the Old World, the United States found itself invited to exercise vast influence there.

How America used its power also mattered tremendously. A country founded in liberal political principles created a comparatively liberal geopolitical system. It promoted an open world economy and gave U.S. friends access to the lucrative American market. It created alliances that protected dozens of major countries, turning killing fields in Western Europe and East Asia into zones of relative peace.[11] The combination of geography and democracy made America a fairly benign superpower, which gave other countries an interest in supporting its hegemony.

China is cursed by comparison. The Eurasian landmass is a big but crowded space; it is home not to one major power but many. A country that dominates Eurasia would pose a mortal threat to the sovereignty, even survival, of countries located in its shadow, which means that the rise of one powerful nation cannot fail to stimulate a reaction from others. For centuries, aggressively expansionist states within Eurasia have precipitated—sooner or later—counterbalancing by anxious neighbors, who typically compensate for their own relative weakness by aligning with strong offshore allies such as Great Britain and, more recently, the United States.

This is what spelled doom for every Eurasian country that tried to become a global superpower in the modern era. Napoleon's France conquered much of Europe but fell victim to a combination of rivals led by Great Britain. In the twentieth century, Germany was destroyed (twice) when its European enemies made common cause with the United States. During the Cold War, the Soviet Union was thwarted by a ring of rivals from Northeast Asia to Western Europe, all backed by Washington. Hegemonic ambitions have long been the ruin of countries situated within Eurasia: The odds of being cornered and killed by a pack of enemies are high indeed.

China is especially exposed to this predicament. America has land borders with two friendly countries. China is surrounded by *twenty* nations and faces historical rivals in every direction: Russia to the north, Japan to the east, Vietnam to the south, and India to the west. China's neighbors include seven of the world's fifteen most populous countries, four countries armed with nuclear weapons, five countries that have waged wars against China in the past eighty years, and ten that still claim parts of Chinese territory. Additionally, China has America as a neighbor, due to the U.S. alliances, strategic partnerships, and military deployments that dot Asia's map. China may once have been a Eurasian empire. But today, one Chinese scholar writes, it "suffers from the harshest global geopolitical security situation among the great powers."[12]

In fact, geography creates a strategic trap for China. The perception of danger everywhere drives a strong impulse to expand: Only by pushing outward can China secure its frontiers, protect its supply lines, and break the bonds a punishing environment imposes.[13] Yet the same impulse will eventually fuel the anxieties of other countries, tempting them to combine against Beijing. And because the CCP exercises power so ruthlessly at home, it faces an inherent challenge in convincing other countries that it would use preeminent power responsibly abroad.

A rising China thus faces a high probability of being encircled and defeated, unless it can somehow escape the fate that has befallen self-aggrandizing Eurasian states in the past. For years, Beijing was fortunate—and skillful—in this respect, but now its luck is running out.

## THE END OF CHINA'S STRATEGIC HOLIDAY

China's strategic holiday began as a matter of Cold War realism: The enemy of America's enemy became its friend. But hard-boiled realists would have had trouble predicting what happened next. China's strategic holiday lasted a full generation after the Soviet threat vanished—and after Tiananmen Square demonstrated that the CCP was still willing to take the most abhorrent measures to preserve its rule. Washington's approach, wrote former State Department official Thomas Christensen in 2015, had been "nearly the opposite of our containment policy toward the Soviets throughout the Cold War."[14] Perhaps the most astonishing aspect of China's rise was how long it took the world to start pushing back.

The United States wasn't entirely asleep at the switch. After the Cold War, a few sharp-eyed observers realized that a flourishing China could one day become a regional and perhaps a global rival. Several administrations hedged against this possibility by retaining powerful air and naval forces in the Pacific. Yet the United States continued to fuel China's explosive growth; American officials encouraged Beijing to become *more* active and influential in global affairs. Far from trying to "hamper and delay" Beijing's rise, Christensen writes, American policy emphasized economic and diplomatic engagement that helped China keep moving up.[15]

One reason for this complacency was greed. In the early 1990s, an engagement policy seemed logical because China was a minor military threat and a massive money-making opportunity. With 1.3 billion people, a long coastline in the heart of East Asia, and an authoritarian regime that was willing to repress dissent and trash the environment to make way for big business, China was simply too good to pass up as a consumer market and a low-wage production platform. So Western multinational companies and financiers pressed their governments to integrate China further into global supply chains. Those governments happily obliged, arguing—when they talked about the CCP's grotesque human rights violations at all—that a more economically open China would eventually become more politically open. "Trade freely with China," George W. Bush explained, "and time is on our side."[16]

That assurance related to a second reason China's holiday continued—the overweening Western confidence, even hubris, of the post–Cold War era. Aggressively containing China seemed almost gratuitous at a time when America was so dominant. Given that China was still relatively poor and technologically weak—the joke in the 1990s was that it would take a "million-man swim" for the PLA to reach Taiwan—there was no need to suppress its growth. Given that the American-led global economy was making China wealthier, surely Beijing would come to see the value in supporting that system. And given that so many authoritarian regimes had recently fallen to the global march of democracy, surely China would eventually do likewise. America would transform China—turning it into a "responsible stakeholder" or perhaps even a liberal democracy—long before China had a chance to transform the American-led order.[17]

There were moments when the engagement paradigm wobbled. When the PLA provocatively splashed missiles around Taiwan in 1995–1996, the Pentagon sent two aircraft carrier strike groups to make Beijing back off. China might be "a great military power," Defense Secretary William Perry remarked, but "the premier—the strongest—military power in the western Pacific is the United States."[18] On the campaign trail in 2000, Bush called China a "strategic competitor" and promised to take a hard line once in office.[19] But it mostly didn't happen, thanks to a third factor—distraction.

The 9/11 attacks diverted U.S. attention for a decade, while making Washington more dependent on Chinese diplomatic support in the war on terror. The Obama administration then sought to recoup lost ground with its "pivot to Asia," only to be whipsawed by the rise of ISIS and another multiyear war in the Middle East. China remained the problem of tomorrow, or perhaps a generation hence, because today's problems were so consuming. "China is like that long book you've always been meaning to read," a U.S. intelligence official commented, "but you always end up waiting until next summer."[20]

Give credit where credit is due: Chinese strategy encouraged American procrastination. Deng's hide-and-bide policy eased fears of a "China threat." The PRC skillfully played the world's democracies off each other, threatening to buy airplanes from Europe's Airbus rather than America's Boeing if Washington got too tough. Even as Chinese strategy gradually became more aggressive, the CCP warned that an American move toward competition would get in the way of bilateral cooperation on nuclear proliferation or climate change. "Cold War thinking," as Xi's diplomats derisively phrased it, would obstruct "win-win cooperation."[21]

The strategy worked remarkably well, and the CCP exploited its twenty-year grace period to the fullest. China sucked up Western technology and capital, dumped its products in foreign markets while keeping its own market relatively closed, installed Chinese officials atop international organizations, and proclaimed its peaceful intentions while building up its military. It was a master class in how to use the illusion of win-win diplomacy to conceal a ruthlessly win-lose approach to global politics.[22] Yet it couldn't go on forever.

America's policy of integrating, rather than isolating, a potential rival had been critical to China's success. But that policy endured after the Cold War only because Washington was so assured in its primacy and so confident that engagement would move China in the right direction. By the aftermath of the global financial crisis, China's growing power was weakening the first of these pillars while its more muscular, autocratic behavior was eviscerating the second. The pendulum of America's China policy was set to make another swing, as the CCP began activating all the geopolitical anxieties that had previously lain dormant.

China's surge of maritime coercion in Asia made it hard to believe that Beijing was reconciling itself to the existing order in the western Pacific. A country that was throwing up a "great wall of sand" in the South China Sea, one U.S. admiral quipped, was not becoming a responsible stakeholder.[23] After roughly twenty years, China's military buildup had reached an alarming level. Respected think-tanks reported that the Pentagon was losing its edge in the Taiwan Strait and other hot spots.[24] American military superiority was being "challenged in ways that I have not seen for decades," Under Secretary of Defense Frank Kendall agreed in 2014. "This is not a future problem. This is a here-now problem."[25]

These weren't the only wake-up calls. Tech gurus such as former Google CEO Eric Schmidt warned that Washington could lose the race for supremacy in artificial intelligence (AI).[26] Meanwhile, Chinese cyberattacks and intellectual property theft were robbing American firms of tens of billions of dollars annually in what recently retired National Security Agency director Keith Alexander called "the greatest transfer of wealth in history."[27] The launch of BRI in 2013 yielded still more evidence that China was not integrating into the American-led system but creating its own. Finally, the stunning centralization of power under Xi brought a decisive end to the era of reform. If engagement had been meant to produce a mellower, freer China, it seemed to have created a more belligerent, mightier autocracy instead.

In 2015, the Sinologist and sometimes-government adviser Michael Pillsbury captured the new mood. In his best-selling book, *The Hundred Year Marathon*, Pillsbury argued that America had been duped by CCP hawks who were well embarked on a quest for global dominance.[28] Before long, Washington would be immersed in a full-blown "who lost China" debate, with critics deriding the engagement policy as a historic blunder.

It's true that engagement failed to tame or transform the CCP. But China had failed, too, by scoring such a catastrophic success. The country's rise had, finally, destroyed the welcoming global environment that had allowed it to rise in the first place. Countries around the world began bringing China's long holiday to a close. Leading the way was its one-time ally, the United States.

## GRADUALLY, THEN SUDDENLY

In Ernest Hemingway's *The Sun Also Rises*, a character quips that he went bankrupt in "two ways. Gradually, then suddenly." That's a good way to describe the collapse of U.S.-China relations.

American officials didn't wake up one day and discover that China was geopolitical enemy Number 1. Even as Washington was touting the "responsible stakeholder" thesis in the early 2000s, the George W. Bush administration was quietly (and very modestly) strengthening America's military posture in the Pacific. Obama's Asia pivot involved upgrading American alliances, moving more air and naval forces to the region, and opposing—not very effectively—Beijing's island-building campaign. But through 2016, engagement was still hanging on: The White House even prohibited the Pentagon from talking publicly about China as a rival.[29]

The rupture in U.S.-China relations came only in 2017, when a most unconventional president—Donald Trump—shattered the engagement paradigm and ushered in full-spectrum competition. Strategy documents of the Trump era bristled with rhetorical fury. In December 2017, Trump's National Security Strategy described China as an international outlaw that was reshaping the world in ways "antithetical to U.S. values and interests." A month later, the Pentagon's National Defense Strategy proclaimed that "long-term, strategic competition" with "revisionist powers" was America's strategic lodestar. Reports by the National Security Council laid out detailed plans for preventing the CCP from seizing the commanding heights of technological innovation, menacing free societies, and turning the western Pacific into a Chinese lake.[30]

Not to be outdone, the State Department—emulating George Kennan's famous "Long Telegram" at the dawn of the Cold War—issued an even longer missive arguing that the CCP was toxically aggressive by nature. Secretary of State Mike Pompeo called for a global alliance of democracies to keep China in its "proper place."[31] This was the most dramatic change in U.S.-China relations since Nixon visited Beijing, and it wasn't just talk.

A significant bump in defense spending allowed the Pentagon to initiate its largest naval and missile expansion in a generation. Trump

hit China with America's most sustained and aggressive use of punitive tariffs since World War II. Washington layered on the tightest
investment and technological restrictions since the Cold War, seeking
to cripple Huawei and turn the world away from Chinese 5G providers. The U.S. Congress created the International Development Finance
Corporation, a $60 billion answer to BRI, while the FBI was unleashed
to go after China's pervasive espionage and influence campaigns. The
bureau, director Christopher Wray announced, was "opening a new
China-related counterintelligence case about every 10 hours."[32] CIA
director Gina Haspel steered that agency away from a generation-long
preoccupation with counterterrorism to focus on the problems presented by big, threatening states.[33] The U.S. national security bureaucracy was training its unrivaled capabilities squarely on China.

In multiple areas, U.S. policy became sharp, even confrontational.
The United States imposed sanctions on CCP officials engaged in the
destruction of Hong Kong's political freedoms in 2019–2020. The State
Department declared that China's program of mass incarceration, forced
sterilization, and systematic abuse of the Uighur population amounted
to genocide. The U.S. Navy ramped up its freedom of navigation operations to challenge China's claims in the South China Sea; arms sales
and military support to vulnerable frontline states increased. Trump's
ever-rotating cast of Cabinet officials traveled the world, admonishing
audiences in Europe, Africa, and Latin America about the specter of
Chinese neo-imperialism. Even trade deals became competitive weapons: The U.S.-Mexico-Canada trade pact, signed in 2019, effectively
prohibited its signatories from signing separate free-trade agreements
with Beijing. If it seemed that America was racing to make up for lost
time in competition with China, that's because Trump's aides saw matters in exactly that light.[34]

Admittedly, American policies weren't always effective or coherent, which was why Xi's regime saw as much opportunity as threat in the Trump era. The president's abrasive, "America First" approach to the entire world—a product of his belief that Washington was being victimized by allies as well as enemies—undercut his anti-China instincts. Upon taking office, Trump withdrew from the Trans-Pacific Partnership trade deal, which two previous administrations had seen as a counterweight to Chinese influence. He started trade wars against America's closest democratic sidekicks, while taking gleeful, destructive pleasure in trashing decades-old alliances. Most bizarre of all, Trump the self-styled strongman admired and occasionally praised Xi's domestic brutality, even as his administration was seeking to punish those very crimes.[35] But whatever the contradictions, Trump had irreversibly broken the mold of U.S.-China relations—and most of Washington applauded him for it.

COVID-19 finished the work Trump had started. The CCP's breathtakingly cynical behavior—first trying to cover up the plague of the century, then exploiting the chaos COVID-19 created to batter its rivals—devastated China's international reputation. According to leaked Chinese government reports and independent Western analyses, negative views of China soared to highs not seen since Tiananmen Square. The percentage of Americans who saw China unfavorably rose from 47 percent in 2017 to 73 percent in 2020.[36] The 2020 presidential election became a contest in China-bashing. And when Trump lost that election, the basic thrust of U.S. policy hardly changed. President Joe Biden, who had once bragged about his close relationship with Xi Jinping, now pledged to prosecute "extreme competition" against the CCP.[37]

Biden proceeded to act like he meant it. The Pentagon formed an emergency China task force charged with sprinting toward better solutions for countering the PLA's buildup, as U.S. officials sought to rally allies for a potential defense of Taiwan. The president maintained most of Trump's sanctions on China, while proposing a $50 billion effort to boost the American semiconductor industry; he began kicking Chinese firms with ties to the PLA and CCP intelligence organs out of U.S. capital markets.[38] China-focused legislation, aimed at increasing U.S. investments in scientific research, cutting Beijing out of key supply chains, and otherwise strengthening America's hand, attracted broad bipartisan support. Biden also threw down the ideological gauntlet, declaring that an epochal struggle between democracy and authoritarianism was under way. Washington must link arms with fellow democracies—on tech, trade, defense, and other issues—to defeat Beijing's repressive model.[39] "It seems that a whole-of-government and whole-of-society campaign is being waged to bring China down," the PRC's deputy foreign minister complained in July 2021.[40]

Admittedly, these measures were merely down payments on a strategy for competition. Yet the harsh reality, from Beijing's vantage point, was that the CCP had made itself the primary target of a global superpower. "A united front has formed in the United States," one Chinese military expert wrote: Hostility toward China had become a point of bipartisan accord in Washington.[41] And just as the U.S. turn toward China opened so many doors from the 1970s onward, the U.S. turn away from China has helped to close them. Countries that have benefited from the American world order are starting to understand the risks of a system run by Beijing. Almost everywhere China is pushing for advantage, a growing cast of rivals is pushing back.

## ON EVERY FRONT

For starters, China has lost any chance of reclaiming Taiwan without a fight. For decades, Beijing thought that it could buy reunification by forging economic links with Taiwan while bribing countries to cut diplomatic relations with the island. But prospects for peaceful reunification are fading fast: It turns out most Taiwanese don't want to live in a belligerent, neo-totalitarian state.

In 2020, a record 64 percent of the island's population identified solely as Taiwanese and not Chinese, up from 55 percent in 2018.[42] Popular support for unification with China has plunged during the past decade; the Kuomintang political party, seen to favor cozy ties with Beijing, has been repeatedly punished at the polls. Taiwan is also trying, belatedly, to turn itself into a strategic porcupine. In 2020, after watching China swallow Hong Kong, Taiwan's government approved a 10 percent hike in military spending and a bold new defense strategy.[43] Under this plan, Taiwan would acquire huge arsenals of mobile missile launchers, armed drones, and mines; prepare its army to surge tens of thousands of troops to any beach in an hour; back those regular forces with a million-strong reserve force trained to fight guerrilla-style in Taiwan's cities, mountains, and jungles; and set up a huge network of shelters and massive stockpiles of fuel, medical supplies, food, and water for a population psychologically prepared to ride out a bloody conflict for months. "We will defend ourselves to the very last day," Taiwan's foreign minister declared.[44] If this plan, which was bolstered by another supplemental defense spending package in 2021, is fully executed, it would make Taiwan extremely difficult to conquer.

The United States is facilitating all of these changes. When the United States and China reestablished diplomatic ties in the 1970s, it seemed certain that Washington would eventually jettison Taiwan. But the relationship endured and has, thanks to Chinese pressure, significantly tightened. America increasingly treats Taiwan as an independent nation in all but name, and the U.S. government is backing up this stance by helping Taiwan's military.

The Trump and Biden administrations both made it easier for

American officials to visit Taiwan; Congress passed a law in 2020 requiring the U.S. government to help Taipei strengthen its presence in international organizations. At the same time, the Trump administration sold nearly $20 billion worth of weapons to Taipei, including missile launchers, mines, and drones that could help an island country repel an amphibious attack. Under Trump and Biden, the Pentagon has put the defense of Taiwan at the center of its military planning; U.S. officials have called their support for the island "rock solid" and hinted ever-less-subtly that America would respond to a Chinese invasion with force.[45] The military balance in the Taiwan Strait has changed in China's favor, but Taipei and Washington are digging in.

So are countries throughout maritime Asia. Japan, the target of Chinese coercion in the East China Sea, is engaged in its most concerted military buildup since the end of the Cold War. It has increased defense spending ten years in a row and made plans to use missile launchers and high-quality submarines, situated in the narrow seas along the Ryukyu Islands, to choke off China's access to the Pacific.[46] The overall balance of naval tonnage now favors Beijing, but Japan still has more large surface combatants than China, including amphibious ships that have been repurposed as carriers for Japan's rapidly expanding arsenal of stealth F-35 fighters armed with long-range anti-ship missiles.[47] Chinese strategists dream of breaking the "First Island Chain"—the strategic cordon of American allies and partners in the western Pacific—but Tokyo can make that a bloody endeavor.

The U.S.-Japan alliance has also assumed an anti-China bent. A succession of American presidents has clarified that the alliance covers the disputed Senkaku Islands, threatening to turn any Japan-China war over those islands into a U.S.-China war. Japan, for its part, has reinterpreted its constitution to allow the Self-Defense Forces to play a more active role in fighting alongside the United States.

Japanese warships and planes often serve as escorts for American warships and planes as they pass through China's near seas. American F-35s are practicing landings on Japan's quasi-aircraft carriers.[48] Most alarming for China, Japan agreed in 2021 to cooperate closely with America in the event of a Chinese attack on Taiwan. Japan's deputy prime minister declared that such an attack would constitute a threat to the survival of Japan itself, and Washington and Tokyo began drawing up a joint battle plan that reportedly involves U.S. Marines deploying deadly long-range artillery on the southernmost Ryukyu Islands, just 90 miles from Taiwan.[49] Meanwhile, Japan has led regional opposition to Chinese economic hegemony by preserving a rump Trans-Pacific Partnership after U.S. withdrawal in 2017. When Chinese leaders gaze across the East China Sea, they see not a small, vulnerable enemy, but a major regional adversary backed by the world's greatest power.

The countries around the South China Sea are weaker and so are their anti-China efforts. But they are not defenseless, and they are developing military capabilities and strategic friendships to keep Beijing at bay. Vietnam is acquiring mobile shore-based anti-ship cruise missile batteries, Russian attack submarines, advanced surface-to-air missiles, new fighter aircraft, and surface ships armed with advanced cruise missiles.[50] With these weapons, Vietnam could destroy ships and aircraft operating within 200 miles of its coast—an area that encompasses the western third of the South China Sea and China's huge military base on Hainan Island.[51] Hanoi has also hosted U.S. warships, and its relationship with America is closer than ever. To the south, Singapore has quietly become America's major military hub in Southeast Asia, hosting maritime surveillance planes, fast littoral combat ships, and other Pentagon assets. That city-state may not be an American treaty ally, a senior U.S. naval commander once remarked, but it acts like one.[52]

Elsewhere around the South China Sea, Indonesia increased its defense spending 20 percent in 2020 and an additional 16 percent in 2021 so it could buy dozens of F-16 fighters and new surface ships armed with long-range anti-ship cruise missiles.[53] In March 2021, the Indonesian government signed a pact to acquire Japanese defense equipment and jointly develop islands in the South China Sea that China claims as its own. In May, the government announced that it would triple its submarine fleet and buy new corvettes in response to Chinese maritime incursions.[54] For good measure, Jakarta declared that it would sink foreign vessels that fish or drill in its claimed waters and has occasionally made good on the threat by blowing up seized Chinese fishing boats on national television.

On the east side of the South China Sea, the Philippines—the primary victim of Chinese coercion in the area—wavered between appeasement and resistance under President Rodrigo Duterte. But the Chinese economic payoffs Duterte sought for selling out Filipino sovereignty never materialized, and frustration with Beijing has increased. In early 2021, Foreign Secretary Teodoro Locsin, Jr., went on a profanity-laced Twitter rant about Chinese bullying. In response, the famously foul-mouthed Duterte, who once called Barack Obama a "son of a whore," decreed that only *he* was allowed to use obscenities as tools of statecraft.[55] Nonetheless, Manila has been ramping up air and naval patrols, conducting military exercises with the United States, and moving to purchase BrahMos cruise missiles from India.[56] It also received, under the Trump and Biden administrations, firmer guarantees of what Washington will do to back up Philippine forces if shooting breaks out.[57]

In short, China has made military gains in the South China Sea, but only by turning many of its neighbors against it. Its assertiveness has also made the fate of that regional waterway a source of global concern: Countries from Japan to Australia to the United Kingdom have sent naval patrols and otherwise opposed China's dominance of a sea through which one-third of the world's shipping passes. And American allies in the region are signing defense cooperation agreements that bring them closer to each other at the same time that they draw closer to the United States.

In fact, as China seeks greater arcs of influence, it is confronting greater arcs of hostility. Australia weathered an economic coercion campaign China unleashed upon it in 2020, coming away more determined to harden its society against foreign interference. Its leaders have largely abandoned the pleasant illusion of not having to choose between America and China, in recognition that the alternative to aligning with Washington is subordination to Beijing. Australia is now engaged in its biggest defense overhaul in generations, expanding northern bases to better accommodate U.S. ships and aircraft, investing in long-range conventional missiles, and fighting Chinese influence in the strategically located islands of the South Pacific.[58] In 2021, Australia's defense minister termed it "inconceivable" that his country would not assist America in a war over Taiwan.[59] That same year, Canberra concluded a landmark deal with Washington and London to build nuclear-powered attack submarines with U.S. technology. That pact would make the Royal Australian Navy a force to be reckoned with in the Indian Ocean and South China Sea; it would also bind the three English-speaking nations together in an anti-China entente. "Panda huggers" have become an endangered species in Australian politics, while "panda sluggers" roam freely.

The same goes for India, the primary bulwark against Chinese power in continental Asia. Fear of China has gradually been pushing New Delhi toward Washington for a generation, but the pace has undoubtedly quickened. "In every sector of India's forward march,"

Modi declared, "I see the U.S. as an indispensable partner."[60] In 2017, India agreed to revive the Quad, which had been moribund for a decade. The Indian Navy has sent warships alongside those from Vietnam through the South China Sea. It is installing missile launchers on the Andaman and Nicobar Islands—a staging point for a wartime blockade of Chinese commerce—and building vessels armed with some of the most advanced anti-ship missiles in the world.[61] Non-alignment is still a powerful ideology in India, but it is no longer a plausible strategy: New Delhi is pursuing an unbalanced triangular relationship in which it leans toward Washington to offset the looming threat from Beijing.

Looking beyond the Indo-Pacific, China's global ambitions are provoking a global response. In 2019, the European Union labeled Beijing a "systemic rival," while many member states have banned or quietly excluded Chinese technology from their 5G networks.[62] Italy, which had shocked its allies by signing on to BRI, effectively reversed that decision in 2021. Western Europe's three great powers—France, Germany, and the United Kingdom—have started sending naval patrols to the South China Sea and Indian Ocean. France conspicuously led a Quad military exercise in 2021; in October, naval forces from America, Britain, Japan, Canada, New Zealand, and the Netherlands all converged and trained together in the Philippine Sea. In Tokyo, Canberra, London, and Paris, high-ranking officials are starting to whisper about coming to Taiwan's aid if China attacks.[63] The turnaround has been particularly sharp in the United Kingdom. In 2015, Prime Minister David Cameron heralded a "golden age" of ties with China; through 2019, the United Kingdom was in peril of becoming a technological appendage of Beijing by allowing Huawei to control its 5G networks. Since 2020, however, the tide has turned: Boris Johnson's government put competition with China at the heart of its "global Britain" strategy while announcing defense spending hikes to match.[64]

It's not just the big guys that are fighting back. In 2020, the Czech Republic—a country that knows what it means to be sacrificed on the altar of appeasement—unexpectedly joined the U.S. assault on Huawei. The leader of the Czech Senate visited Taipei and declared, in language reminiscent of John F. Kennedy's celebrated trip to West Berlin, "I am Taiwanese."[65] The following year, Canada launched a 58-country diplomatic initiative to isolate countries that seize foreign nationals as diplomatic hostages—precisely what China had done to two Canadian citizens in 2018.[66] Lithuania allowed Taiwan to open a diplomatic representative's office (a step short of an embassy) in Vilnius, while undertaking a campaign against Chinese influence in Central and Eastern Europe. At the same time, a transregional group of democracies struck at the heart of the CCP's rule by imposing sanctions on regime officials involved in the genocide in Xinjiang.

Beijing, true to form, reacted furiously: The CCP slapped countersanctions on European officials and even on European think-tanks. The upshot was to derail an EU-China investment deal that Beijing had hoped to use as a wedge between America and Europe. This is "how China loses," one scholar has perceptively written—through high-handed, reflexive pugnacity that reminds so many countries how much they will hate living in a CCP-led world.[67]

## CHINA'S LENGTHENING ODDS

It is important not to get carried away. Counter-China cooperation has remained imperfect and halting, mostly because so many countries are still hooked on trade with Beijing. China's economic presence is pervasive in Southeast Asia, Africa, South America, and other developing regions. Singapore's prime minister Lee Hsien Loong pointedly advised Washington in 2019 not to expect countries to simply sever ties to Beijing. "Where is your part of the world, and who will be in your system?" he asked.[68]

Even close U.S. allies, such as France and Germany, sometimes seem wishy-washy. Still scarred by the memory of one cold war, these countries are eager to avoid a second that once again splits the world down the middle. China exacerbates this hedging by using its economic influence to divide and neutralize regional groupings, whether ASEAN or, on occasion, the European Union. Moreover, what governments want is one thing and what businesses want is another: As Washington and Tokyo sought to limit dependence on China in 2020–2021, U.S. and Japanese investment flowed *into* that country.[69] When it comes to military matters, multilateral consultations on defending Taiwan and securing the western Pacific are still immature—nothing like the deep cooperation, developed through decades of training and fighting, that the Pentagon enjoys with America's NATO allies. Balancing against China often has the feel of two steps forward, one step back.

China, for its part, has been pursuing hedges against strategic isolation. It has built an entente with Putin's Russia, another angry, revisionist autocracy with a penchant for aggression and a talent for making enemies. That partnership features deepening economic, technological, diplomatic, and military cooperation beyond what most Western observers would have predicted a decade ago. It features a tacit agreement that Beijing and Moscow won't make trouble for each other along their once-contested border, so that they can maximize the trouble they make for the United States and its allies across Eurasia and beyond. On the eve of Russia's invasion of Ukraine, Xi Jinping and Vladimir Putin declared that their friendship had "no limits"; Moscow's subsequent attack, and the global security crisis it precipitated, underscored that the balance of power is under strain in Europe and Asia simultaneously.

If China and Russia have traditionally struggled to tame their historical rivalry for long, for now their anti-U.S., anti-democracy agendas are binding them together.[70]

The strategic effects of this alignment are potentially quite important. Just as Germany and Japan—two ambivalent, distrustful partners with fundamentally different long-term visions for the world—profited from the chaos and pressure each other's advances created in the run-up to World War II, China and Russia benefit from the fact that America cannot fully concentrate on either of its great-power rivals. Sino-Russian ties could get even tighter in the coming years. If Russia faces prolonged isolation thanks to its assault on Ukraine, it will become more dependent, economically and strategically, on China. If Beijing experiences a more energetic form of containment at the hands of Washington and its allies, then calm, productive relations with Russia will become all the more valuable. It is no longer absurd to imagine a scenario in which America's parallel great-power rivalries, against China and Russia, merge into a single contest against a more coherent autocratic axis spanning a large part of Eurasia.[71]

Yet even here, not all is well for Beijing. Perhaps Putin is Tojo to Xi's Hitler—or perhaps he is Mussolini, the weaker but truculent ally whose missteps blow back on the stronger.[72] The Russian invasion of Ukraine created problems for China, bringing down international scrutiny and suspicion on Xi for his close relationship with Putin.[73] A China that stays close to Russia will be a China that grows more estranged from much of the world. And as Putin's attack heightens fears of autocratic aggression around the globe, it could precipitate more strenuous balancing against Beijing, as well.

Indeed, the overall trends are clear and, from the CCP's perspective, ominous. An assortment of actors is joining forces to check China's power and put it in a strategic box. Expect more of this in the future.

Groups of the world's most innovative countries could set technological standards that discriminate against Chinese companies and perhaps even exclude them from Western production and digital networks. A shifting coalition of democracies could begin protecting liberal systems worldwide while naming, shaming, and sanctioning China for human rights abuses. An expanded Quad could coordinate intelligence and military action in the event of Chinese aggression, while a revitalized Anglosphere could pursue deepening technological and security cooperation at Beijing's expense. A coalition of wealthy Western countries, perhaps centered on the Group of 7, could pool their development and infrastructure resources to compete with BRI. In the wake of COVID-19, supply chain alliances that seek to move production from China to friendly countries such as India or Vietnam may well proliferate.[74]

There probably won't be a single, overarching anti-China coalition akin to NATO or the Grand Alliance during World War II. Yet the world is already on its way to forming multiple, overlapping anti-China coalitions through which like-minded countries address issues of shared concern. And this strategic backlash is something China cannot afford.

China may have passed the United States by some measures of GDP, but by other crucial indices it is still quite weak. Per capita GDP is a crucial measure of how much wealth a country can extract from its population to pursue global power: By this standard, the United States was six times richer than China in 2019.[75] According to estimates of total wealth (as opposed to annual output) issued by the United Nations and the World Bank, America is by far the plusher power—and China's prospects will only worsen if its economy weakens.[76] Even by metrics more favorable to Beijing, Washington and its allies still account for a clear majority of the world's military spending and economic output.

No country, and certainly not a stagnating autocracy, can fight at such a disadvantage forever. The CCP can only achieve its long-term goals if it divides the countries opposing it. But its actions are uniting them instead.

This cruel arithmetic is beginning to dawn on Beijing. In 2021, Defense Minister Wei Fenghe predicted that the coming years would see a contest between "containment and counter-containment": China would seek to break the bonds of American hegemony, while Washington and its allies would work to preserve the existing order.[77] A few observers—those who aren't too terrified of Xi to obliquely criticize him—have been more explicit. Dai Xu, a senior PLA officer, explained how deadly it could be to provoke the hostility of a superpower with dozens of allies. "Don't think that the U.S. imperialist is a 'paper tiger,'" he wrote. "It's a 'real tiger' that 'kills people.'" "Once Imperial America considers you as their 'enemy,'" he added, "you're in big trouble."[78]

Other Chinese analysts, including some with impeccably hawkish credentials, have sent the same message. Retired major general Qiao Liang is considered one of the intellectual fathers of the CCP's approach to contesting American influence. But in 2020 he warned that behaving too aggressively could endanger China's great rejuvenation. COVID-19 may have created a "short tactical window" for China, but that window "is not big enough to solve the strategic dilemma it will face in the future."[79] Yuan Nansheng, a former diplomat and CCP stalwart, likewise argued—by way of the historical analogies that offer a safer means of criticism—that "having enemies on all sides" is a recipe for disaster.[80] America's "multilateral club strategy," agreed Yan Xuetong in July 2021, was "isolating China" and causing severe difficulties for its economic development and diplomatic relations.[81] By late 2021, one American think-tank reported, there was a consensus among Chinese analysts that Washington was "employing multilateral institutions and closer relationships to U.S. allies and partners as a way to contain the PRC."[82]

As veteran China-watcher Richard McGregor has written, Xi is now facing a quiet backlash of his own, with some subordinates worrying about where his policies are taking the country.[83] Chinese officials may be looking covetously at the post–COVID-19 world. But they must also be concerned that China is energizing a collective hostility it cannot overcome.

History does not repeat itself, Mark Twain observed, but it does rhyme: Basic patterns reappear even though the past never looks exactly like the present. Looking to history is particularly fruitful in understanding where all of this leaves China and America today.

China is, in many ways, a power that has already risen: It has, or will soon possess, some truly formidable geopolitical capabilities. But China is also "risen" in the sense that its best days are probably behind it. The CCP is now running head-on into domestic and global problems that will make it devilishly difficult for Beijing to achieve its grandest strategic goals over time. Put simply, it is hard to see how a country with so many metastasizing cancers, and so many wary rivals, can forever outrun all the resistance its behavior has begun to provoke.

That may seem like good news, from an American perspective. But it's not entirely reassuring. As China's problems really take hold in the coming years, the future will come to look darker and darker for Beijing. The twin specters of economic decay and geopolitical encirclement will stalk CCP officials remorselessly. And that's when we should get *really* worried. What happens when a country that wants the world concludes that it might not be able to get it peacefully? The answer, history suggests, is nothing good.

# 4

## Danger: Falling Powers

On the surface, Kaiser Wilhelm II had every reason to be optimistic in 1914. A century earlier, Prussia—the forerunner to Wilhelm's German Empire—had been thrashed by Napoleon. Into the 1850s, a loosely confederated Germany was, one British observer later said, a "cluster of insignificant states under insignificant princelings."[1] Since the unification of those states in 1871, however, Germany had been a great power on the make.

Its factories churned out iron and steel, erasing Great Britain's once-unassailable economic lead. Germany built an army unparalleled in Europe; its growing navy threatened British supremacy at sea. By the early 1900s, Germany was a continental heavyweight pursuing an audacious "world policy" aimed at grabbing colonies and global power. "Germany towered above all the other continental states," historian A. J. P. Taylor wrote; it seemed destined for dominance in Europe and perhaps beyond.[2]

Yet the kaiser and his aides didn't feel confident. In the East, one enemy—Russia—was building up its army, enlarging its fleet, and slashing the time required to ready its forces for war. In the West, another enemy—France—was dramatically enlarging the army it could hurl at Germany. Even worse, a Franco-Russian-British entente had Germany surrounded, while the kaiser's allies, he complained, were dropping away like rotten fruit.[3] Perhaps time was *not* on Berlin's side: If Wilhelm did not make a dash for greatness soon, Germany's military position and hopes for world power might crumble.

Germany must strike to "defeat the enemy while we still stand a chance of victory," the chief of the General Staff, Helmuth von Moltke, declared in 1914, even if that meant "provoking a war in the near future."[4] When a diplomatic crisis broke upon Europe that summer, the kaiser's government did just that—making the decisions and taking the risks that helped turn the assassination of an Austrian prince into the global conflagration known as World War I. If Germany's rise had given it the wherewithal to destroy the balance of power, its impending decline drove the aggressive gamble that plunged Europe into darkness.

This scenario has been more common than you might think. The conventional wisdom among political scientists holds that great powers are either rising or falling; that rising powers push forward whereas declining powers fall back; and that the greatest tensions and most devastating wars occur when a rising challenger surpasses an established superpower—what scholars call a "power transition." The reality is more complicated.

A country can be rising and falling at the same time: States that we look back on as "rising powers" often experienced economic slowdowns and strategic encirclement by hostile actors. It is the resulting fear of decline—not the optimism created by perpetual ascent—that frequently incites risky, belligerent behavior. When growth slows, anxious expansion often follows. When a country is surrounded by enemies, it may try reckless gambits to break the closing ring. Most important, conflict can occur even when there is no "hegemonic transition": The real trap may come once a previously rising challenger realizes it *won't* overtake its enemies. When a dissatisfied power's window begins to close, when its leaders fear that they cannot deliver the glories they have promised, even a low-probability lunge for victory may seem better than a humiliating descent.

In other words, the reason China's trajectory is so alarming is not that it will inexorably overtake America. It is that some of history's deadliest wars were started by revisionist powers whose future no longer looked so bright.

## WAS THUCYDIDES WRONG?

The current understanding of what causes great-power conflict draws heavily from one of the earliest wars on record. In his chronicle of the Great Peloponnesian War between Athens and Sparta from 431 to 405 BC, Thucydides provided the classic formula. The rise of Athens, with its peerless navy and growing empire, threatened Sparta, a land power that had previously led the Greek world. The Spartans watched nervously as Athens grew, armed, and drew other states into its orbit. Sparta found its influence tested in ways that became harder to abide. Amid a series of escalating crises, Sparta resolved to fight before it was too late—"to throw themselves heart and soul upon the hostile power, and break it, if they could, by commencing the present war."[5] The horrific clash that followed devastated both sides and brought the golden age of Greek civilization to an end.

Thucydides is considered the father of the international relations canon, and his explanation of great-power conflict remains at the heart of that discipline. Power transition theory holds that war is likely when a rising country threatens to overtake an established country. As the

challenger grows stronger, it destabilizes the existing system. It pro-
vokes tests of strength with the reigning power. The outcome is a spiral
of hostility. "War is most likely," one political scientist writes, "during
the periods when the power capabilities of a rising and dissatisfied challenger begin to approach those of the leading state."[6]

In 2015, Harvard University's Graham Allison appropriated the
wisdom of the ancients to explain the rivalries of the present. Throughout history, Allison argued, power transitions have led to war. This
danger is particularly acute because China will soon be "the biggest
player in the history of the world."[7] The task of the coming decades will
be managing the rise of a country that is destined to replace America as
the world's leader, without causing a violent cataclysm along the way.
That formula, not surprisingly, appeals to Xi Jinping, who has cited the
"Thucydides Trap" in calling on America to accept Chinese primacy
in Asia and beyond.[8]

There is an elemental truth to Thucydides's thesis: The rise of new
powers inevitably shakes up the world. Twenty-five hundred years ago,
Athens would not have been nearly so threatening to Sparta had it not
become a mighty superpower. Washington and Beijing would not be
locked in rivalry if China was still a weak, impoverished state. Rising
powers *do* typically expand their influence in ways that threaten reigning powers. But the calculus that produces war isn't as straightforward
as it seems.

To see why, go back to the Peloponnesian War. Donald Kagan,
the leading modern historian of that conflict, shows that the rise of
Athens probably caused the *first* Peloponnesian War, fought from
460 to 455 BC. But that war ended in a comprehensive peace settlement. The causes of the *Great* Peloponnesian War (the one Thucydides
chronicled) were more complex. Athens was, in the years before that
conflict, a *risen* power whose influence was no longer expanding. It

made moves that tested and ultimately ruptured the peace because it feared rapid decline.

The cause was a struggle between a Spartan ally, Corinth, and a neutral power, Corcyra, over an obscure place called Epidamnus. Corinth was on the verge of winning that struggle and adding Corcyra's formidable fleet to its own. That would have given Corinth's ally, Sparta, the ability to neutralize Athens's naval advantage, the basis of its power and prosperity. The Athenians, writes Kagan, "were threatened with a deadly change in the balance of power at one stroke."[9] This nightmare drew Athens into the fight between Corinth and Corcyra—and set off a chain reaction that produced the Great Peloponnesian War.

There's a clue here for understanding what drives great powers to desperation. A country whose relative wealth and power are growing, whose position is improving, will surely enlarge its geopolitical horizons. But it should also want to delay a climactic confrontation—to avoid prematurely bringing down the wrath of the reigning hegemon. Such a country should presumably conduct itself as China did for two decades after the Cold War, by hiding its capabilities and biding its time.

Now imagine an alternative scenario. A dissatisfied state has been building its power and ratcheting up its ambitions. Its leaders have stoked intense nationalism; they have promised the people that past insults will be avenged and great sacrifices will be rewarded. But then the country peaks, perhaps because its economy stalls, perhaps because it runs into a coalition of rivals determined to thwart its rise. A window of opportunity now begins to shut; a window of vulnerability looms. In these circumstances, a revisionist power may behave more aggressively, even unpredictably, because it feels an urge to grab what it can before it is too late.

That's the troubling possibility the United States confronts vis-à-vis China today—and it's one that has played out many times in the past.

## HITTING THE WALL

Let's start with economic slowdowns: What happens when fast-rising countries suffer severe stagnation? To answer this question, we looked at every instance during the past 150 years in which a major power's per capita GDP grew at least twice as fast as the world average for 7 years and then slowed by at least 50 percent over the next 7 years.[10] These are countries that were soaring and then fell back to earth. They usually landed hard.

Most of the rising countries that stagnated during the past 150 years tried to revive their economies through mercantilist policies—the use of state power to lock up markets and resources—and international expansion. They cracked down at home and carved out spheres of influence abroad. They built up their militaries and used them more assertively. In many cases, this behavior fueled great-power tensions. In some cases, it triggered major wars.

Why are stumbling great-powers so problematic? The logic is straightforward. Eras of rapid growth fuel a country's ambitions, raise its citizens' expectations, and unnerve its rivals. During a long economic boom, businesses enjoy swelling profits, and citizens get used to the good life. The country achieves greater international power and prestige. Leaders feed these expectations, promising the people a future of prosperity and greatness. Then stagnation jeopardizes everything.

Slowing growth makes it harder for leaders to keep the people fat and happy. Economic underperformance weakens the country and gives its rivals the upper hand. Fearful of unrest, leaders repress domestic dissent. They become determined to restore stronger growth and keep foreign predators at bay. Expansion seems like an escape hatch—a way of grabbing new sources of wealth, rallying the nation around its leaders, and warding off looming threats.[11]

Many countries have followed this path, including some you might not expect. Democratic France, one of America's key NATO allies, had a long post–World War II boom that fizzled in the 1970s. Paris responded by trying to rebuild its old economic sphere of influence in Africa, deploying 14,000 troops in its former colonies and undertaking a dozen military interventions over the next two decades.[12] Democratic Japan grew even more rapidly in the 1950s and 1960s before slumping in the 1970s. Tokyo reacted by ramping up investment in Southeast Asia, in hopes of establishing a geo-economic domain, and by helping Japanese firms snap up global market share in key industries and secure access to critical resources such as oil. Japan did not become militarily aggressive, in this case, but it developed a powerful navy to protect its investments and sea lanes.[13]

Even America once engaged in anxious expansion. In the 1880s, the long post–Civil War economic surge ended, and the 1890s saw a brutal financial panic and a prolonged depression. National unemployment averaged nearly 12 percent from 1894 to 1898. Strikes, lockouts, and other labor battles became frequent and bloody.[14] Beset by domestic strife, American officials also worried that the country was vulnerable to European mega-empires that were eating up the globe. Africa and Asia had already been devoured; the Western Hemisphere might be next. "Our only rivals in peace as well as enemies in war would be found located at our very doors," Secretary of State Richard Olney warned.[15]

Washington didn't gently accept this fate. The government violently suppressed strikes at home and jacked up tariffs on foreign goods while engaging in a burst of global expansion.[16] The United States pumped investment and exports into new markets in Latin America and East Asia while keeping its home market relatively closed against European goods.[17] It built a vast navy and seized key strategic points such as Puerto Rico, the Philippines, and the Panama Canal route. It fought a war against Spain, sent troops to China, and asserted a right to keep foreign powers out of the Western Hemisphere. "The United States . . . stands face to face with the greatest conjuncture that can confront a people," wrote one leading expansionist. "She must protect the outlets of her trade, or run the risk of suffocation."[18]

Fortunately, these were mild cases of anxious aggrandizement. In each case, democratic institutions served as shock absorbers for aggressive urges and internal tensions. In each case, the country still had a relatively open, dynamic economy that could compete in foreign markets. These characteristics made it easier to restore growth by promoting innovation and peaceful commerce, rather than using full-blown military aggression to create a self-contained economic bloc.[19] Finally, because postwar Japan and postwar France lived within a relatively healthy world order led by Washington, they had limited need—or ability—to engage in the worst forms of mercantilist expansion.

But what happens when stagnation hits authoritarian regimes that lack democratic legitimacy and traffic in blustery nationalism? Whose uncompetitive, state-controlled economies rely on crony capitalist networks that profit from mercantilism? That's when countries simply push their way into foreign markets and seize critical resources, even if it means destabilizing world politics.

Consider imperial Russia. That country enjoyed an economic boom from the late 1880s to the turn of the century. Industrial output doubled, while iron and steel, crude oil, and coal production tripled. By 1900, however, a deep slump was under way. Peasants ransacked estates, workers destroyed railways and factories, and dozens of senior officials were assassinated. Russia's rulers feared that its technological backwardness would condemn it to "industrial captivity" by more advanced nations.[20]

A scared, absolutist government cracked down severely: By 1905, 70 percent of the empire was under martial law and more than 10,000 people had been executed. The Russian military grew, with both the naval budget and tonnage of the fleet rising by nearly 40 percent between 1901 and 1905.[21] Government-controlled banks and industries became tools of economic expansion. St. Petersburg pushed hard to strengthen its influence in East Asia, seeking colonial gains in Korea and sending 170,000 soldiers to occupy Manchuria. These moves, however, backfired: They antagonized Japan, which beat Russia in the first great-power war of the twentieth century.[22]

A century later, Vladimir Putin's Russia turned aggressive under similar circumstances.[23] After the global financial crisis and a crash in oil prices ended a run of hydrocarbon-propelled growth, Putin needed new ways of strengthening Russia's position, propping up its resource-dependent economy, and averting challenges to his rule. He criminalized dissent, murdered his political challengers, and steered Russia deeper into autocracy; he dialed up the nationalism and xenophobia toward foreign enemies.[24] Putin sought to create a Eurasian economic bloc centered on Russia—"a new imperial community," one cheerleader called it. He deployed state-owned enterprises, such as oil giant Rosneft, and government-backed mercenaries as tools of state power in overseas regions. Not least, Russia lopped off chunks of two neighbors (Georgia and Ukraine) that were trying to escape its orbit, while also intervening in the Syrian civil war. "We need a small victorious war," one Russian minister argued (foolishly) in 1904. Russia's twenty-first century tsar knows that playbook well.[25]

Indeed, Russian aggression in Ukraine demonstrates the peaking-power dynamic at work. In the early 2010s, the EU threatened Putin's vision for a Eurasian bloc by offering Ukraine a comprehensive free trade agreement that would have barred many Russian products.[26] The agreement also called for integrating Ukraine into the EU's common security and defense policy, a move Russian leaders may have viewed as a slippery slope leading to NATO membership.[27]

Russia aggressively pressured Ukraine to reject the EU's deal, and in November 2013, Moscow had seemingly achieved its objectives when Ukraine's president, Victor Yanukovych, killed the agreement.[28] But that decision sparked protests in Kyiv that eventually forced Yanukovych to flee to Russia. Russian officials warned that Ukraine was about to split in half, that the EU would swallow the western portion of the country, that Russia would lose its gas deals with Ukraine and its naval base in Crimea, and that the resulting chaos might spark domestic unrest in Russia itself.[29] Faced with a Western-leaning Ukraine and the consequences that might follow, Putin chose to use the fruits of a years-long military buildup to vivisect that country instead. Russia annexed Crimea and fomented insurgencies in eastern Ukraine in 2014, a state of open hostility that lasted until Russia launched a full-scale invasion— representing Europe's largest interstate military conflict since World War II—in 2022.

Economic stagnation even helps explain some of the most violent, radically disruptive behavior the world has ever seen. During the 1920s, Japan and Germany grew rapidly before hitting a wall. During the Great Depression, both countries went on expansionist rampages that were fueled by toxic ideologies as well as a desire to seize land, resources, and other assets before enemies—many of them self-created—could move in for the kill.[30]

All of these cases were complicated: There is never just one factor that drives a country to war. Yet there is a clear pattern. If rapid growth gives countries the *ability* to act boldly, stagnation can provide a powerful *motive* for rasher forms of expansion and belligerence. That's why the most dangerous sequence in international politics is a long ascent followed by the prospect of a sharp decline. We see something similar when we look at how revisionist powers have coped with a second challenge: geopolitical encirclement. Some of the most catastrophic gambles in history have come when once-rising powers concluded that their path to glory was about to be blocked.

## THE SOONER THE BETTER: GERMANY AND WORLD WAR I

Imperial Germany is the textbook example. The Anglo-German rivalry of the late nineteenth and early twentieth centuries is often seen as a forerunner to the U.S.-China competition: Both were cases of a fast-rising, autocratic power challenging the liberal superpower of the day. But the more ominous precedent may be this: War came when a cornered, declining Germany realized that it could *not* get past its rivals without a fight.

World War I marked the calamitous coda to an era of remarkable German ascent. Between 1864 and 1871, Wilhelm I and his "iron chancellor," Otto von Bismarck, forged the German Empire through short, brilliantly orchestrated wars against Denmark, Austria-Hungary, and France. The unified state soon became an industrial juggernaut. By 1910, Germany had Europe's leading economy; by 1914, it produced twice as much steel as Britain and had twice as many miles of railroad track. Defense spending multiplied nearly fivefold between 1880 and 1914; Berlin soon commanded Europe's most fearsome army, and its shipyards were building a navy that would nip at Britain's heels. Looking back, historian Paul Kennedy doubted whether the relative power "of any two neighboring states" had ever changed as much "in the course of one man's lifetime as occurred here between Britain and Germany."[31] Not since Napoleon

had Europe seen a country with such potential to dominate on land
while also vying for supremacy at sea.

Yet Germany's rise was always precarious because that country had
potential foes all around. Its location in the heart of a crowded continent provided tremendous influence but ensured the jealousy of states
along its flanks. Germany rose, moreover, at a time when many of the
world's choice colonial possessions had been claimed or were being
snapped up by established empires that were not eager to share. So even
a strong, surging Germany had to tread carefully, lest it provoke what
Bismarck called the "nightmare of coalitions"—the combined hostility
of countries that could tear it apart.[32]

Until the 1890s, Germany played the game with skill. During
the wars of unification, Bismarck deftly prevented Germany's enemies
from ganging up on it. He refused to march all the way to Vienna
after Prussia had routed Austria-Hungary in 1866, for fear of turning a wounded rival into a lasting enemy; he cleverly provoked France
into starting the war in 1870.[33] After unification, Bismarck manipu-
lated Europe's complex alliance politics and limited Germany's global
ambitions to keep the new empire from being surrounded. "My map of
Africa is here in Europe," he explained: Rather than making itself the
target of Europe's imperial rivalries, Germany should pit its competitors against each other by encouraging *them* to expand abroad.[34]

Yet this nineteenth century "hide and bide" strategy didn't last,
because Bismarck himself didn't last. The chancellor was fired by the
more impulsive Wilhelm II in 1890. Under Wilhelm II, Germany
became less abashed in its pursuit of European and global aggrandizement. It embarked on a "world policy" meant to deliver markets,
resources, and an overseas empire on par with those of Germany's rivals.
It envisioned a German-dominated *Mitteleuropa* that would provide
economic security and a platform to project global power. "The days

when Germans granted one neighbor the earth, the other the sea, and reserved for themselves the sky, where pure doctrine reigns—those days are over," foreign minister and future chancellor Bernhard von Bülow announced in 1897: Germany would claim its "place in the sun."[35]

That policy threatened to leave others in the shade. The quest for imperial gains in Africa, the Near East, the Pacific, and the Western Hemisphere drew Germany into rows with London, Paris, St. Petersburg, and Washington. The great strength of the German army posed a mortal peril to a still-seething France. Perhaps most important, Berlin constructed a powerful "risk fleet" of battleships intended to keep the vaunted Royal Navy at bay and thereby give Germany a free hand in Europe and around the globe. Bismarck had assiduously reassured other countries that Germany would respect the existing order. The actions of his successors raised suspicions that Berlin intended to break that order—to seek "a general political hegemony and maritime ascendancy, threatening the independence of her neighbors and ultimately the existence of England," wrote British diplomat Eyre Crowe.[36]

Germany thus began to precipitate the encirclement Bismarck had feared. In 1894, France and Russia concluded a military alliance aimed at Berlin. Britain threw its energies into maintaining an unmatched fleet of battleships and positioning them near Germany. "Germany keeps her whole fleet always concentrated within a few hours of England," Admiral Jackie Fisher remarked. "We must therefore keep a fleet twice as powerful as that of Germany always concentrated within a few hours of Germany."[37] More damaging, Berlin's assertiveness caused London to settle disputes with its other rivals—France, Russia, Japan, the United States—to focus on the menace across the North Sea. Germany had activated the anxieties that could turn Europe's geography into a deadly trap. It faced, in Bülow's phrasing, a "ring of Powers" who sought "to isolate and paralyze it."[38]

It also faced economic containment. Germany's industrial rise had naturally stimulated insecurities elsewhere. "In every part of the globe they are cutting out English traders," the *Saturday Review* warned in 1875, "and even in England they are seizing on whole branches and even centers of trade as their own."[39] As Germany's conduct became more menacing, its rivals threw up protective tariffs and began consolidating their empires against the emerging challenge. The British were out to "destroy" German industry, the kaiser predicted. Germany must "forestall the evil by building a strong fleet."[40]

Berlin's response was to try to break the ring—through tactics that strengthened it instead. When Germany provoked an imperial imbroglio with France over Morocco in 1905, in hopes of showing that the recent Anglo-French entente was toothless, it simply demonstrated how badly the two countries needed each other—and hastened the formation of a Triple Entente linking Paris, London, and St. Petersburg. When Berlin used coercive threats against Russia during crises in the volatile Balkans in 1908–1909 and 1912–1913, Tsar Nicholas II's government concluded that it must stand firm in the future. And when Germany stirred up another colonial dispute in Morocco in 1911, it produced explicit warnings that Britain did not seek peace "at any price."[41] The tendency, Chancellor Theobald von Bethmann-Hollweg (Bülow's successor) lamented, was to "challenge everybody, get in everyone's way and actually, in the course of all this, weaken nobody."[42] All the while, recurring crises were making Europe a geopolitical hothouse. Fears of war were rising on all sides.

Nothing better illustrated this vicious circle than Germany's war plans. To deal with the threat of a two-front fight against France and Russia, the General Staff had developed its Schlieffen Plan, which envisioned a lightning blow against France so that Germany's forces could then pivot to block slow-mobilizing Russian armies in the East. Yet the only way to defeat France quickly was to skirt the heavy fortifications on the Franco-German frontier by knifing through neutral Belgium. That move might well bring Britain into any European war, because London could not tolerate an enemy dominating the Low Countries just across the water. It was an absurd situation: Germany's abundance of enemies produced high-risk military plans that were liable to create even more.[43] The Schlieffen Plan also made Germany hypersensitive to small shifts in the military balance, which would wreck the exquisite timing and the scheme required.

And *big* shifts were coming. In 1912, Russia approved the expansion of its Baltic fleet; in 1913, it began to enlarge the army by 470,000 men. With French financial backing, Russia was also expanding and modernizing its railroads: Its mobilization time would soon fall from six weeks to two. France had passed new conscription laws that, by extending the term of service from two years to three, threatened to negate the numerical advantage that Germany's larger population provided. The United Kingdom announced that it would build two battleships for every one by Berlin.[44] Germany was still Europe's foremost military power. But by 1916–1917, it would be hopelessly outclassed by the enemy coalition. "I believe a war to be unavoidable and: the sooner the better," Moltke declared in late 1912: Better to fight now than suffer slow suffocation or outright destruction.[45]

There was plenty of cause for fatalism. Germany's isolation had caused it to lean ever more heavily on its principal ally, Austria-Hungary. Yet that multinational empire was being torn apart by ethnic tensions and challenged by a Russian-backed Serbia in the Balkans. Other potential allies, such as Italy and the Ottoman Empire, were fading. Before long, Germany might be all alone.[46]

The economic pressure was also intensifying. Prior to World War

I, Russia was growing at almost 10 percent annually, meaning that Germany was losing ground. London was blocking Germany from accessing the oil its navy needed in Persia, while France was obstructing crucial exports of iron ore. German exporters were petrified that Russia would launch a crippling tariff war. Germany, industrialist Walther Rathenau commented in 1913, was too much at "the mercy of the world market."[47] Its enemies might choke off the markets and resources Germany needed to thrive in a cutthroat world.

At home, too, conditions were flammable. The socialist Left was advancing as labor strikes multiplied. The prestige of the kaiser and the German military was ebbing, and the autocratic political system was under strain. The government had stoked nationalist passions that it was now in danger of disappointing; it had promised triumphs that were not materializing. Even increased repression could not stabilize the situation: The kaiser's aides began to see a brief, victorious war as a last-gasp way of rallying the population behind a faltering regime. "I need" a "declaration of war for reasons of internal politics," Bethmann-Hollweg said.[48] On the eve of World War I, Germany was a mighty state that had become terrified of the future.

The result was a now-or-never mentality. Berlin must strike soon to cripple France as a great power, set Russia back by a generation, and carve out the vast domain—a *Mitteleuropa* stretching from Western Europe to Ukraine, as well as new colonies far afield—it was being denied. It must exploit the closing window of opportunity that its military strength still provided before a window of vulnerability opened wide. "If we do not conjure up a war into being," one of Germany's diplomats quipped, "no one else certainly will do so."[49] Bismarck had once compared preventive war to committing suicide for fear of death. Yet this was the risk German leaders were now willing to take.

The opportunity arose after Serbian radicals assassinated Franz

Ferdinand, the heir to the Austro-Hungarian throne, on June 28, 1914. It didn't initially seem that a global war would erupt: Many European leaders stuck to their summer vacation plans. Yet as more candid German officials later admitted, Berlin did nothing in the subsequent crisis to prevent a major war—while doing much to precipitate one.[50]

The timing was right: Germany's military position might never again be as good. The contours of the crisis were favorable: An enraged Austria-Hungary was sure to align with Germany.[51] The fact that the quarrel had started in a relatively remote corner of Europe provided a fatal glimmer of hope, encouraged by London's initial irresolution, that Great Britain might stay on the sidelines. The politics also looked promising: The government might whip up a patriotic fervor by portraying the clash as a war of necessity against predators closing in for the kill. So Berlin first issued a "blank check" to Austria-Hungary, pushing it to crush Serbia and pledging to back it even at risk of war with Russia and France. As the crisis spiraled, the German government deflected opportunities for a peaceful settlement, while the military prepared to implement the Schlieffen Plan despite the obvious dangers. "This war will turn into a world war in which England will also intervene," Moltke acknowledged—but the alternative was for Germany to be contained and its ambitions extinguished.[52]

At the last minute, the kaiser waffled, fearful of a great catastrophe. But he ultimately pushed ahead rather than disrupt the elaborate timing of the Schlieffen Plan—delaying the public announcement of Germany's mobilization just enough to make it appear that Russia had decided for war first. "The government has succeeded very well in making us appear as the attacked," one military official wrote.[53] What ensued was not the unifying victory Wilhelm sought, but a four-year slugfest that destroyed his regime, toppled empires, and introduced the world to industrial-age mass slaughter. "Lord yes, in a certain sense it

was a preventive war," Bethmann-Hollweg admitted in 1915, motivated by the belief that "today war is still possible without defeat, but
not in two years!"[54]

World War I, like every war, had many causes. But at root it was
a German preventive war, launched because the kaiser's government
saw no other way of escaping the trap it had laid for itself. Germany
was a revisionist power whose rise had been stunted by the blowback
from its own designs. So it wagered and lost everything on a showdown
that—as Moltke rightly predicted—would "annihilate the civilization
of almost the whole of Europe for decades to come."[55]

## "CLOSE ONE'S EYES AND JUMP": JAPAN AND WORLD WAR II

In some cases, economic slumps cause major powers to lash out instead
of accepting a new, disappointing normal. In others, expansionist states
provoke their own containment and then go for broke. Imperial Japan
experienced *both* dynamics in the 1920s and 1930s. What ensued was
a ghastly Pacific War within World War II.

For more than a half-century after the Meiji Restoration in 1868,
Japan was rising impressively. The creation of a modern economy and a
strong military allowed Japan to defeat the Qing Dynasty in one war,
rout tsarist Russia in another, and accumulate colonial privileges in
Taiwan, Korea, and China. During World War I, Japan seized German holdings in China and the Pacific. Yet Japan was hardly a hyper-
belligerent rogue state. It allied with Great Britain from 1902 to 1923;
it accepted American influence in the Philippines in exchange for
Washington blessing Japanese control of Korea. All the while, Japan's
economy was zipping along at 6.1 percent annual growth from 1904
to 1919. The value of Japanese exports tripled during World War I.[56]

Into the 1920s, Japan looked like a responsible stakeholder. Voting rights expanded and the political system became more democratic. The Japanese government signed a set of treaties, known as the Washington System, in which it joined America, Britain, and other countries in creating a stable balance of naval power, pledging to respect the sovereignty and territorial integrity of China, and forswearing unilateral expansion in the Asia-Pacific. In 1923, Franklin D. Roosevelt commented that America and Japan "had not a single valid reason . . . for fighting each other."[57] And as long as the global economy was working relatively well for Japan, it had good reason not to cause too much trouble. Japan needed "the great market of China," Japanese foreign minister Kijūrō Shidehara explained. But if it chased the "territorial expansion" favored by some military officials, it would "merely destroy international cooperation."[58]

The trouble began when the prosperity ended. Japanese growth dropped to 1.8 percent annually during the 1920s.[59] A major earthquake and a banking collapse rocked the economy. Rising American tariffs battered Japanese silk exports. Then the Great Depression struck. Markets slammed shut and Japanese exports fell by 50 percent in a single year.[60] More than 2.6 million citizens lost their jobs; farmers resorted to selling their daughters.[61] Communist and anarchist influences proliferated. "Unemployment is increasing daily. The family is breaking up. Starving people fill the streets," one government official wrote.[62] Above all, the global turn to protectionism made Japan's pursuit of integration seem quixotic—and made a quest for expansion and autarky more attractive. "The economic warfare in the world," future foreign minister Yosuke Matsuoka observed, "is tending to create larger economic blocs." A "suffocated" Japan needed "room that will let us breathe."[63]

The depression made Japan especially sensitive to changes in

China. During the late 1920s, a nationalist movement under Chiang Kai-shek had begun attacking Japan's economic privileges and contesting its influence. Chiang's Soviet-trained army was on the march. Other rivals were, simultaneously, prowling: The Soviets sent 100,000 troops to retake a crucial railway that had been seized by a Manchurian warlord, then secured an agreement that allowed their goods, but not Japan's, to pass through the region duty-free.[64] Eighty percent of Japan's overseas business investment was in China. Tokyo relied on Manchuria for 40 percent of its trade and critical resources such as coal, iron, and grain.[65] The region was a crucial buffer against foreign encroachment. As Japan stagnated, other powers seemed primed to pounce.

Tokyo's answer was fascism at home and violence abroad. From the late 1920s onward, the military conducted a slow-motion coup, while ultranationalist zealots murdered prime ministers and other officials deemed insufficiently patriotic. The government outlawed dissent, jailed its critics, and built a pervasive police state. It exerted greater control over banks and industries to harness the nation's resources for rivalry. An ascendant military faction preached the need for "total war" and began mobilizing society for conflict.[66] By 1941, one Western observer wrote, Japan had walked "a long way on the road to totalitarian statehood."[67]

It had also become a serial aggressor. The army seized control of Manchuria in 1931, making it a Japanese puppet state. In 1932–1933, Japanese troops pushed farther down China's coast and into its interior. In 1934, Tokyo declared East Asia its exclusive domain—a reverse Monroe Doctrine that, U.S. ambassador Joseph Grew wrote, "places China in a state of tutelage under Japan."[68] Withdrawing from the Washington treaties, Japan also began a massive military buildup featuring aircraft carriers, monster battleships, and state-of-the-art fighter planes. And by 1936, Japanese officials had drawn up plans for a vast Asian empire that would make Japan a superpower by giving it copious resources, markets, and geopolitical space.

Under this plan, Manchuria would be developed and large swaths of China would be seized. Japan would grab European colonies in Southeast Asia that were rich in oil, rubber, and other resources; it would claim strategic islands throughout the western and central Pacific. All of this would require preparations for war with the countries that would surely resist Japanese dominance of such a large, vital region—the Soviet Union, the United Kingdom, and America.[69] Unless Japan got what it demanded, Japanese prime minister Fumimaro Konoye had earlier written, it must "destroy the status quo for the sake of self-preservation."[70]

Konoye was a man of his word. In 1937, Japan launched a massive, brutal war in China, using up to 800,000 troops in a bid to force Chiang into submission. In 1938, Konoye announced the creation of the "New Order," a Japanese-dominated Asia in which all roads led to Tokyo. Konoye's government put the country on a war footing to support this expanding imperial project, while allying with other fascist powers—Nazi Germany and Italy—seeking empires of their own. "The era of democracy is finished," Matsuoka declared. "Totalitarianism . . . will control the world."[71]

Yet war in the expanses of China turned into a quagmire: Even before Pearl Harbor, Japanese forces had paid a blood price of 600,000 casualties.[72] It forced food shortages and other sacrifices on a restive population. Perversely, expansion also left Tokyo *more* reliant on its potential enemies for resources to keep the war machine humming. Before World War II, Japan "imported 80 percent of its oil, 90 percent of its gasoline, 74 percent of its scrap iron, and 60 percent of its machine tools" from America.[73] "We are aiming to put an end to seventy years' dependence on Britain and America commercially and economically," army officials had vowed—but an interminable war in China had the opposite effect.[74]

It simultaneously put a target on Japan's back. The push into Manchuria and northern China eventually incited a brief but punishing war with the Soviet Union, in which Stalin's Red Army pounded Japan's Sixth Army. Japan's viciousness in China and covetous gaze toward Southeast Asia alienated the United Kingdom and other European powers. And while America had reacted weakly to the conquest of Manchuria, the audacity of Japan's drive for regional dominance and the sheer horror of the war in China—the terror bombing, the deliberate massacre and rape of civilians, the use of biological weapons—began to make Washington an enemy.[75]

"The present reign of terror and international lawlessness," FDR declared, threatened "the very foundations of civilization."[76] By 1940, the United States was floating Chiang's government financially and constricting the export of aviation materials, high-octane gasoline, scrap metal, and other goods to Japan. America was also responding to threats in Europe and Asia by making itself a military superpower. That year, the U.S. Navy placed orders for 9 battleships, 11 aircraft carriers, 8 heavy cruisers, 31 light cruisers, and 181 destroyers. FDR set a target of producing 50,000 airplanes per year; Congress raised the authorized manpower of the U.S. Army by nearly 1 million men.[77] And when Japan signed the Tripartite Pact with Italy and Germany, while also occupying northern French Indochina in September 1940, U.S. officials concluded that Tokyo had cast its lot with vile gangsters who were destroying the world.

By this point, a strategic noose was tightening around Japan's neck. In view of the "total war" clique, Japan had to keep pushing—especially into Indochina and the Dutch East Indies—to build its autarkic empire. Yet doing so meant marching toward war with Britain and with America, a country whose economy was *twelve times* the size of Japan's.[78] The United States could throttle Japan by turning off the oil shipments that fueled its army and navy; America could mobilize unmatchable military power. "Anyone who has seen the auto factories in Detroit and the oil fields in Texas knows that Japan lacks the national power for a naval race with America," Admiral Isoroku Yamamoto warned.[79] Like Wilhelm's Germany, Japan had cornered itself: Expansion had led to isolation that could only be overcome by a humiliating retreat—withdrawal from China and abandonment of the New Order—or by staking everything on a wild dash for victory.

What made the bet-the-house option more appealing was that Japan had, in late 1940 and 1941, a narrow window of military opportunity. Germany's blitzkrieg in Western Europe had broken France and left Britain fighting for its life, creating "the opportunity of a century" in Southeast Asia.[80] FDR was distracted by the undeclared battle with Hitler for control of the Atlantic. Japan's nonaggression pact with the Soviet Union in April 1941, followed by Hitler's invasion of the country in June, temporarily neutralized any threat from the north. Not least, Japan still had a military lead thanks to its early rearmament: It possessed ten aircraft carriers to the three that Anglo-American forces had across the entire Pacific.[81] The question was how long the window would stay open.

The answer came in the second half of 1941. After Japanese forces moved into southern Indochina, FDR imposed a full oil embargo that threatened to leave Japan's ships and planes running on fumes. Japan was "like a fish in a pond from which the water was gradually being drained away," its leaders believed.[82] America was bulking up its defenses in the Philippines with B-17 bombers and P-40 fighters. Military staff talks with the British and Dutch, and economic sanctions coordinated with them, made the Japanese fear that their encirclement was nearly complete. And with American rearmament accelerating, the U.S. Navy would, by 1942–1943, have "four times the tonnage and four times the air power of Japan's."[83] At that point, Japan would have no hope of hegemony in Asia. Its leaders would be totally discredited: All the blood the nation had shed, all the privations it had endured, would be for naught. America would "demand more and more concessions," Japanese leaders concluded, "and ultimately our empire will lie prostrate at the feet of the United States."[84]

In the fall of 1941, the Japanese government decided to seize the Dutch East Indies, Philippines, and other possessions from Singapore to the central Pacific, even though this meant war with Britain and America. Few Japanese officials believed that the country could win an all-out struggle. "We can give you a wild show for six months to a year, but if the war drags on to two and three years, I cannot be confident of the outcome," Yamamoto predicted.[85] But they feared that the alternative was a sharp decline that would leave Japan impotent before its enemies. And they hoped that a series of lightning blows could so demoralize the United States that it might sue for peace rather than continue the fight. At best, war would bring terrible risks; at worst, it might cause national destruction. But sometimes, said Hideki Tojo, the general who ultimately led Japan into war, "one must conjure up enough courage, close one's eyes, and jump."[86]

This was the genesis of the surprise attack on Pearl Harbor. If war was inevitable, then why not buy more temporary military advantage—and more time to digest Japan's new conquests—by devastating the U.S. Pacific Fleet? The irony was that the attack was so devastating and, in American eyes, so treacherous, that it galvanized the country to destroy Japan whatever the cost. "The Japanese," one congressman thundered, "have gone stark, raving mad, and have, by their unprovoked attack committed military, naval, and national suicide."[87]

World War II would prove nearly suicidal for Japan. The cause, however, was not insanity but the desperation of a country whose revisionist dreams were about to be shattered. Japan had been on an aggressive tear for a decade. It became most dangerous when it realized that time was running out.

Historians typically think of pre–World War I Germany and pre–World War II Japan as rising countries. Japan had gone from weakness to strength in the decades after 1868; its empire grew rapidly in the 1930s. Germany was a vastly more formidable contender in 1914 than it had been in 1871. Both countries had risen far enough, fast enough to fundamentally challenge the global status quo.

Yet at the climactic moment, imperial German and imperial Japanese leaders did not feel like they were moving up. Stagnation, encirclement, or some combination convinced them that their moment was slipping away. A revisionist power that has begun to fear the future may well act more impulsively than one that thinks tomorrow will be better than today. That's the real trap we ought to worry about—the trap in which an aspiring superpower peaks and then refuses to bear the painful consequences of descent.

China's present-day leaders would be outraged to hear the CCP compared to imperial Germany, let alone to imperial Japan. In fairness, China hasn't embarked on anything like the military aggression that Japan perpetrated for a decade prior to World War II.

But don't take too much comfort. Imperial Germany didn't wage a major war for four decades after 1871, yet in 1914 it did much to thrust the world into a catastrophe on an almost unimaginable scale. World War I was "the deluge . . . a convulsion of nature," said Britain's David Lloyd George, "an earthquake which is upheaving the very rocks of European life."[88] When revisionist powers see the writing on the wall, things can get ugly quickly—with consequences that might have seemed inconceivable not long before.

Here's another reason for concern: Like Japan, China checks a lot of worrying boxes. It is dealing with a prolonged economic slowdown that will be extremely difficult to escape. It is encountering a ring of rivals that are working, albeit incrementally, to stymie Beijing's advance. China also has an authoritarian system and an economic model that make mercantilist expansion more attractive. Its trade expectations are turning starkly negative. Indeed, China is already engaging in the practices—the military buildup, the search for spheres of influence, the effort to control critical technologies and resources—we would expect from a state in its position. If there is a recipe for aggression by a country that has risen remarkably but is now struggling to deal with stagnation and encirclement, China has all the critical ingredients. So let's now look closely at what moves a more combative China might make.

# 5

## The Gathering Storm

The Chinese H-6K bomber took off from an airfield on the mainland, with two advanced fighter jets as escorts. It flew east, between Taiwan and the Philippines, en route to the open Pacific. When it came within range of its target, it released a precision-guided missile that ripped into Andersen Air Force Base on Guam, triggering massive explosions and ravaging the central hub for U.S. airpower in the western Pacific. The attack was a devastating salvo in the long-feared Sino-American war.

Fortunately, the incident was only a video simulation, released by the People's Liberation Army Air Force (PLAAF) in September 2020 to show off its improving skills and capabilities. In the best tradition of Chinese intellectual property theft, the PLAAF even spliced in footage from the Hollywood films *Transformers* and *The Rock*. But the video—call it "Wolf-Warrior cinematography"—was just the latest warning about a scary shift in Chinese strategy.

Future historians will say we should have seen it coming. Xi Jinping has been telegraphing a Chinese turn to the dark side since he took power in 2012. His internal speeches on national security have consistently stressed two themes: First, China faces worsening threats. Second, the CCP must preemptively crush those threats before they destroy its rule and derail its grand plans for the future. The primary threats Xi worries about are the ones we've described—slowing growth and foreign hostility—and the response he advocates resembles that of past peaking powers: a surge of mercantilism, repression, and revanchism.

What will this look like? China probably won't expand on all fronts in a mad frenzy or impose North Korea–style lockdowns on its population. Xi and his cronies are too smart for that. They know what happened when Germany and Japan tried to run the table in Eurasia, and they saw how rigid totalitarianism and autarky doomed the Soviet Union. But China's leaders also know that surrendering to a "new normal" of sluggish growth and strategic encirclement would expose them to foreign predation and domestic unrest. So the CCP will engage in calculated coercion and expansion to keep rivals at bay and secure the Chinese dream. Xi has already started to implement key elements of this strategy—and it's not a pretty sight.

For starters, China will redouble its efforts to forge an economic empire across Eurasia and Africa. Awash in excess production capacity at home and confronted by rising foreign protectionism, China is intensifying a massive campaign to carve out exclusive economic zones where its firms will enjoy privileged access to markets and raw materials. At the same time, China is racing to claim technological primacy and spread its digital influence around the world. These efforts are meant, in Xi's words, to make China "invincible"—to give Beijing leverage to lord over enemies and vassals.[1] Collectively, China's actions threaten to balkanize the global economy and fuel a new Cold War.

An insecure China will also more zealously roll back the frontiers of freedom. The CCP won't export a specific "China model," but it will try to protect its regime by shifting the global balance between autocracy and democracy. Beijing is quickly becoming a potent anti-democratic force, armed with more advanced tools of surveillance and punishment than Mao Zedong ever could have imagined. And it is working hard to prop up dictators and destabilize liberal societies just as the democratic world is suffering its greatest crisis since the 1930s.

Finally, China is gearing up for war. Its ongoing military buildup is unlike any since World War II. Although China's neighbors and the United States are belatedly beefing up their militaries, many of their new weapons systems won't be operational for years. In the meantime, China will have a chance to seize contested territory in East Asia and blast through the chain of U.S. alliances along its maritime flank.

In each of these areas, China is trying to sprint through near-term windows of opportunity before they close and longer-term windows of vulnerability open. In so doing, China is walking a familiar path of ambition, desperation, and aggression. Whereas a rising China could afford to tolerate some dissent, forgo some opportunities for expansion, and de-escalate crises—confident that its wealth, power, and status were rising—a peaking China will be more desperate to score geopolitical wins and primed to overreact to slights and setbacks. Having spent decades building up its military and developing powerful tools of economic influence, China now looks ready to cash in on those capabilities while it has the chance. The results could be disastrous for the world.

## CHINA'S HAIR-TRIGGER SECURITY STRATEGY

In 2014, China produced a formal national security strategy for the first time and established a new National Security Commission to orchestrate it.[2] Xi left no doubt about why. In a series of speeches, he said that China faced "the most complicated internal and external factors in its history"[3] and "confronted increasing threats and challenges."[4] To underscore the peril, Xi quoted from the *Book of Changes*, a classic text from the Warring States period (500–200 BC) in which China collapsed into internecine strife: "One should be mindful of possible danger in times of peace, downfall in times of survival, and chaos in times of stability."[5]

Foreign observers might dismiss Xi's warning as paranoia or a ploy to justify strongman rule. But China's leaders saw this dark period coming years ago. In 2002, the official mantra, coined by then-president Jiang Zemin, was that China would enjoy a two-decade "period of strategic opportunity" marked by peaceful international relations and steady economic development. Now those twenty years are up, and the CCP's new catchphrase is that China is witnessing "profound changes unseen in 100 years," a slogan that connotes both tantalizing opportunity and grave threats.[6] A century ago, the global balance was in flux, as old empires crumbled and rising powers emerged. Yet those rising powers were eventually destroyed in a global war. Moreover, China spent part of the 1920s mired in its so-called Warlord Era—a period every bit as bad as it sounds—which erupted after foreign powers and Western-educated Chinese revolutionaries brought down the Qing Dynasty.

Today, CCP leaders know that their nation again faces big problems, in the form of slowing growth and foreign encirclement. China's new national security strategy is designed to address those threats in two ways.

First, the strategy "integrates security into every domain and every process of national development."[7] Whereas regime security used to be one of many government priorities (albeit the most important), now it is *the* priority.[8] All other issues—economic development, technological innovation, environmental policy—are adjuncts to the prime directive of keeping the party in power. As a result, every issue is a matter of national security. A trade war is no longer just an economic disagreement; it is an assault on China's comprehensive national power and a possible prelude to a shooting war. This securitization of policy making is dangerous, because it elevates every concern to the level of a vital national interest and justifies extreme responses. If a competing power tries to hurt China's economy, for example, all options are on the table, including military retaliation.

Second, China's strategy embraces preventive solutions. Whereas previous Chinese administrations espoused a doctrine of "stability maintenance," the new policy focuses on "preventing and controlling" threats before they metastasize. Chinese documents compare national security threats to cancerous tumors that need to be cut out quickly before they spread to vital organs of the state. Rival ideologies, such as liberalism and Islamism, are infectious diseases against which China's population must be immunized. As Sheena Chestnut Greitens has shown, these medical metaphors justify targeting and "treating" people long before they display threatening symptoms.[9] The clearest illustration is in Xinjiang, where China has extrajudicially locked up more than 1 million Uighurs in concentration camps.[10] But China is applying preventive logic in foreign affairs, too, in ways that previous peaking powers would find familiar.

## THE LENIN TRAP

China's main challenge isn't the Thucydides Trap; it's what Vladimir Lenin called imperialism, a process he predicted would lead to economic ruin and war.[11] Lenin defined imperialism as a capitalist country's attempt to secure new markets and resources abroad when its home economy becomes oversaturated with production capacity.[12] Unless the country finds new markets, Lenin theorized, it would suffer economic stagnation. Growth would cease, jobs would vanish, and domestic unrest would spike. To avoid this fate, a country must carve out an exclusive economic zone abroad—aka, an empire—where its firms will have easy access to consumers and cheap raw materials. The late nineteenth century "scramble for Africa" in which European powers colonized 90 percent of the continent in thirty years was exhibit A for Lenin's theory.

In a twist of fate, "Communist" China now looks primed for capitalist imperialism. Its economy is glutted with excess capacity generated by decades of subprime lending. The main markets where it used to dump its products—North America, Europe, and Japan—are increasingly unwilling to absorb an endless flood of Chinese goods. Since 2008, China has responded to these trends with a two-step plan. First, lend more than a trillion dollars to foreigners so they buy enough Chinese goods and services to keep CCP Inc. in business.[13] Second, use the proceeds to become a technological powerhouse by pumping investment into R&D, buying and stealing foreign technology, and using subsidies and trade barriers to protect Chinese firms from foreign competition. The resulting surge of innovation, Beijing hopes, will reinvigorate China's economy and boost its power.

As Lenin predicted, however, expanding abroad while practicing protectionism at home tends to incite foreign opposition. When a great power dumps products overseas while keeping its market relatively closed, it antagonizes trade partners. The result is vicious competition—sometimes military conflict—over markets, resources, and status. In addition, when an imperial power saddles developing nations with debt and coerces them to buy its products, nationalist movements rise up to resist. The CCP is experiencing these dynamics today, as rich countries rethink economic engagement with China while poor countries demand better terms for their BRI contracts or quit the initiative entirely. But China is trapped: It cannot abandon economic imperialism or truly reform its economy without endangering the crony capitalism that sustains its political system.[14] If it gives up on creating spheres of influence, it will be strategically naked before its rivals. So Beijing is doubling down on a quest for empire.

Part of this quest will involve old-fashioned tools. As resistance to China's neocolonial development projects grows, Beijing may feel compelled to use heavier-handed methods—even military intervention—to protect its informal empire. As China worries more about the availability of resources and the security of long supply lines, it could strive harder to build additional military bases, deploy a global navy, and plunder contested areas such as the South China Sea. As China becomes more dependent on its empire, in other words, it will become more likely to defend that empire through rough methods that invite international conflict.[15] That's a worrying possibility—but just as worrying is the reality posed by a new form of Chinese imperialism, symbolized by a policy called "dual circulation."

"Dual circulation" is an innocuous sounding program with portentous implications. The basic goal is to enhance China's economic self-reliance (the "great internal circulation") and then pry open foreign markets and extract foreign technology and resources from a position of strength (the "great international circulation").[16] By producing more of what it needs at home, and by dominating the production of linchpin technologies and resources, China can dictate terms economically and geopolitically. China already has a record of exploiting pockets of economic leverage to turn the screws on foreign countries and companies.[17] Now it is gearing up to wield economic coercion on a massive scale by becoming *the* supplier of vital products and services. China must "successfully fight tough battles for the key core technologies," Xi declared in 2020. In another speech, he said that Beijing must "enhance our superiority across the entire production chain."[18]

Like much of China's statecraft, dual circulation sits at the intersection of opportunity and vulnerability. During the 2010s, China bolted out to a lead in areas such as 5G telecommunications by using heavy state subsidies to help Huawei and other firms develop key products and gobble up global market share. "We were asleep at the switch," admitted Mike Brown, director of the Pentagon's Defense Innovation Unit.[19] While the United States was gradually realizing the strategic implications of technologies such as artificial intelligence and synthetic biology, and while the U.S. government had a frosty relationship with major tech firms, Beijing was starting a major, state-backed push—Made in China 2025—to zoom ahead in key areas of competition.[20]

But these initial gains haven't yet allowed China to overcome its deep dependence on foreign technology and resources. In today's hostile geopolitical climate, that dependence could prove fatal. Washington and its allies are trying to "decapitate" Huawei by blocking its access to high-end computer chips.[21] China's aviation industry is being grounded by U.S. and allied restrictions on jet engines and avionics.[22] American tariffs have crimped China's exports: Trump's "trade protectionism and economic hegemony," Xi admitted, were "having a great impact."[23] And there remain many more pressure points for China's rivals to squeeze: China imports roughly 70–80 percent of its oil, computer chips, high-end sensors, and advanced medical devices as well as 90 percent of its advanced manufacturing equipment.[24] This dependence, *People's Daily* has written, is China's "Achilles' Heel."[25]

"Dual circulation," then, is more than a buzzword. It is an effort to wring maximum strategic advantage out of China's initial technological advances before foreign rivals smother Beijing's rise. Confronted with growing global animosity, China's only option is to become less dependent on foreigners—and to make them more dependent on China.

The first step, according to government documents, is to dominate production of "choke-point" technologies and fill "empty spots" that could cause Chinese supply chains to break "during crucial times."[26] China's latest five-year plan, made public in March 2021, mandates 7 percent annual increases in R&D spending, a rate of growth faster than what is planned for the military budget. China's banks have set aside tens of billions of dollars to lend to more than 1,000 Chinese firms in strategic industries, including artificial intelligence, quantum computing, semiconductors, advanced robotics, and synthetic biology.[27] The objective is for China to produce 70 percent of key components in strategic industries by the end of the decade. To meet that goal, Beijing is pressing private tech firms into national service, tapping their data, and obliging them to develop new technologies and hand them over to the government—part of another innocuous-sounding doctrine called "civil-military fusion."[28]

China's attempt to hoard global data is particularly telling. In 2013, shortly after coming to power, Xi declared: "The vast ocean of data, just like oil resources during industrialization, contains immense productive power and opportunities. Whoever controls big data technologies will control the resources for development and have the upper hand."[29] Since then, Beijing has become the world's most powerful data broker by walling Chinese data off from the world while buying and stealing other countries' data. A web of new laws requires all firms operating in China to store their data locally and grant full access and control to the CCP. Foreign firms can't even send a memo about data from China to their home headquarters without Beijing's blessing. As a result, Apple, Tesla, and other major tech firms are rushing to build dedicated Chinese data centers. Meanwhile, China is sucking up data from abroad by hacking multinational corporate databases and buying foreign companies. It is a nakedly mercantilist strategy to dominate the most important resource in the world.

China's efforts to harness data are part of a broader push for primacy in artificial intelligence (AI). AI is "one of the most important things humanity is working on," Google CEO Sundar Pichai said in 2018. "It is more profound than . . . electricity or fire."[30] Hyperbole aside, experts generally agree that AI will create vast increases in economic productivity, perhaps doubling growth rates in the next twenty years. It could change how countries fight, by allowing the most advanced militaries to better understand the battlefield, enhance their speed of decision, and coordinate complex operations. Whoever harnesses AI could "have a decisive advantage . . . for years to come," warned Secretary of Defense Mark Esper in 2020.[31] AI will enable new, paradigm-shifting forms of espionage and disinformation; it is already being integrated into new mechanisms of social control.

No wonder Xi seeks to make China the world leader in AI by 2030.[32] Beijing is betting that AI dominance will give it great geopolitical leverage and freedom of action—perhaps allowing it simply to leapfrog countries blocking its advance.

The second step in China's economic strategy is to wire the world by installing 5G networks, fiber-optic cables, and satellite systems in dozens of countries worldwide, as part of its Digital Silk Road.[33] By laying down vital communications networks, Beijing will be able to track and store the data that passes through them, reaping enormous espionage opportunities, both corporate and strategic, and opportunities to coerce countries by threatening to manipulate or shut down their networks. When the United Kingdom was considering letting Huawei build its 5G network, for example, the Trump administration warned that America wouldn't share sensitive intelligence with a country whose communications were so susceptible to being compromised.[34] For Beijing, that was presumably the point: How can countries help America contain China if they have become dependent on technologies provided by companies in thrall to the CCP?

China is well on its way to dominating global networks. It is the world's largest provider of telecommunications technology. It has already become a landing point or supplier for 12 percent of the world's submarine cables, which carry 95 percent of international data. Huawei claims to have cloud computing contracts with 140 countries; another Chinese company, Hengtong Group, has installed 15 percent of the world's fiber optics.[35] China's BeiDou satellite network has been adopted by dozens of countries and provides greater coverage over 165 of the world's capital cities than does the U.S. Global Positioning System (GPS).[36] China's gains in global networks could be long-lasting, because telecom and satellite infrastructures are extremely expensive to replace. Once a country adopts China's systems, it is basically locked in.

Think of this as a counter-encirclement strategy: If China can draw countries throughout Eurasia and beyond into its technological grasp, it can escape the economic and geopolitical trap in which it has become ensnared.

Finally, China is racing to set international technical standards for next-generation technology such as advanced microchips, the internet of things, cloud computing, big data, 5G, intelligent health care, and AI.[37] In most of these industries, there will be only one set of global standards, and the country that sets them will likely rule the market because its products will already meet the required specifications. The Chinese recognize this advantage and have a saying: third-tier companies make products, second-tier companies make technology, top-tier companies set standards. The CCP also has a plan, China Standards 2035, dedicated to dictating international technical standards. As of 2021, Beijing led four of the fifteen science- and technology-related agencies of the United Nations (compared to one led by the United States) and submitted more standard-setting proposals to international bodies than any other country. "Global technical standards are still in the process of being formed," said Dai Hong, a member of China's National Standardization Management Committee, in 2018. "This gives China's industry and standards the opportunity to surpass the world."[38]

The boldness here is remarkable: If this modern-day imperialism succeeds, China will rule over a new "sinosphere," in which global networks of trade and innovation once dominated by the West will cluster around Beijing. This scenario keeps many American strategists up at night. But another scenario that could be just as troubling is if Beijing's efforts succeed only partially, leaving China strong enough to scare and pressure many countries, but not strong enough to feel secure about its long-term prospects. The world would then face a more muscular but still distressed China, a combustible combination.

China's leaders know this partial-success scenario is a distinct possibility: The international backlash against Huawei threatens their scheme to install the guts of global telecommunications. Nor can the CCP have much confidence in its new innovation initiative, given that Beijing spent a decade and tens of billions of dollars on a domestic microchip industry, yet still relies on imports for 80 percent of the country's computing needs.[39] China also spent tens of billions of dollars on biotech, yet its COVID-19 vaccines were lapped in quality by the wonder drugs produced in America and other democratic countries.[40] And while Beijing has made great progress in a relatively narrow swath of AI applications, such as surveillance, it still lags significantly behind the United States across a wider array of AI subfields and uses.[41] Given the obstacles China faces in breaking free of Lenin's trap, the CCP is hedging its bets by honing other tools of influence, including powerful ideological weapons.

## DEMOCRACY PREVENTION

At the darkest moment of World War II, there were perhaps a dozen democracies in the world.[42] As late as 1989, there were twice as many autocratic governments as democracies. Twenty years later, however, democracies outnumbered autocracies 100 to 78, and the share of the world's population living under autocracy had fallen by half. From a U.S. perspective, democracy's global advance was one of the most hopeful developments of the postwar era. From the perspective of China's leaders, it was a clear sign that the liberal world order was rigged against their form of government and needed to be changed before it destroyed their regime.

According to Beijing's narrative, the problem started at the beginning of the postwar period, when the United States exploited its dominant position to inject radical liberal ideas into international institutions. For example, the UN's 1948 Universal Declaration on Human Rights was modeled on the U.S. Bill of Rights. It states that all humans are born free and have the right to overthrow governments that fail to respect that freedom. In later decades, America helped foster democratic institutions in numerous countries, including some of China's neighbors: Japan, South Korea, and Taiwan. The expanding global posse of democracies subsequently used military force, economic sanctions, and an array of media and human rights organizations to undermine dozens of autocracies—not just tin-pot dictators, but also the Soviet Union and nearly China itself in 1989. "Capitalist forces will always use subversion to exterminate socialist countries and the socialist system," CCP officials wrote.[43]

Although PRC leaders long chafed at this ideological pressure, it was bearable so long as China enjoyed a booming economy and a stable periphery. With a GDP growing three times faster than the democratic average in the 1990s and 2000s, it was easy for Beijing to persuade people at home and abroad that authoritarianism was best for China, if not for other countries.[44]

But now, with a slowing economy and brewing international hostility, autocracy is no longer an easy sell. China's citizens were willing to forgo political rights when their bank accounts and their country's international status were swelling, but it's an open question whether they would do so under harsher conditions. That question is especially pressing with regard to China's millennials, who have known nothing but upward economic and international mobility. When that cohort was being born in the 1980s, Deng Xiaoping warned that opening the "window" to breathe the "fresh air" of Western commerce would also allow in "flies" in the form of seductive ideas and corrupting influences.[45] What he did not say, but knew very well, was that rapid growth and engagement with the West could also change the Chinese people, raising their expectations in ways that the regime might one day struggle to satisfy.

China's rulers also have long understood what political scientists have proven empirically: Autocracies often fall in waves, as revolutionary activity in one country inspires popular uprisings in others.[46] A democratic domino effect brought down Communist regimes across Eastern Europe in 1989. A fruit vendor who immolated himself in Tunisia in 2011 set much of the Middle East aflame in revolt. The lesson is that revolution anywhere can be a threat to autocracy everywhere—even to regimes that seemed stable weeks or even days before.[47]

This lurking threat is why the CCP has become so much more repressive in the past decade—why it has worked proactively to jail dissidents, mobilize security forces, censor information, and preempt popular unrest. Yet China is now strong enough that it has options besides hunkering down against foreign pressure. Xi believes that the CCP's domestic power will be enhanced if authoritarianism is prevalent and democracies are dysfunctional, because fellow despots won't punish China for human rights abuses, and the Chinese people won't want to emulate chaotic liberal systems. He thinks that preventing anti-authoritarian revolts in other countries will reduce the possibility that they might erupt in China. And he believes that silencing critics abroad will limit the challenges the CCP faces at home. So Xi is moving to secure his regime by rolling back democracy overseas.

China has gone on the ideological offensive in recent years and taken its repression global. Beijing now spends billions of dollars annually on an "anti-democratic toolkit" of NGOs, media outlets, diplomats, advisers, hackers, and bribes all designed to prop up autocrats and sow discord in democracies.[48] Whereas China once worried about insulating itself from foreign popular unrest, it now aims to prevent that unrest from breaking out in the first place.[49] The CCP provides fellow autocracies with guns, money, and protection from UN sanctions. Chinese officials offer their authoritarian brethren riot-control gear and pointers in how to build a surveillance state. Beijing also runs interference for authoritarian regimes by using a vast array of global media to tout the accomplishments of illiberal rule, argue that democracy is a neocolonial imposition, and highlight hyper-partisanship in the United States.

It might be tempting to dismiss China's democracy prevention efforts as "world politics as usual." After all, autocrats have been colluding to hold liberalism at bay ever since Russia, Austria, and Prussia helped crush the French Revolution. Vladimir Putin's Russia is pursuing a similar agenda in the former Soviet Union and beyond. But China's ideological assault is more profound, for three reasons.

First, it capitalizes on a disturbing recent trend. The long arc of history may have bended, since World War II, toward greater freedom. But according to the statistics compiled by Freedom House, authoritarianism has been spreading, and democracy receding, every year since 2006.[50] The causes of democratic backsliding remain disputed, but it didn't help that leading democracies spent the first two decades of the new millennium waging an ugly war on terror and reeling from the worst financial crisis since the Great Depression. The resulting "democratic recession" has given China a window of ideological opportunity. The anti-liberal critique Beijing offers has become more persuasive to disillusioned democrats, and more useful to aspiring autocrats, the world over.[51] China's iron fist is knocking on an open door.

Second, China's global reach is more pervasive than that of any prior illiberal power. Beijing's success in taking leadership positions in major international organizations now allows it to turn organs of the liberal order into tools of anti-democratic influence. A case in point: When Belarus flagrantly violated international norms by forcing down an airliner that was carrying a wanted dissident in 2021, guess which country headed the International Civil Aviation Organization and helped protect that brutal regime from censure?[52] In addition, Beijing's 1.4 billion consumers give it an ability—which the Soviets never had—to export its repressive practices to the world.

In 2020, for example, Beijing retaliated against Australia—which had committed the affront of asking for an international inquiry into the origins of COVID-19—not just by imposing sanctions on its economy but also by demanding that Canberra gut its democracy by silencing critical newspapers and think tanks. Likewise, when China applies sanctions against European politicians and analysts who condemn the repression in Xinjiang, when it compels Marriott to fire an American employee who likes a tweet referring to Tibet, or when it passes a law that threatens to punish anyone, anywhere in the world, who supports political freedom in Hong Kong, it is using its market power to attack free speech—the very foundation of democracy—in some of the most advanced societies in the world.[53]

The third and most important factor supercharging China's efforts is the ongoing digital revolution.[54] Think of the data-collection and messaging power of Apple, Amazon, Facebook, Google, and Twitter. Now imagine that in the hands of the CCP. By combining AI, big data, and cyber, biometric, and speech- and facial-recognition technologies, the Chinese government is pioneering a system that will allow dictators to know everything about their subjects—what people are saying and viewing; whom they hang out with; what they like and dislike; and where they are located at any given time. That system will allow regimes to discipline citizens instantly by restricting their access to credit, education, employment, medical care, telecommunications, and travel—as well as to hunt people down for more medieval forms of punishment.

This technological revolution threatens to upend the global balance between democracy and authoritarianism by making repression more affordable and effective than ever before.[55] Instead of relying on expensive (and potentially rebellious) armies to brutalize and brainwash a resentful population, an autocrat will now have cheaper and more insidious means of control. Millions of spies can be replaced with hundreds of millions of unblinking cameras. Facial-recognition and artificial intelligence technologies can rapidly sort through video feeds and identify troublemakers. Bots can deliver propaganda tailored to specific groups or individuals. Malware can be installed on computers through seemingly innocuous apps or links, and then government hackers can crash the computer networks of dissidents or gather data on their operations. That information, in turn, can be used to coopt resistance movements by bribing their leaders or meeting their more innocuous demands. Alternatively, authorities can print out an AI-assembled list of alleged activists and kill everyone on it.

The evil genius of this "digital authoritarianism" is that most people will be seemingly free to go about their daily lives. In reality, the state will censor everything they see and track everything they do. With old-school authoritarianism, one at least knew where the oppression was coming from. But now people can be nudged and cajoled by invisible algorithms delivering personalized content through social media. In past eras, autocrats had to make tough choices between funding death squads or delivering economic growth. Today, however, repression is not only affordable, it may be profitable, because the same "smart-city" technologies that facilitate strict social control can also be used to improve infrastructure, diagnose diseases, and make the trains run on time.

Needless to say, these technologies are a tyrant's dream. "Dictators may not want China's ideology," says U.S. under secretary of defense for policy Colin Kahl, "but they do want its methodology." Recognizing this demand, Chinese companies were already selling and operating surveillance systems in more than 80 countries, as of 2020.[56] As the CCP feels increasingly threatened at home and abroad, there is every reason to expect Beijing to export digital authoritarianism farther and wider. Many countries already want it, and China has powerful tools to compel those that don't. Want access to China's market? Let Huawei install the core components of your 5G network. Want a Chinese loan? Accept Chinese surveillance technology in your capital.

As more governments partner with Beijing, the reach of China's global surveillance-state will grow.[57] Existing autocracies will become more totalitarian, and some democracies will drift into the authoritarian camp. The liberal belief, so common in the 1990s, that democracy would inevitably spread around the world will be upended.

So will the comforting myth that humanity has evolved past the point of mass atrocities. Digital authoritarianism is not a substitute for gulags and genocide; it is an enabler. Political scientists have shown that when dictatorships ramp up digital repression, they also engage in more torture and murder.[58] The reason is simple: With machines handling day-to-day bookkeeping and surveillance, foot soldiers are free to focus on the physical aspects of authoritarian rule, such as ethnic cleansing and beating dissidents into submission.

Just look at Xinjiang, where smart cities exist side-by-side with concentration camps.[59] Chinese security officers man the camps and handle the "reeducation" and forced sterilization, while cameras, biometric scanners, and mandatory cell-phone apps feed data into computers that keep tabs on everything that happens in the province. Algorithms match camera footage with snapshots, blood samples, and DNA swabs taken by police at "health checks." When Uighurs reach the edge of their neighborhood, their cell phones automatically alert authorities. When they pump gas, the system checks whether they are the car's owner. If they try to flee the province, police are dispatched to the doorsteps of their family and friends. If they somehow make it abroad, they aren't guaranteed an escape: China's authoritarian allies, even those in Muslim-majority countries such as Egypt, are starting to use Chinese surveillance technology to track down and deport Uighurs back into Beijing's clutches.

Some experts still cling to the belief that China doesn't actually pose a major threat to democracy, because it doesn't really care—as the Soviet Union did—whether other countries are ruled by Communists.[60] Or they argue that rich and consolidated democracies such as the United States will endure as islands of liberty, even if some weak, partial democracies disappear behind a digital iron curtain.

This couldn't be more wrong. Digital authoritarianism is creeping into the heart of the liberal world. The use of digital tools to manipulate public opinion, demonize opponents, and mobilize violent mobs of supporters is just as alluring for someone seeking power in a democracy as it is for a dictator. That is especially true in the tribal political climate that prevails in many democracies today. Across the liberal world, partisan divisions have surged to historic highs, public trust in democratic institutions has sunk to lows not seen since the 1930s, and major parties are openly advocating anti-democratic laws.[61] The political soil is ripe for elements of authoritarianism to take root, and China and Russia are fertilizing it with digital disinformation, churned out by bots and mainlined into the Facebook feeds of millions around the world.[62] As the intensity of the U.S.-China rivalry spikes, so will Beijing's incentive to use AI-enabled deep fakes and other forms of disinformation to weaken and undermine its adversary.

Even if America and other leading democracies don't fall prey to this ideological offensive, their power and security would be diminished in a more authoritarian world. It is no coincidence that the strongest links in the strategic chain America is trying to wrap around China are democracies. Nor is it a coincidence that Beijing counts tyrannies such as Russia and Iran among its closest friends—and indeed, Chinese and Russian efforts to disrupt and degrade the world's democracies go hand-in-hand. Democracies all need an international environment conducive to preserving their liberal institutions. Authoritarians all need a world that protects them from the subversive forces of freedom. Different versions of domestic order produce different visions of international order.[63] If China succeeds in pulling more countries into the authoritarian camp, it will shift the strategic balance and weaken the coalition mobilizing against it.

Most fundamentally, autocracies have a vested interest in demonizing democracies. Dictators don't want their people admiring democratic institutions and demanding freedom. The best way to rally citizens around an authoritarian regime is to inspire hatred of leading democracies, and that requires a steady stream of ideological conflict. It's entirely predictable that the world's most notorious strongmen—Xi, Putin, Khamenei, Kim, Assad, Erdogan, Orbán, Lukashenko—portray themselves as defenders of tradition, hierarchy, and order against a decadent democratic West. As China enlarges the ranks of authoritarians, the world will become a shabbier place for the United States and its democratic allies.[64] International conflicts will proliferate, and not just at the level of ideas, but also in the military realm, because blood-and-soil nationalism goes hand-in-hand with violent revanchism. That dynamic, worryingly, is already playing out.

## WINDOWS AND WAR

Russia's full-scale invasion of Ukraine in February 2022 shocked the world, by reminding leaders everywhere that geopolitical competition can all-too-easily turn into outright military conflict on an epic scale. But Russia isn't the only revisionist state—or even the most powerful one—capable of catastrophic aggression. China will also feel the urge to strike as this decade goes on.

There is no mystery about what the CCP wants geopolitically, because it has wanted the same things for decades: to make China whole again, turn the East China and South China Seas into Chinese lakes, and grab regional primacy as a springboard to global power. These goals are fixed: The question is how China will pursue them.

In the 1990s and 2000s, Beijing's approach was mostly peaceful and patient. Confident in a growing economy, and wary of prematurely picking a fight with the West, China pursued its aims primarily through nonconfrontational means. By flaunting its vast market, China wrested territory from foreign rivals without firing a shot. The British handed back Hong Kong in 1997. Portugal gave up Macao in 1999. Half a dozen countries settled their territorial disputes with China between 1991 and 2019, and two dozen other countries cut diplomatic ties with Taiwan to secure relations with Beijing. China carried out a "peaceful rise" strategy, and it worked well.[65]

Those days are over. Other countries are becoming less enthralled by the money to be made in China and more concerned about Beijing's predation. Globally, the mood has shifted from cautiously welcoming China's rise to fearing and opposing it, and *that* has raised a pivotal question for Xi: If the peaceful route to reclaiming territory and expanding influence is closing, is it time to start flexing the military muscle China has spent $3 trillion building over the past three decades?

That's what past peaking powers did, and China's history suggests it will follow in their footsteps. Numerous studies have analyzed when and why the PRC uses force, and they all reach the same conclusion: China fights, not when it is rising, but when its security is deteriorating and its bargaining strength is declining.[66] In other words, the CCP typically uses force to exploit a closing window of opportunity or avoid an opening window of vulnerability. When cornered by rivals, China does not wait to be attacked. Instead, it usually shoots first to gain tactical advantage before its strategic situation gets even worse. In fact, China often starts wars against superior foes with little expectation of winning the biggest battles. The goal may simply be making an enemy back off by fighting hard and demonstrating a willingness to inflict— and suffer—enormous casualties. That message is usually directed as much to rivals standing on the sidelines as it is to the enemy tangling with China in the ring.

Just look at any of the PRC's wars. In late 1950, waves of Chinese soldiers attacked U.S. forces in Korea for fear that the Americans would conquer North Korea and build military bases there. China suffered almost a million casualties but to this day celebrates its defense of North Korea as a glorious victory. In 1962, the PLA attacked Indian forces, ostensibly because they built outposts in Chinese-claimed territory in the Himalayas, but really because China felt it was being encircled by the Indians, Americans, Soviets, and Chinese Nationalists. By attacking India, China "killed a chicken to scare the monkeys," as the old Chinese saying goes, coercing several enemies by making an example out of one.

The Soviets didn't get the message and continued to mass forces on China's borders while asserting their right to use military force to beat back "counterrevolution" in any socialist state, as they did in Czechoslovakia in 1968. Fearing invasion, China ambushed Soviet forces on their shared border in 1969. Ten years later, Beijing again went to war, this time to "teach Vietnam a lesson," as Deng said, after it signed a defense agreement with Moscow and conquered Cambodia, one of China's only allies. In addition to these wars, China has launched artillery or missile barrages at or near Taiwanese territory on three occasions (1954–1955, 1958, and 1995–1996), each time hoping to prevent Taipei from tightening its relationship with the United States or edging toward independence. The record is clear: When China feels vulnerable, it gets violent.

Today, there are plenty of chickens to kill and teachable moments to exploit. The PLA already brawled with India in the Himalayas in 2020, seeking—unsuccessfully—to drive a wedge between Washington and New Delhi. It might try again as India draws closer to the United States. But if the CCP really wants to roll back the emerging anti-China coalition, it must break the ring of U.S. alliances and partnerships off its coast.

An obvious target would be Japan. Tokyo is a hated historical enemy that currently administers the Senkaku Islands, which China claims and calls the Diaoyu Islands. The U.S.-Japan alliance is the linchpin of America's containment strategy in East Asia. Taking Japan down a peg while straining its alliance with Washington might appeal to an encircled PRC.

China already sends armed coast guard cutters into the territorial waters around the Senkakus to contest Japan's control. China's next move up the escalation ladder could be to land soldiers on the islands; declare a fifty-mile exclusion zone around them; and wrap them with swarms of ships, submarines, warplanes, and drones—backed by missiles based on the Chinese mainland. Japan then would either have to acquiesce to China's annexation or go to war with a nuclear power over a few tiny rocks covered in bird droppings. America would face the same dilemma. Would it respond with economic sanctions and feeble diplomatic protests? Or would it honor the pledges made, in 2014 and again in 2021, to help Japan defend the Senkakus? The former response might wreck the U.S.-Japan alliance. The latter approach, according to wargames conducted by U.S. think-tanks, could end in World War III.[67]

If China isn't ready to rumble with a regional power such as Japan, it could instead muscle one of its weaker maritime neighbors in the South China Sea. Although Beijing would surely like to knock Vietnam down, an even juicier target would be the Philippines, which meets all the criteria of a perfect enemy.

Militarily weak? Check. The Philippines may be slowly turning against China, but for now its capabilities are pathetic, and Beijing could wipe out the Filipino navy and air force in a single skirmish. Symbolically important? Check. In 2016, Manila took Beijing to the Permanent Court of Arbitration (aka, the World Court) and won, with the tribunal ruling that China's South China Sea claims were null and void. China responded by declaring that it would not be bound by the rulings of a "puppet" court half a world away. Ejecting Filipino forces from their isolated, indefensible South China Sea outposts or simply building military bases on rocks and reefs that Beijing has already seized but not yet developed would be a great way for China to back up that declaration.

Strategically important? Check. The U.S.-Philippines alliance is critical to regional security but has often been shaky since the Cold War. And while Washington has pledged to defend Filipino possessions in the South China Sea, Beijing might not believe it. "Would you go to war over Scarborough Shoals?" the chairman of the Joint Chiefs of Staff was overheard saying in 2016.[68] If China bludgeoned Filipino forces, it would force the United States into a very tough choice: defend an ambivalent ally over its territorial claims or stand aside as China makes a mockery of international law, expands its control of the South China Sea, and wrecks the credibility of U.S. alliance commitments in Asia.

## TARGET: TAIWAN

As bad as those scenarios are, they pale in comparison to what is likely to be the main event of a Chinese revanchist campaign: the conquest of Taiwan. Grabbing Taiwan is China's top foreign policy goal, and preparations to reclaim the island reportedly consume roughly one-third of the PLA's budget.[69] If China subdued Taiwan, it would gain access to its world-class semiconductor industry and free up dozens of ships, hundreds of missile launchers and combat aircraft, and billions of defense dollars to wreak havoc farther afield. China could use Taiwan as an "unsinkable aircraft carrier" to project power into the Pacific, blockade Japan and the Philippines, and fracture U.S. alliances in East Asia. Not least, successful aggression would eliminate the world's only Chinese democracy, removing a persistent threat to the CCP's legitimacy. Taiwan is the center of gravity in East Asia—and the epitome of a place where

China's leaders might think that near-term aggression could radically improve their country's long-term trajectory vis-à-vis the United States.

Taiwan is Beijing's most inviting target for other reasons, as well. The geographic asymmetry is severe: The defense of Taiwan would require U.S. forces to fight less than 100 miles off China's coast and travel hundreds or even thousands of miles from a few fragile bases and aircraft carriers. With many of its forces stationed in other regions, America would be fighting with one hand tied behind its back. China, by contrast, could throw most of its military into the war and use its homeland as a giant base. Chinese forces would have secure, land-based lines of communications and resupply. They could shoot, scoot, and reload from countless mainland sanctuaries; the entire nation could support the war effort by housing, feeding, supplying, and transporting Chinese troops.

Compare those home-field advantages to what China would face in a war in the East China or South China Seas. Chinese air and naval forces would have to travel hundreds of miles between the battlefield and the mainland to refuel and reload, a commute that would slash PLA combat power on the front lines and force Chinese units to rely on vulnerable communications satellites. Chinese forces would also have to run a gauntlet every time they pass by Taiwan on their way to and from the combat theater, giving the PLA's foes copious chances for harassment and attrition.

Finally, Taiwan is where China faces its most rapidly closing window of opportunity. The possibility of peaceful reunification is disappearing fast: Fewer and fewer Taiwanese want to be part of mainland China, and the United States is strengthening its military and diplomatic ties with Taipei. In response, China is considering military options.

In September 2020, the PLA began carrying out the most aggressive show of force in the Taiwan Strait in a quarter century. Incursions into Taiwan's air defense identification zone skyrocketed. Chinese military task forces, some involving more than thirty combat aircraft and a half-dozen naval ships, roamed the strait roughly every other day. Many of them breached the median line between Taiwan and China, a boundary that both sides had respected for decades. Several of these patrols simulated attacks on U.S. aircraft carriers and destroyers sailing between the Philippines and Taiwan. By crushing the pro-democracy movement in Hong Kong in 2020, China also suggested that the days of peaceful persuasion vis-à-vis Taiwan are finished.

Could a military attack succeed? Until recently, the answer was no. In the 1990s, Taiwan's geographic and technological advantages over China made it virtually unconquerable. The Taiwan Strait is perilous—typhoons and twenty-foot waves are common—and the island is a natural fortress. Its east coast consists of steep cliffs, and its west coast is dominated by mud flats that extend miles out to sea and are buffeted by severe tides. There are only a dozen beaches on Taiwan where an invading force could even land—and U.S. and Taiwanese fighter aircraft and naval armadas could have made sure that China's army never got close.[70]

Since then, however, China has outspent Taiwan 25-to-1 on defense. It has churned out new warships, combat aircraft, and missiles, along with amphibious craft that can ferry thousands of troops. China's military is now ten times larger than Taiwan's. China's long-range air-defense systems can shoot down aircraft over Taiwan. China's land-based missiles and combat aircraft could potentially wipe out Taiwan's air force and navy and destroy U.S. bases in East Asia. China's cyber and anti-satellite capabilities threaten to render U.S. forces deaf, blind, and dumb by crippling their vital sensors and satellites. Chinese anti-ship missiles can make the western Pacific a very dangerous place for any large U.S. surface combatant. For a quarter-century, the PLA has focused relentlessly on preparing to conquer Taiwan.

The U.S. military, by contrast, spent most of this period fighting terrorists in the Middle East. More recently, it has funneled troops and weapons into Europe to shore up NATO's eastern flank. The Obama, Trump, and Biden administrations all hoped to pivot U.S. forces to Asia to counter China. But those plans were overtaken by events in other regions, including the rise of ISIS and Russia's invasion of Ukraine. As a global power, the United States hasn't had the luxury of preparing for a single military contingency. Consequently, its air force and navy haven't kept pace with China's military modernization.

America's armed forces in Asia still consist predominantly of small numbers of large warships and short-range combat aircraft operating from exposed bases—precisely the kind of forces China could destroy in a surprise missile attack. The United States only has two air bases within 500 miles of Taiwan—the maximum distance unrefueled fighter aircraft can fly before they run out of gas. If China disables those bases, U.S. forces would have to operate from aircraft carriers and from Guam, located 1,800 miles from Taiwan. The extra distance and midair refueling would cut the number of U.S. air sorties in half, giving China an opportunity to dominate the skies over Taiwan. Worse, China now has bombers and ballistic missiles that can strike Guam and potentially hit moving aircraft carriers more than 1,000 miles from the mainland. If these "Guam-killer" and "carrier-killer" missiles work as advertised, China could cripple U.S. military power in East Asia.[71]

Taiwan isn't ready to pick up the slack.[72] As part of its transition from a conscript army to a more professional all-volunteer military, Taiwan has cut its active-duty force from 275,000 to 175,000 troops and reduced the length of conscription from one year to four months. Recruits receive only a few weeks of basic training, and training for reservists is infrequent and inadequate. Taiwan also has gutted its logistics force, which now routinely fails to resupply combat units or perform basic maintenance. Consequently, soldiers avoid training with their weapons for fear of accidents or wasting precious ammunition; Taiwan's pilots fly for less than ten hours per month. More than half of Taiwan's tanks and attack helicopters are dysfunctional, and many Taiwanese soldiers suffer low morale.

The bottom line is that China, like Germany in 1914 or Japan in 1941, has a favorable but finite military window. It could, Taiwan's own government has assessed, "paralyze" the island's defenses.[73] As we detailed in chapter 3, Taiwan and the United States have awoken to the threat, identified the key problems they must solve, and started retooling their militaries accordingly. But between now and the early 2030s—when U.S. and Taiwanese defense reforms will begin to make a major impact—China has its chance.

In fact, the cross-strait military balance will temporarily shift further in China's favor in the mid-2020s, when many U.S. cruisers, guided-missile submarines, and long-range bombers will be retired.[74] In many ways, the U.S. military is still the force that Ronald Reagan built. U.S. Navy and Air Force modernization, in particular, has been postponed for decades. Now the problem is acute.[75] Many of the Pentagon's workhorse ships and combat aircraft are literally falling apart or bursting into flames. Their aging hulls and airframes can't withstand another upgrade, let alone accommodate the modern engines, sensors, and munitions they would need to compete with China's new forces. These U.S. capabilities have to be retired. And when they are, the U.S. military will have hundreds fewer vertical-launch missile tubes—the sine qua non of modern naval firepower—floating around East Asia. Meanwhile, China will bring online hundreds of additional anti-ship and land-attack missiles, dozens of long-range bombers and amphibious ships, and a rocket launcher system that can hit most or all of Taiwan from mainland China.

This is the geopolitical equivalent of a ticking time bomb. In the mid to late 2020s, China will never have a better chance to defeat its enemies and satisfy its revisionist appetites. It is during this period that America risks—as one former Pentagon official has said—getting "its ass handed to it" in a Taiwan fight.[76]

Seeing these trends, a chorus of retired Chinese military officers and state-run news outlets is urging the CCP to invade Taiwan immediately. The Chinese public seems to be aboard: According to a 2020 survey by the state-run *Global Times*, 70 percent of mainlanders strongly support using force to unify Taiwan with the mainland, and 37 percent think it would be best if the war occurred by 2025.[77] Behind closed doors, Chinese officials have told Western analysts that calls for an invasion are proliferating within the CCP, and that Xi is surrounded by hawks and yes-men who tell him that the PLA could pull it off.[78] Perhaps for that reason, Xi has staked his legitimacy on liberating Taiwan. In 2017, he announced that reunification is "an inevitable requirement for realizing the great rejuvenation of the Chinese nation."[79] In 2020, the CCP moved up the date at which it plans to field a "modernized" military from 2034 to 2027.[80] In March 2021, Admiral Philip Davidson, then the commander of U.S. forces in the Indo-Pacific, warned that China could invade Taiwan within the next six years.[81]

The Chinese have several options for squeezing Taiwan and trying to make it surrender: Seizing one of the exposed offshore islands controlled by Taipei but located just miles from the Chinese coast, enacting a naval and air blockade, or simply pummeling Taiwan with guided missiles. But these options would give the United States and Taiwan time to react, something the Chinese have no intention of granting.

They saw how Saddam Hussein's forces got massacred in the 1990–1991 Persian Gulf War when the Pentagon had weeks to assemble an iron mountain of weapons nearby and rally a giant international coalition. They know their best chance of winning is to hit Taiwanese and U.S. forces hard and early, before they can fight back. That's why China's military doctrine calls for disarming opponents quickly through Pearl Harbor–style attacks.[82] And that's why we should worry about a truly dire scenario.

In the most likely contingency, the war would start with thousands of ground- and air-launched Chinese missiles raining down on Taiwan, American military bases on Okinawa and Guam, and the U.S. carrier strike group that has its home port in Japan. All over Taiwan, undercover Chinese special forces and intelligence operatives would emerge, detonating bombs at military facilities and assassinating Taiwanese leaders. Chinese cyberattacks would cripple Taiwan's critical infrastructure. The PLA would also use cyberattacks and, potentially, ground-launched missiles to destroy the satellites that allow U.S. forces to communicate with each other and with Washington—thereby rendering America unable to respond or even reliably know what is happening for days or weeks.[83] The PLA's cyber units would simultaneously stir up trouble on the American home front, unleashing disinformation campaigns to sow confusion and exacerbate political disputes in the United States.

Meanwhile, a Chinese flotilla previously engaged in military exercises in the Taiwan Strait would dash for Taiwan's beaches while hundreds of thousands of Chinese troops on the mainland start piling into ships and helicopters in preparation for the main assault. Small amphibious assault craft could emerge from civilian ferries in the strait and try to seize a key port or beach before Taiwanese forces can respond. The United States, having lost many of its forward-deployed forces in China's surprise attack, would have to surge aircraft and war-ships from thousands of miles away and fight through a hail of missiles, smart mines, and electromagnetic interference to get anywhere close to Taiwan. Summoning those assets, moreover, might require wrenching them away from other important priorities, such as protecting NATO's Eastern flank from an aggressive Russia. The United States might find itself facing dire security challenges against two-nuclear armed great powers—with a military resourced to cope only with one.[84]

America would confront agonizing global trade-offs, and U.S. forces in the Pacific would incur losses unlike anything since the Viet-nam War or possibly World War II. American leaders might even find themselves up against an awful dilemma—whether to accept a humili-ating military setback or threaten to use nuclear weapons if China doesn't stand down. The United States, a blue-ribbon commission of defense experts concluded in 2018, could suffer "a decisive military defeat" unless it resorts to strategies that risk nuclear apocalypse.[85] Geopolitics doesn't get any more dangerous than this.

The "terrible 2020s" will be a nasty decade because China has reached a nasty geopolitical juncture—the point at which it can and must act boldly to avoid decline.[86] A peaking revisionist typically looks for chances to act while it still has some prospect of success. And China, thanks to several near-term windows of opportunity, sees tantalizing possibilities.

Boldness isn't the same thing as insanity. The fact that China's power has plateaued doesn't mean that it will lash out violently in all directions. It does mean that China will become more coercive and aggressive, particularly in areas where it thinks risk-taking now will create a better long-term reality. If China grabs Taiwan, then the First Island Chain is broken, and Beijing's strategic geography improves enormously. If China creates a high-tech empire, it might stave off economic stagnation and foreign encirclement. If the CCP rolls back democracy, it can entrench its regime and reduce its international isolation. Perhaps, China's leaders tell themselves, a bit of audacity can rescue them from a grimmer fate.

That's one possibility. Another is that these gambits will end in tragedy. Chinese neo-imperialism could fuel conflicts around the world. Aggression in the western Pacific could cause cataclysmic escalation. Peaking powers don't lose their ability to reason: Most Japanese leaders in 1941 understood that Tokyo was likely to lose. But their behavior usually becomes more erratic, because they are willing to accept higher risks to avert a terrifying future.

Washington thus has its work cut out for it. America needs a long-term strategy for dealing with an assertive, authoritarian China for a generation or more. But it also needs a shorter-term strategy for navigating a period of high tension during the current decade. If the United States is to win the twilight struggle peacefully, it must first traverse the danger zone. Here again, history can be instructive.

# 6

---

# What One Cold War Can
# Teach Us About Another

George Kennan got paid to take the long view, but in May 1947, he had only the shortest window in which to do it. A year earlier, the U.S. diplomat had made a name for himself by authoring his famous "Long Telegram" from America's embassy in Moscow. In that document, Kennan had described the Soviet Union as an implacable foe in the emerging Cold War, while also arguing that the balance of strengths and weaknesses would favor America in the end. By May 1947, however, Kennan was in a new role as director of the State Department's Policy Planning Staff (PPS)—its small, elite unit dedicated to big-picture strategy—and time was a luxury neither he nor the free world had.

Europe was in the grips of an existential crisis. The continent was still devastated, economically and politically, from World War II. A harsh, record-breaking winter had compounded the misery. The continent that had once ruled the world was now on the precipice of starvation, chaos, revolution. It had been reduced, in Winston Churchill's phrasing, to "a rubble heap, a charnel house, a breeding ground of pestilence and hate."[1] If America didn't quickly restore hope and prosperity, then well-organized Communist parties might seize power or win it at the ballot box. Once they had power, they could deliver the continent into Soviet dictator Joseph Stalin's hands. "The patient is sinking while the doctors deliberate," Secretary of State George C. Marshall—Kennan's boss—had concluded. Decisive action was needed "without delay."[2]

Marshall gave Kennan, Under Secretary of State Dean Acheson, and other State Department officials two weeks to solve the problem. What emerged, after three weeks rather than two, was perhaps the most famous foreign policy initiative in American history: The Marshall Plan. "The best answer we can give today," explained Kennan in a memo outlining the program, "is perhaps more useful than a more thoroughly considered study one or two months hence."[3] Formally known as the European Recovery Program, the Marshall Plan was meant to combat the desperation that was softening up the continent for Communist takeovers, and then to jump-start the economic recovery required for lasting stability and strength. Marshall announced the nascent idea in a speech at Harvard in June; U.S. and European officials scrambled, over the summer and fall, to turn a vague ambition into the four-year, $13 billion aid package that brought a dying region back to life. The policy that ultimately did as much as any other to win the Cold War for America was hastily thrown together to meet a challenge that would not wait.

The problem America faces vis-à-vis China today is scary, but not unprecedented. During an earlier twilight struggle, America's best strategic thinkers realized that time was on the free world's side—that a pathologically repressive, economically irrational Soviet system would struggle to keep up forever. For the first few years, however, it wasn't clear that this would matter, because Moscow had near-term windows of opportunity in which it might overturn a tenuous global balance of power.

Winning the Cold War required crossing a danger zone in which America might easily have lost that contest instead. No less, it required exploiting the urgency created by crisis to make bold moves that would strengthen the Western world for decades to come. "Fools learn by experience," Bismarck said, "wise men learn by others' experience."[4] Revisiting the early Cold War provides lessons that can help America fashion a new danger-zone strategy today.

## THE COLD WAR DANGER ZONE

Historical analogies are never exact, and the U.S.-China contest is not a carbon copy of the early Cold War. The China of the 2020s is not the Soviet Union of the 1940s, even if Xi is taking on distinctly Stalinist tendencies. Nor was the Soviet Union on the precipice of severe stagnation, as China is today.[5] In the aftermath of World War II, Moscow was looking forward to a much-needed economic recovery; the Red Army was the military juggernaut that had defeated Hitler and marched halfway across Europe. "Russia will emerge from the present conflict as by far the strongest nation in Europe and Asia—strong enough, if the United States should stand aside, to dominate Europe and at the same time to establish her hegemony over Asia," wrote U.S. intelligence analysts in 1945.[6]

Yet the late 1940s also presented dynamics that resonate today. Even at the dawn of the Cold War, America's shrewdest observers realized that the façade of Soviet power was more impressive than the foundation. The combination of Communist ideology, autocratic insecurity, and traditional Russian expansionism meant that there could be no lasting accommodation between the Kremlin and the capitalist world, Kennan argued: Moscow deemed it essential "that the internal harmony of our society be disrupted, our traditional way of life be destroyed, the international authority of our state be broken, if Soviet power is to be secure." Compared to the Western world, however, the Soviets were "still by far the weaker force."[7]

Moscow, Kennan believed, would find it hard to dominate captive peoples in Eastern Europe perpetually. The vicious totalitarian absurdities of its politics and the inherent limitations of its command economy would severely handicap the Soviet Union in any long race. Decline was inevitable, Kennan argued in 1947: Soviet power "bears within it the seeds of its own decay" and "the sprouting of those seeds is well advanced." The United States—a vibrant democracy that accounted for nearly half of world production—could undertake "with reasonable confidence" a "policy of firm containment," blocking Soviet advances until that decay destroyed the system from within.[8]

There was less cause for confidence in the near term, because the Soviets had not one but two windows of opportunity. The first was economic and political. The world was in chaos in the late 1940s. Economic devastation and human misery were the rule rather than the exception: "More people face starvation and even actual death for want of food today than in any war year and perhaps more than in all the war years combined," President Harry Truman reported in 1946.[9] The war had created power vacuums and sparked political radicalism from Western Europe to Southeast Asia; Communist parties loyal to Moscow were swelling with new adherents to the faith. "The way of life we have known," Marshall would remark, "is literally in balance."[10] If the Soviet Union or its proxies could exploit this chaos to grab political control of key countries, Stalin might dominate much of Eurasia without firing a shot.

The second window was of a military nature. The United States had cut a fighting force of some 12 million men in 1945 to one of well under 2 million by 1947. Its overall military *potential* was still vastly greater than that of the Soviet Union, but its existing military *power* had melted away. And while Washington had an insurance policy in the atomic bomb, it didn't have nearly enough of those weapons to stop a Soviet offensive into Western Europe, the Middle East, or any other hot spot along the East-West divide. Once the Soviets built their own atomic bomb in 1949, America had lost this trump card—and Pentagon planners worried that it might well lose a global war.[11] Even short of that horrifying scenario, an imbalance of military power might let Moscow expand its influence through bullying and intimidation: "The shadow of Soviet armed strength," Kennan acknowledged, could "have a paralyzing effect" on the free world.[12]

The Truman years were, consequently, a period of unrelenting insecurity. There were multiple war scares: During a showdown over Turkey in 1946, after Communist forces seized power in Czechoslovakia in 1948, and after Stalin blockaded the western sectors of a divided Berlin later that year. A Soviet proxy, North Korea, did start a major conflict by trying to conquer South Korea in 1950. "It looks like World War III is here," Truman wrote.[13] There were also profound, disconcerting shifts in the military balance, particularly after the United States lost its atomic monopoly and had to face its glaring conventional inferiority. Most of all, there was a pervasive sense that America must run a gauntlet of imminent threats just to reach a longer Cold War in which its economic and political advantages might be decisive. "In general . . . time is on our side," wrote the Joint Chiefs of Staff in 1951. But "the critical period" would be "the next two or three years."[14]

The United States would make it through this critical period. The Truman administration pursued landmark policies that helped America avoid defeat in the near term while positioning it for victory in the long term—even as it also suffered severe setbacks and made glaring mistakes. The Truman Doctrine of aid to Greece and Turkey in

1947 shored up endangered outposts at the gateway to two continents while making clear that America would resist Communist expansion. The Marshall Plan and the creation of NATO changed Europe from a source of alarming weakness to a pillar of Western strength. The revival of Japan and West Germany turned recent enemies into some of America's best allies; the Berlin airlift kept another great European city from slipping entirely behind the Iron Curtain. The U.S. intervention in Korea prevented a collapse of the world's psychological balance of power, while the subsequent buildup of American military strength reinforced the physical balance at a crucial time. Other initiatives, some famous and some now forgotten, allowed America to survive the early Cold War and thrive in the protracted struggle that followed.

"When history says that my term of office saw the beginning of the cold war," Truman could brag as he retired in 1953, "it will also say that in those 8 years we have set the course that we can win it."[15] Indeed, the early Cold War is perhaps the best historical example of a successful danger-zone strategy. The specific policies America followed back then can't simply be replicated now. But America's experience does reveal four strategic insights about what crossing a danger zone requires.

## FIRST THINGS FIRST

First, *prioritize ruthlessly*. Thinking clearly about where to bet big and where to conserve resources is always important; it can be a matter of life and death when the level of threat is high and the margin for error is low. The key is to prevent near-term breakthroughs that can dramatically shift the longer-term balance of power—and to make early investments that create lasting legacies of strength. The United States mostly obeyed this rule during the early Cold War, although doing so was harder than it seemed.

The basic problem, then as now, was that America was under pressure almost everywhere. In 1946–1947, the Truman administration faced crises along an arc of instability running from the Atlantic coast of Europe all the way to the Pacific. Communist advances seemed possible, even likely, in France and Italy, Greece and Turkey, Iran and Indonesia, China and Korea, and other locales. The question was how Washington would respond.

Truman gave one answer in March 1947, when he went before Congress to request roughly $400 million in emergency aid for Greece and Turkey, the former menaced by a Communist insurgency and the latter facing Soviet territorial demands and military coercion. "At the present moment in world history nearly every nation must choose between alternative ways of life," Truman declared. The United States must "support free peoples who are resisting attempted subjugation by armed minorities or by outside pressures."[16]

The stark phrasing was deliberate. "This was America's answer to the surge of expansion of Communist tyranny," Truman later wrote. "It had to be clear and free of hesitation or double talk."[17] The United States must rally domestic support for containment by vividly explaining what was at stake in the Cold War; it must signal that America would stand with countries resisting totalitarian aggression. But the implication of Truman's message was that America would respond equally to Communist probes everywhere, and the president soon realized this was impossible. "Our resources are not unlimited," he admitted. A refusal to economize anywhere would lead to weakness everywhere.[18]

Truman's team spent much of 1947 hashing out which theaters of the competition were truly vital—where immediate setbacks might give Moscow a lasting advantage, and where wins today might give the West an enduring edge. The vital sites were Japan and, especially, Western Europe. If these two centers of industrial might fell under

Soviet control, the entire global balance might tip in Stalin's favor. If they could be revived and tied to the non-Communist world, the Kremlin would be at a grave, possibly insurmountable, deficit. "That means peace in the world, if we can get recovery in Europe," Truman commented: The region was the center of gravity in the Cold War.[19]

Western Europe and Japan were crucial in another respect: They were the areas that most highlighted the asymmetry of U.S. and Soviet aims. For Moscow to gain the upper hand, it would have to control countries where most people preferred to remain free of Communist domination. For the United States to preserve its position, it had only to deny the Soviets that control. Washington could work *with* "local forces of resistance" to maintain their independence, as Kennan put it, whereas the Soviets had to work *against* them to snuff it out.[20] This dynamic created a tremendous force-multiplier for America—an ability to capitalize on the exertions of free, friendly nations—that the Soviets never enjoyed.

The late 1940s saw a brutal sorting of commitments. The United States poured historic amounts of aid—equal to 5 percent of U.S. gross national product in 1948—into Western Europe and Japan.[21] Washington thereby began the process of turning Tokyo into an anti-Communist bastion in the Pacific. Meanwhile, American officials made clear that they were willing to go to nearly any length—whether by unveiling the Marshall Plan or breaking with 150 years of diplomatic precedent by establishing a peacetime military alliance, NATO—to protect Western Europe. "If anything happens in Western Europe," Acheson would comment after replacing Marshall as secretary of state, "the whole business goes to pieces."[22] There would be no uncertainty about the U.S. commitment: Any Soviet attack on Western Europe would mean all-out conflict with the United States.[23]

At the same time, Truman opted *not* to make an all-out effort to prevent Communist victories in places considered less important or promising. Case in point: Washington did little to prevent Mao's Communists from defeating Chiang's Nationalists, on the assumption that an underdeveloped, poverty-stricken China didn't weigh heavily on the scales of global power. Truman also withdrew U.S. forces from South Korea, then an unstable, impoverished nation; Acheson publicly announced that the country was outside America's defense perimeter in the Pacific. Not going all-out in peripheral areas was the cost of being effective at the core of the Cold War.[24]

It wasn't always easy to distinguish between vital and secondary areas. America could not rebuild Europe without ensuring that Middle Eastern oil remained in friendly hands—or rebuild Japan without protecting its access to markets and resources in places such as Indochina.[25] The fall of China to Mao's forces in 1949 may not have been a strategic disaster for America, but it was a political disaster for Truman, who then became less willing to write off other exposed positions in Asia. That reluctance, in turn, led to a gradual expansion of U.S. commitments and led America down a long road to tragedy in Vietnam.

A more immediate problem was that announcing what the United States would *not* defend could entice enemies to advance there—and that nonvital interests could suddenly become vital when they were attacked. This is what happened in Korea. Acheson's declaration that South Korea was on its own in January 1950 helped persuade an opportunistic Stalin to approve the North Korean invasion in June. To Stalin's surprise, Truman then decided to enter the fray. He did so not because South Korea itself was vitally important (it wasn't), but because a failure to thwart blatant aggression there might shatter the confidence Washington was seeking to build in more important areas. "You may be sure that all Europeans to say nothing of the Asiatics are watching to see what the United States will do," one State Department official wrote: The United States could hardly build a stable geopolitical balance if Stalin's minions simply destroyed the psychological balance.[26]

Truman's decision to intervene was the right one: It saved South Korea from destruction and reassured anxious allies that the West was not entering another age of appeasement. "Thank God this will not be a repetition of the past," the French foreign minister exclaimed.[27] Unfortunately, it also consigned the United States to fighting a bloody, draining conflict in a strategic backwater—a conflict that would escalate dramatically when the United States tried and failed to reunite the entire peninsula in late 1950.

For the most part, though, the administration kept its eye on the ball. Truman and Acheson used the sense of emergency fostered by an out-of-the-way war to fortify America's position in more crucial theaters: At the height of the fighting in Korea, the United States dispatched four additional divisions of troops to Western Europe and concluded a peace treaty and security pact with Japan. That country, Acheson explained, was "the heart of the whole Far Eastern situation."[28] As Korea showed, a superpower can never concentrate on just one problem: Sometimes an enemy does something so shocking and brazen that it demands action in an unexpected place. But getting through a danger zone requires prioritizing areas where the near-term consequences of weakness could be catastrophic—and the long-term benefits of strength can be transformative.

## ROUGH AND READY

Second, *combine strategic purpose with tactical agility*. A period of high tensions is no time to be wandering without aim, but neither is it a time to be rigid and dogmatic. When caught in the danger zone, a country needs clear, well-articulated objectives, as well as a rough-and-ready approach to achieving them. It should make the most of good-enough solutions—and friends—that are available today, rather than waiting for ideal ones that may not come along until too late.

Kennan knew this well. The PPS director was at the center of a massive strategic planning effort in the late 1940s. Kennan's PPS was charged with sorting out priorities and defining long-range goals. The Joint Chiefs of Staff conducted detailed studies to determine which areas were most important to American security. From all this emerged a clear, elegant strategic concept: America would hold the Soviet Union in check until its internal weakness brought it down, and it would do so primarily by building positions of Western strength along the Kremlin's Eurasian flanks. America's goal, stated Marshall, was "the restoration of balance of power in both Europe and Asia," and "all actions" would be viewed in this light.[29]

Yet Kennan also realized that dexterity would be required to stay on top of a dynamic rivalry. Just weeks after taking charge at the PPS, he had already concluded that it was impossible to come up with perfect answers to an avalanche of problems. "The only way we could ever hope to solve them would be if we could persuade the world to stand still for six months while we sit down and think it over," he said. "But life does not stand still, and the resulting confusion is terrific."[30]

What did this mean for U.S. policy? For one thing, speed was at a premium: American officials fast-tracked big initiatives. The Truman Doctrine involved a historic decision to aid Greece and Turkey and commit the United States to shoring up an endangered world. Which made it all the more noteworthy that Truman's aides drew up the initial outlines of the plan in a few days, and then worked out the details over three hectic weeks, after British officials dropped a Friday afternoon bombshell by informing the State Department that a bankrupt London was leaving Athens and Ankara to their fate. The administration instantly grasped, as one British diplomat wrote, that "no time must be lost in plucking the torch of world leadership from our chilling hands."[31]

American officials also had to get creative with the tools at hand. In early 1948, Italy's future hung in the balance: A Communist electoral victory was a real possibility. In response, the CIA, the State Department, and other agencies mounted an everything-but-the-kitchen-sink campaign to keep Italians from voting their country into totalitarianism. Washington delivered bags of cash to favored politicians. The State Department orchestrated a letter-writing campaign by Italian-Americans to their families in the old country. The United States used newsreels, stamps, and prayer cards as vehicles for anti-Communist propaganda. American officials even arranged a strategically timed shipment of British coal to help head off economic and political disaster. "Every action of the U.S. will have a direct bearing on the outcome," the U.S. ambassador wrote—so Washington must make the most of whatever weapons it had available.[32]

The same went for assembling the free-world coalition. Truman may have labeled the Cold War a contest between democracy and totalitarianism, but he never let the perfect be the enemy of the good in rounding up an anti-Soviet posse. In the late 1940s, America quickly pivoted from punitive military occupations of Japan and Germany—the countries that had just terrorized the world—to programs that rebuilt them as Cold War allies. In 1945, U.S. bombers had pulverized Berlin; in 1948, they kept its citizens alive through the allied airlift. Truman even used good Communists to check bad ones: After Stalin had a venomous falling out with Yugoslavia in 1948, Washington enlisted that Communist country as a tacit ally.

Not least, getting through the danger zone required sacrificing tradition for the sake of innovation. The best example of this was a departure so radical that it was opposed even by Kennan—the creation of NATO. That alliance was a strategic watershed: It signaled, as unambiguously as America's constitutional processes allowed, that the United States was fully committed to the freedom of Western Europe.[33] NATO was not, however, part of any grand American plan.

As late as early 1948, the Truman administration had no intention of creating an "entangling" peacetime alliance. NATO was a European idea pressed upon U.S. officials. It was also a frantic response to fast-breaking crises—namely the Czech coup in February 1948 and the Berlin blockade in June—that terrified the Europeans and convinced the Truman administration that nothing short of a formal defense treaty could buck them up against Soviet pressure. The Soviets were becoming more aggressive; the chances of war were rising. Only through unprecedented steps could America hold the line. The Europeans were "'completely out of their skin, and sitting on their nerves,' and hope must be recreated in them very soon," Marshall said.[34]

Re-creating that hope required overcoming one of the most venerable aspects of America's strategic heritage—the idea, as an isolationist senator had once put it, that "we want America for Americans and Europe for Europeans, and that is a good American doctrine."[35] It would also require working feverishly, in the years that followed, to change NATO from an alliance that existed mostly on paper to a military coalition that could put up a serious fight against Soviet aggression. The United States generally knew what it wanted in the late 1940s—a stable, secure Western Europe—but had to be flexible in figuring out how to get it.

American officials weren't just making things up as they went along. Yet the most important initiatives, such as NATO, were often improvised solutions to imminent problems. The United States used the tools it had to prevent an unstable situation from collapsing entirely.

It relied on new and sometimes motley crews that came together in unusual circumstances. It moved with urgency and adaptability in meeting pressing threats. If the Truman years are now remembered as a golden age of policy innovation, it was because Washington thought deliberately—and acted quickly.

## RISKY BUSINESS

Third, *a little offense is the best defense.* Danger-zone strategies involve taking the fight to the enemy by probing its weaknesses or throwing it off-balance. They require bold measures to close off potentially fatal vulnerabilities. But every step must be measured, because heedless provocation can be deadly. The key is to take calculated risks—and avoid reckless ones that convince a rival it has no better option than to go for broke.

This calculated risk-taking infused U.S. policy, because the only way to protect the free world was to make moves that antagonized powerful enemies.[36] Launching the Marshall Plan meant kicking obstructionist, fifth-column Communist ministers out of Western European governments, and thereby incurring the wrath—in the form of strikes, riots, and violence—of the radical Left. Undertaking the Berlin airlift, after Stalin cut off ground and rail access to that isolated city, meant gambling that the Soviets would not shoot down American planes or take advantage of the West's military weakness. The Truman administration decided, correctly, that these risks were worth running, because weakness could prove more provocative than strength, and because U.S. intelligence analysts doubted that Moscow would start World War III until it had recovered from World War II.[37] But the experience underscored an inherent dilemma of danger-zone strategy: There is no entirely safe course of action.

This was why the United States did something even more forward-leaning: It tried, albeit modestly, to undermine the Soviet bloc. In the early days of the Cold War, American officials believed that harried efforts to shore up Western positions had to be paired with selective efforts to weaken Soviet positions. U.S. policy, explained Kennan, involved "holding our own world together" and "increasing the disruptive strains in the Soviet world."[38]

To that end, the United States initially offered Marshall Plan aid to Eastern Europe as well as Western Europe—the calculation being that a hyper-suspicious Moscow would force the satellite states to decline and thereby destroy its own moral authority in the bloc. Washington subsequently beamed radio broadcasts into Eastern Europe to play up the crimes and failings of the Soviet-backed regimes. It waged economic warfare, denying Moscow critical goods that might feed its war machine. The U.S. and UK intelligence services even dropped paramilitary operatives behind the Iron Curtain in hopes of stirring up violent resistance. The last initiative was eventually ditched because it produced too much provocation at too little benefit. But traversing the danger zone meant finding ways of putting the enemy on the defensive.[39]

American risk-taking became most pronounced, ironically, after a gamble that went awry. During the late 1940s, Truman had kept military expenditures far below what his military chiefs deemed prudent. But Moscow's success in developing the A-bomb in 1949 shifted that calculus. The United States, a highly classified report known as NSC-68 concluded in April 1950, might face a "year of maximum danger" as soon as 1954. When North Korean forces, with Stalin's blessing, invaded South Korea two months later, Truman concluded that the Communists would "now use armed invasion and war" to subjugate their enemies.[40]

U.S. forces blunted, at heavy cost, North Korea's drive down the peninsula. In September, General Douglas MacArthur turned the tide with a brilliant amphibious landing behind North Korean lines. Truman then allowed MacArthur to race north toward the Yalu River, hoping that he could reunify all of Korea without provoking Chinese or Soviet intervention. The wager did not pay: In late 1950, Mao's forces jumped overextended American units near the Chinese border, inflicting one of the worst military defeats in U.S. history and casting the shadow of a new global war. If such a conflict erupted, warned General Omar Bradley, the chairman of the Joint Chiefs of Staff, "we might be in danger of losing."[41] It was now clear, as NSC-68 had argued, that America must urgently close the window of vulnerability that had opened wide.

From 1950 onward, the United States would settle for a ferocious draw in Korea while undertaking a massive military buildup and a worldwide diplomatic offensive. Pentagon spending nearly quadrupled, the American atomic arsenal roughly tripled, and the size of U.S. conventional forces more than doubled.[42] Washington sealed military alliances with Japan, Australia, New Zealand, and the Philippines. It sent more troops and planes to Europe and assigned General Dwight Eisenhower to whip the alliance into a real fighting force. Truman and Acheson even brought West Germany—the country that had invaded and savaged the Soviet Union a decade before—into NATO and began preparing to rebuild its military. All of these measures would anger the Soviet Union. But as Acheson put it, "the only thing that was more dangerous than undertaking this program was not undertaking it."[43]

Indeed, it is hard to overstate the impact that Korea had on American strategy. Things that were not possible before, whether dramatic growth in U.S. military spending or the rearmament of former aggressors, became possible amid global crisis. Previous political and diplomatic constraints on American policy fell away. "Korea saved us," Acheson later remarked: The United States capitalized on the sense of shock and urgency created by autocratic aggression to make investments that ultimately strengthened its position nearly around the globe.[44]

Yet American risk-taking was not limitless. It could be counter-productive to threaten or corner the Soviet Union too fully—to make it feel that it had no choice but to use force. Stalin might opt for war, U.S. analysts had written in 1948, "when the Soviet Government is convinced that measures short of war will fail to secure its objectives."[45] This made a careful balancing act essential: The United States had to make the free world more resilient, while avoiding moves that might encourage a now-or-never mentality in Moscow. The experience of 1941—when the American oil embargo convinced Japan to wage war immediately, before the United States was ready—was not one Truman wished to repeat.

This prospect acted as a brake on U.S. policy in the late 1940s and early 1950s. The United States never tried to roll back the Soviet bloc in Europe militarily: The likelihood of starting a major war was just too great. When it came to rearming the free world, American planners envisioned a carefully constrained West German military that could only operate within NATO, rather than a fully rearmed, autonomous West Germany that could pose "a grave threat to the security of the USSR."[46] Most important, while Truman occasionally mused in private about issuing ultimatums to the Soviets, in public his administration shut down every argument that it should deal with a hostile, aggressive Soviet Union by bringing matters to a head.

When Winston Churchill argued that the United States should threaten the Soviet Union with nuclear destruction if it didn't evacuate Eastern Europe in 1948, and when Douglas MacArthur called on Truman to dramatically escalate the war against China in 1951, the response was the same. "The whole purpose of what we are doing is to prevent world war III," Truman explained.[47] The aim of a danger-zone strategy was to strengthen the American position by taking necessary risks—not to bring on the apocalypse by taking foolish ones.

Nor, for the same reason, did Washington fully close the door to diplomacy. Truman believed that there was little hope of reaching a comprehensive settlement with the Soviets. But diplomacy could still play a role in American strategy. It could assure Soviet leaders that the United States did not *want* war even as it built up the free world. It could de-escalate crises once Washington had showed it could not be bullied. In 1951, for instance, after U.S. and allied forces had stopped the Chinese onslaught, talks between American and Soviet diplomats began the long, painful process of ending the Korean War.[48] If the United States could "create strength instead of weakness," Acheson remarked, then one day the Soviets would "recognize facts."[49] Until then, even episodic diplomacy could buy time for American strategy to work.

## GETTING TO THE LONG GAME

This relates to the fourth and final lesson. *Danger-zone strategy is about getting to the long game—and ensuring you can win it.* A smart danger-zone strategy won't necessarily allow you to defeat a tough competitor quickly. But it can build a bridge to a more manageable stage of the rivalry, while creating advantages that pay off in the end.

At the end of Truman's presidency, this was starting to happen. Only a half-decade prior, the Soviets had a plausible path to victory in the Cold War. As two French officials described that scenario, a demoralized capitalist world would fall into a "profound depression," which would cause Washington to turn inward. European economies would "disintegrate" and "economic, social and political chaos" would follow.

This "catastrophe" would allow the Soviets "to take over the Western European countries with their well-organized Communist Parties."[50] America would wake up one day to a hostile Eurasia. This nightmare seemed real enough in 1947. Within years, however, America and its allies were blocking Moscow's axis of advance and establishing patterns of strength that would one day deliver Western triumph.

By the early 1950s, Western Europe was recovering economically and regaining its self-confidence. NATO was emerging as a powerful bloc of democracies. On the other side of Eurasia, Japan was beginning its remarkable run of postwar prosperity. And while the post-1950 military buildup never gave Washington outright military dominance, it did create what Eisenhower called a "real deterrent to aggression" by ensuring that the Soviets would have to pay an apocalyptic price to wage war against the West.[51] The free world, an assessment by the National Security Council concluded, now had "such strength" as to prevent decisive Soviet advances—and perhaps, over time, to "cause that system gradually to weaken and decay."[52]

Nothing was guaranteed. The Korean War and Truman's military buildup had raised defense spending to an eye-popping 14 percent of GDP, a rate the incoming Eisenhower administration thought might bankrupt the country.[53] Some of the most hair-raising Cold War crises would come in the late 1950s and early 1960s, when Nikita Khrushchev sought—again—to force the West out of Berlin and stationed nuclear missiles in Cuba. As the Cold War spread into the Third World, there would be quiet struggles, gruesome proxy wars, and high-stakes crises. The Cold War never ceased being a dangerous, demanding competition. For decades, it would test American power, strategy, and resolve.

There were even times when the outcome seemed very much in doubt. In the 1970s, American alliances were under strain, and the free-world economy was reeling from oil shocks and other disruptions. Moscow had run off a series of victories in the Third World, while Washington had suffered embarrassing defeats in locations from Vietnam and Angola to Iran and Nicaragua. Soviet military power had continued to grow: Some American strategists worried about a new "window of vulnerability" in which Moscow might batter and bully its enemies. Predictions of American decline were ubiquitous. Even those officials, such as Ronald Reagan, who were most confident in America's long-term prospects never took it for granted that the United States would win the Cold War.

But whatever the challenges of this period, America's danger-zone strategy had succeeded in one fundamental respect: Never again would the balance of power be as precarious as it was in the late 1940s and early 1950s. Eisenhower's secretary of state, John Foster Dulles, had lambasted Truman's policies during the 1952 campaign, but in private, he acknowledged that America's alliance system had "staked out the vital areas of the world" and tied them to Washington.[54] Periodic crises notwithstanding, the free world had now laid the basis for sustained economic dynamism well beyond anything the Communist world could offer: By the 1980s, per capita income in the West was *nine times* greater than in the Soviet bloc.[55] The balance of power remained fluid; the Soviet Union could still menace the free world. But Moscow's odds of decisively winning the contest were mostly decreasing over time.

Two other important things happened as the United States crossed the danger zone. One was that America could downshift: It could move from an extremely high-cost strategy geared toward meeting a point of maximum peril to a somewhat lower-cost strategy geared toward meeting a less acute but ongoing challenge. By the end of the 1950s, American defense spending had fallen to around 9 percent of gross national product. On average, it continued to fall over the rest of the Cold War.[56]

The other development was that it became possible to occasionally decrease U.S.-Soviet tensions. Stalin's death in March 1953 brought the period of greatest Soviet hostility to the West to an end. By the mid-1950s, the superpowers had started negotiations to control the arms race. During the 1960s and after, Moscow and Washington would agree to limit nuclear testing, cap their nuclear arsenals, and reduce the chances of confrontation in a few hot spots. They would even cooperate to eradicate smallpox and limit the spread of nuclear weapons. Tensions still rose and fell; during the late Cold War, the *Bulletin of the Atomic Scientists* placed the hands of its famous "doomsday clock" at just two minutes to midnight. But in retrospect, the Cold War was becoming a "long peace."[57]

It would stay peaceful even as the Soviet Union finally hit the terminal decline Kennan had predicted. By the 1980s, the Soviet growth model was exhausted. Communist ideology was discredited; the regime had become a corrupt gerontocracy whose legitimacy was draining away. Under Reagan, a U.S. geopolitical assault—the counteroffensive following the setbacks of the 1970s—was pressuring exposed Soviet positions in the Third World, increasing the regime's moral and diplomatic isolation, and shifting the balance of military power and geopolitical momentum decisively in the West's favor. Wrote one U.S. intelligence official, "History is no longer on Moscow's side—if it ever was—and Soviet leaders sense they lack the wit, the energy, the resources, and above all the time, to win it back."[58] Yet if the resulting fears made Soviet leaders anxious and prickly, they ultimately accepted that decline, choosing, under Mikhail Gorbachev, to negotiate the terms of geopolitical surrender to the West rather than lashing out against it.

This was in part because American leaders, especially Ronald Reagan and George H.W. Bush, took pains to avoid humiliating a superpower in distress, even as they happily pocketed its concessions. A Soviet Union that changed its behavior, slashed its military arsenal, and tore down the Iron Curtain, Reagan and Bush reassured Gorbachev, would not be attacked: It would be welcomed back into the world community.[59] Yet this achievement also happened because the "situations of strength" that Truman, Acheson, and their successors had built meant that the Soviets had no feasible options for improving their position through war.

Germany could dream, in 1914, of a short, victorious conflict that would set its enemies back a generation. Its leaders could hope, however unrealistically, that Britain might stay out of a continental war. The Soviets, by contrast, confronted a ring of free-world alliances that were backed by decades of U.S. military investments and countless public affirmations that Washington would fight to defend its friends. These pledges were all the more credible thanks to the U.S. buildup of the Reagan era, which made it impossible for Soviet leaders to imagine that conflict would result in anything but catastrophic defeat.[60] The United States avoided a hot end to the Cold War because it reduced the desperation a declining Soviet Union felt, while also destroying any hope that a gamble for resurrection might succeed.

Prioritize ruthlessly; thwart near-term breakthroughs that can have devastating long-term effects. Be strategically deliberate and tactically agile; don't make the perfect the enemy of the good. Firm up the defense by playing some offense; take prudent risks but not unduly provocative ones. Think of danger-zone strategy as something that helps you win in the future by avoiding disaster in the here and now.

These insights from an earlier era are again becoming very relevant. The United States can't simply go back to the Cold War playbook for every policy: Run away from anyone who tries to tell you that the answer to a bellicose China is a "new Marshall Plan" or an "Asian NATO." But America will need a strategy that reflects the larger lessons of one Cold War if it hopes to make it through another today.

# 7

---

# Into the Danger Zone

In February 2021, Joe Biden used the White House as a backdrop to declare a technological cold war on China. Just weeks after taking office, the president signed an executive order that mandated a top-to-bottom review of U.S. technological supply chains. The United States, the thinking within the administration went, would need secure sources of rare earths and other critical inputs in a protracted contest with Beijing; it required long-term investments to preserve its dominance in advanced semiconductors and other technologies.[1] In the accompanying photo op, Biden squeezed, between his thumb and index finger, a microchip that an aide had procured that morning from a nearby plant. Across the river, at the Pentagon, Biden's defense team was working to reboot a military that had spent two decades chasing terrorists. The PLA, as Pentagon leaders now put it, will be America's "pacing challenge" for years to come.[2]

Since 2017, two U.S. administrations, one Republican and one Democratic, have called China the defining danger of the twenty-first century. American officials have been piecing together strategies to keep America ahead economically, militarily, and diplomatically.

"Great-power competition" and "long-term rivalry" have become go-to catchphrases in D.C. policy circles; "marathon" metaphors are ubiquitous.[3] Biden himself put the issue in generational terms: Future historians "are going to be doing their doctoral thesis on the issue of who succeeded, autocracy or democracy."[4]

But if American officials now understand the stakes of the competition, they don't always grasp the urgency. During the Cold War, winning a long contest against the Soviet Union first required not losing the crucial early battles. To triumph in the struggle for the twenty-first century, Washington must once again withstand a strategic onslaught in this decade. Fortunately, many of the principles that helped America survive the early Cold War can help it thrive in a new danger-zone scenario today.

First, prioritize ruthlessly. A danger-zone strategy must deny China any easy escape from its economic and strategic problems by thwarting near-term successes that could radically change the balance of power. The most pressing matters are China's efforts to forge a high-tech economic empire, spread digital authoritarianism, and shatter the geopolitical status quo by taking Taiwan. To be clear, Washington shouldn't ignore other areas of competition; it will have to make long-term investments in innovation, the health of its own democracy, and the vitality of an international order that has served America well. But in the next few years, the United States must focus on issues where the dangers are acute and the consequences of failure would be felt for decades. When time is short and competition is intense, picking your battles wisely is just as important as fighting them well.

Second, don't make the perfect the enemy of the good enough. A danger-zone strategy is a race against the clock, and the China threat is escalating faster than business-as-usual in Washington can keep up. Securing U.S. interests will require embracing second-best solutions, adapting old capabilities for new purposes, and assembling imperfect coalitions on the fly. Think of this as "strategic MacGyverism"—using the tools we have or can quickly summon to defuse geopolitical bombs that are about to explode.[5]

Third, playing defense requires a good offense. The United States cannot get through the danger zone without calculated risk-taking. It must be willing to anger China, bait it into strategic blunders, and selectively roll back its power. The CCP won't abandon its lofty ambitions anytime soon, so Washington must focus on selectively degrading China's capabilities and blocking its opportunities for aggrandizement. Seduction and integration are out; coercion and attrition are in. Yet American officials must also avoid backing China into corners where its only option is to lash out violently. Urgency, not stupidity, is the order of the day.

Finally, a danger-zone strategy is a way of getting to the long game—and ensuring that America can win it. The crisis-driven measures of the Truman years didn't end the Cold War, but they did a great deal to determine its outcome by shifting the balance of power so markedly in the free world's favor. In the same vein, America will still have far to go even if it deftly navigates the 2020s. But by taking the steps necessary to avoid disaster, America can simultaneously build the advantages and coalitions that will help it win in the end. Danger-zone strategies emerge in response to pressing perils. When done right, they can also create situations of enduring strength.

## ANTI-IMPERIALISM IN THE DIGITAL AGE

One such peril is China's emerging high-tech empire. The United States doesn't need to counter every Chinese infrastructure project around the world; doing so would be financially ruinous and strategically exhausting. It *does* need to prevent China from monopolizing what the Pentagon calls "critical" technologies, meaning those with the potential to produce massive economic and military gains, and using that dominance to ensnare nations around the globe.[6]

History shows that whoever dominates the critical technologies of an era dominates that era.[7] Britain was able to build an empire on which the sun never set largely because it mastered steam, iron, and the telegraph before other nations. American hegemony today is due in no small part to U.S. superiority, first in steel, electronics, aerospace, and chemicals and more recently in information technology. Now China aims to use preeminence in artificial intelligence, telecommunications, quantum computing, and synthetic biology to leap ahead of its competitors and force other countries to do its bidding.

Permanently denying China a high-tech sphere of influence could take decades, involving long-term investments in American innovation and painstaking efforts to revamp the institutions (namely the World Trade Organization) that govern the global economy. Yet these initiatives won't deliver results for years, if ever: China has demonstrated an impressive aptitude for stealing the fruits of American R&D and circumventing international trade agreements. It also has made clear that it won't change its predatory economic practices anytime soon; subsidies and espionage are too central to its growth model.

For now, the United States needs to give up on trying to make Beijing play by the rules of a fair and open economic order, whether by browbeating it with tariffs or enticing it with new trade agreements. Instead, the thrust of U.S. policy should be sharper and narrower: weakening Beijing's relative technological capabilities. That's the path to thwarting an authoritarian empire in this era, just as America thwarted a series of authoritarian empires during the twentieth century.

The best way of doing this is to forge an informal economic alliance that excludes and outcompetes China. The gold standard for such cooperation occurred during the Cold War, when the United States gathered the world's most economically advanced democracies together, country-club style, in an exclusive trade and investment network. Members shared technology, pooled R&D funds, and integrated their supply chains, allowing each member to specialize in areas of comparative advantage. They coordinated export controls to curtail the Kremlin's access to strategic commodities and high-tech goods. The sum of these collaborative efforts far exceeded what America could have achieved alone, and the Western alliance left the Soviets in the dust. "Globalization was not global," the political scientists Stephen Brooks and William Wohlforth note, "it took sides in the Cold War."[8]

Today, the United States needs to reestablish a free-world economic bloc, this time aimed at China. This is not a sweeping call for *de-globalization*; bloc members would still trade with China in most sectors and could reduce tariffs on low-value Chinese goods.[9] Nor is it a call for the sort of economic unilateralism the Trump administration often practiced. Rather, it entails *re-globalization*—deepening integration among the United States and its allies—to blunt Chinese economic leverage and pursue a strategic, multilateral decoupling in the technologies and resources that matter most.[10]

To make this strategy work, U.S. officials first need to forget about universalism. In an ideal world, members of the free-world bloc would unanimously adopt common trade and investment standards, many of which have already been developed in existing accords such as the Comprehensive and Progressive Agreement for Trans-Pacific Partnership (CPTPP), United States-Mexico-Canada Agreement (USMCA), and the EU-Japan economic partnership agreement. They would thereby revive the aspiration of the post–Cold War era—a seamless, liberal economic order—this time with China on the outside. In reality, there's no time for this, and even a patchy collection of mini-lateral agreements would build multilateral resilience against Chinese pressure by reorienting strategic supply chains away from Beijing. America can still promote a global rules-based trade system as a distant aspiration, but its immediate focus should be on power politics.

This also means accepting that small can be beautiful. Over the long term, the United States should seek to bring as many countries as possible into this bloc. But the collective-action challenges of big clubs can be paralyzing, so for now, Washington should start with a small but powerful group. If the United States can enlist just seven countries, all of which are close treaty allies—Australia, Canada, France, Germany, Japan, South Korea, and the United Kingdom—it would have a potent economic alliance. These countries collectively outspend China on R&D, account for nearly a quarter of the global economy, and produce most of the choke-point technologies that the United States does not already dominate.[11] Such a vibrant core could also attract other partners in the future.

At the same time, the United States and its partners need to put function ahead of form. This informal alliance would not become a full-fledged "economic NATO" where members sign a formal, binding treaty pledging to defend each other from Chinese economic coercion. Instead, it would have a network-based structure that allows members to create flexible, issue-based partnerships. For example, a semiconductor coalition would ideally include Germany, Japan, the Netherlands, South Korea, Taiwan, and the United States—countries that comprise almost the entire manufacturing supply chain of advanced chips. A quantum computing and next-generation encryption coalition could be spearheaded by the Five Eyes intelligence alliance, comprising Australia, Canada, New Zealand, the United Kingdom, and the United States. At the level of operations, a free-world economic alliance would really be a set of overlapping power blocs that coalesce around key challenges.

Succeeding in these areas, in turn, requires running faster *and* slowing the opponent down.[12] Each ad hoc coalition would pursue the positive goal of outpacing Beijing in critical technologies by engaging in collaborative R&D and setting international technical standards.[13] At the same time, these coalitions would kneecap Chinese innovation, imposing strict export and investment controls that deny Beijing access to cutting-edge technologies (members would be free to sell China older models) and the money that has too often fueled companies in cahoots with the CCP.[14] In essence, the coalitions would act as mini-CoComs, tailored versions of the Cold War–era Coordinating Committee for Multilateral Export Controls, which embargoed advanced technology to the Soviet bloc. The United States and its allies have already crimped China's access to advanced semiconductors and related manufacturing equipment, with devastating effects on Huawei's ability to fulfill its telecommunications contracts. Similar multilateral embargos are needed to hobble Beijing's momentum in other areas—cloud computing, advanced robotics, machine learning, and many others.[15]

As all this indicates, digital anti-imperialism involves attacking the core of Beijing's techno-bloc as well as competing at the periphery. To date, much of the U.S. policy debate has focused on how to prevent countries, particularly in the developing world, from adopting Chinese technology in 5G telecommunications. The challenges here are real: When Secretary of Defense Mark Esper told one international gathering not to rely on Chinese tech in 2020, a rejoinder from the audience—"Are you offering an alternative?"—drew laughter and applause.[16]

The United States has recently notched some victories by offering financial incentives for regional powers such as Ethiopia to jilt Huawei.[17] If a free-world bloc can multi-lateralize this approach, while also developing cheaper, good-enough alternatives to Chinese products, it may be able to fight a selective rearguard action in developing countries where price is the decisive factor. But it will be hard to win a worldwide subsidy war against a mercantilist CCP, especially when the battlefield—in regions from Southeast Asia to Latin America—is densely populated with corrupt leaders and regimes. The more proactive approach is to go to the source by using the blend of offensive and defensive measures we advocate to keep Beijing from dominating key industries in the first place.

China certainly will bristle at these attacks. And to some degree that's a good thing, because it provides opportunities to bait Beijing into strategic blunders. Recall what happened in March 2021, when the United States, European Union, United Kingdom, and Canada sanctioned four Chinese officials for human rights abuses in Xinjiang. The sanctions were slaps on the wrist, but they triggered a self-defeating wolf-warrior outburst: Beijing unleashed a tirade of vituperative statements and sanctioned four EU entities and ten EU officials, including five members of the European Parliament. The European Union responded by freezing the pending China-EU Comprehensive Agreement on Investment that had been concluded just three months earlier. The lesson is that America and its allies can goad China in subtle ways that don't risk war but do trigger the type of blustery overreaction through which Beijing isolates itself.

Bait-and-bleed strategies, however, require resilience. When Chinese state media threatened, in March 2020, to plunge America into "a mighty sea of coronavirus" by denying it pharmaceuticals, it underscored Beijing's capacity for ugly retaliation.[18] A final requirement of this strategy, then, will be rapidly developing free-world production networks for critical resources that China currently dominates, including rare earths and emergency medical supplies. The Quad's collaboration to produce COVID-19 vaccines shows how an ad hoc coalition can quickly generate alternatives to Chinese products, when the requisite sense of urgency is there. A forum that had previously focused on maritime security was rapidly repurposed, using U.S. biotechnology, Indian production, Japanese financing, and Australian logistics, to provide 1 billion doses of vaccine to Southeast Asia.

Can this strategy of collective anti-imperialism really work? Some observers believe genuine counter-China cooperation will remain the exception rather than the norm, because major U.S. allies are too dependent on China's economy. Berlin, the key player in Europe, is wary of incurring Beijing's wrath given that one in three German cars is sold in China. Many traditional U.S. allies were also scarred by four years of tariffs and scorn from Donald Trump. Surveys in late 2020 showed that majorities in Germany, France, and the United Kingdom believe the American political system is broken and that their governments should remain neutral in U.S.-China competition.[19]

Yet U.S. allies were often appalled by American politics during the Cold War; they were simply far *more* horrified by the prospect of Soviet hegemony. Today, China's predatory economic tactics, wolf-warrior diplomacy, and humanitarian outrages have kept hope alive for a free-world bloc. Nearly 75 percent of thought leaders in Europe and Asia support collaborative efforts to reduce economic dependence on China, and as of late 2021, twenty-four of the twenty-seven member countries of the European Union had restricted or banned Chinese firms from their telecommunications networks.[20] A variety of Asian countries, such as India, Bangladesh, and Vietnam, would love to grab pieces of China's role in global supply chains. Washington can channel this anti-China sentiment into allied cooperation in several ways.

One is by exercising convening power, not coercive hegemony. The United States doesn't have to be the leader or even a member of every anti-China coalition. The overarching goal of a free-world economic bloc is to achieve collective resilience through diversity, preventing Chinese dominance by fostering an array of alternative products and supply chains. An example is U.S. promotion of a telecommunications policy called "Open RAN."[21] Under this approach, policy makers are developing common industry standards that foster greater compatibility between different types of 5G equipment. The goal is to prevent Huawei—or any other 5G equipment provider—from dominating global telecommunications infrastructure. American firms (particularly those that make relevant software) would benefit from this approach, but so would Huawei's competitors in Finland, South Korea, and other countries.

America also has an unparalleled ability to cajole allied cooperation. The U.S. consumer market is as large as that of the next five nations combined; half of world trade and 90 percent of international financial transactions are conducted in dollars and pass through institutions under the thumb of the U.S. Treasury Department. American firms create one-third of the value in global high-tech industries. No country has more carrots and sticks.[22] In addition, the globalized nature of tech supply chains has increased the number of choke points under U.S. control by virtually guaranteeing that an American firm occupies at least one critical node in the chain.[23]

These advantages bestow massive convening power on the United States. The semiconductor example is illustrative. Washington was able to persuade allies to cut China off from high-end chips and manufacturing machines because U.S. firms produce critical components for those machines, allies increasingly fear China, and allies depend more on America's market (and America's protection) than they do on China's.[24]

Selective multilateral decoupling is, therefore, achievable—at a cost. The economic expense should not be exaggerated—even if American exports to China fell by half, it would be the equivalent of less than one-half of 1 percent of GDP—but specific U.S. and allied companies could lose billions of dollars in China-based revenue.[25] That's why multilateral decoupling is not a money-making scheme; it is damage limitation. Decoupling will not re-shore millions of American jobs, but it will save many existing jobs and companies from Chinese predation. American and allied firms might lose access to China's market, but they will gain protection from Chinese coercion and espionage, the latter of which costs U.S. firms between $225 billion and $600 billion every year.[26] The costs of decoupling are great, but they pale in comparison to the costs of "business as usual" with Beijing.

Even as China's high-tech empire crumbles, however, Beijing has other tools at its disposal, including potent ideological weapons. While resisting China's economic influence, the United States and its friends must also secure their democratic institutions from authoritarian assault. If democracy *promotion* has a bad name, democracy *protection* is becoming indispensable.

## DEMOCRACY PROTECTION

At its core, democracy protection requires what military planners call "defending forward"—safeguarding democratic systems by actively weakening an opponent's ability to damage them.[27] In other words, the United States should do whatever it can to shore up democracy at home and abroad, but the immediate priority must be to blast holes in the digital iron curtain Beijing is drawing around large swaths of the globe. If the world is indeed at an "inflection point" in the struggle between democracy and autocracy, as President Biden has said and President Xi clearly believes, America won't tip the balance by remaining on the defensive.[28]

For example, getting "America's democratic house in order" is a wonderful idea, but it will take years and will only counter China's ideological offensive over an extended time horizon. Contesting China's control of human rights bodies in the United Nations and policing autocratic financial networks are crucially important tasks, but success here will mainly affect Beijing's strategy at the margins. Forming a giant alliance of democracies to combat authoritarian political meddling is a worthy objective for a long cold war, but such a large, unwieldy group might deliver endless debate instead of decisive action. In 2000, the Clinton administration created the "Community of Democracies," which ultimately included 106 countries. After years of meetings, its sole accomplishment was a bland statement criticizing Myanmar.

Instead of building a sprawling organization, the United States should mobilize rough-and-ready gangs to attack China's digital authoritarianism on multiple fronts. This impromptu, offensive approach accommodates the varying capabilities and interests of democratic states; it allows for selective cooperation with imperfect democracies and even a few friendly non-democracies. Like digital anti-imperialism, it allows Washington to build on existing groups; it emphasizes function over form by zeroing in on specific threats.[29] Most important, it takes the fight to the enemy, actively degrading and deterring China's political warfare initiatives, rather than meekly patching holes in democratic defenses, which inevitably will remain porous given the open nature of liberal societies.

Step one is for America and its allies to aggressively hack digital authoritarian systems, thereby undermining their effectiveness. One redeeming quality of high-tech police states is that they have myriad points of failure.[30] Any government computer or goon is a potential entry point for malware. Hackers can stealthily feed "adversarial inputs" into AI-enabled surveillance systems by changing a few pixels in certain images. They can "poison the data" authoritarian regimes use to train their algorithms with fake inputs; they can enter malicious code into the patches authoritarian technicians use to fix faulty systems.

Basic hacks can spring leaks in censorship systems, allowing prohibited news stories to go viral; they also can trick surveillance systems or
social credit schemes into overlooking dissident activity or misclassify-
ing regime loyalists as enemies of the state.

Democratic governments don't even need to attack authoritarian
states directly; they can post spoofs online and let dissidents around the
world weaponize them. And defenders of democracy need not disrupt
every digital authoritarian regime—just a few high-profile flubs might
be enough to dampen demand for Beijing's products. Think of this as
ideological cost-imposition: The more time, energy, and money China
spends fixing bugs in its surveillance state at home, the less it has to
manipulate democratic politics abroad.

Autocrats constantly seek to enhance their internal security systems, so another vital task is to slow the spread of repression-relevant
technology. In part, that means producing affordable alternatives to
Chinese telecom and smart-city products, such as low-earth-orbit satellites that provide global broadband. More important, it means barring
U.S. and allied firms from transferring certain technologies—such as
advanced speech- and facial-recognition, computer vision, and natural
language processing technologies—to authoritarian regimes, as well as
barring foreign firms involved in authoritarian repression from raising
capital in democratic financial markets.[31] The export control coalitions
we discussed previously could make that happen, while also generat-
ing leverage to prevent democratic backsliding by tenuous members of
the free world. If Hungary's increasingly thuggish government wants
continued access to U.S. and Western European markets, for example,
it would have to dispense with digital systems provided by Beijing.

More broadly, fostering economic cooperation among democracies
would reduce China's ability to play divide-and-conquer, punishing
one outspoken democracy to scare others into silence. China's coercive

campaign against Australia in 2020 was indicative of the challenge. To recall, the CCP hit Canberra with steep tariffs on coal, beef, wheat, wine, and other goods, while also demanding that it stifle domestic voices that had been "unfriendly" to Beijing, after Australia called for an international COVID-19 inquiry.

To its credit, Canberra didn't cave, and it slowly found alternative markets, in part by launching a "fight communism, buy Australian wine" public relations campaign. The Biden administration informed Chinese officials that bilateral tensions would not subside as long as the CCP was beating up on American allies, and it helped Canberra exact some revenge by promising to supply it with nuclear propulsion technology to power cutting-edge attack submarines.[32] But Australia's economy suffered a blow—and, awkwardly, firms from other democracies grabbed some of the resulting market share. Denser economic ties among democracies (and also with friendly quasi- or non-democracies that fear Chinese coercion, such as Vietnam and Singapore) are crucial to reduce the costs of future resistance. It would be even better if rich democracies, such as the eight-nation bloc that might take on Chinese digital imperialism, agreed to inflict reciprocal pain on Beijing through coordinated counter-sanctions. China could still try to censor democratic speech in foreign countries, but only at the cost of its own economic growth.

Most audaciously, the United States and its allies could preemptively split the Internet by creating a digital bloc in which data and products flow freely, while excluding China and other countries that do not respect freedom of expression or privacy rights. The CCP currently enjoys the best of both worlds. It runs a closed network at home that prevents Chinese citizens from reaching foreign websites and limits Western companies from entering China's digital market. Yet it also selectively accesses the global Internet to steal intellectual property, meddle in democratic elections, spread propaganda, and hack critical infrastructure. It's a digital-age version of the Soviet Union's infamous Brezhnev Doctrine: What's mine is mine, and what's yours is up for grabs.

To counter this exploitation, Richard Clarke and Rob Knake have proposed forming an "Internet Freedom League."[33] Under this system, countries that adhere to the vision of a free and open Internet would stay mutually connected, while countries opposed to that vision would face restricted access or be shut out. In essence, the league would be a digital version of the Schengen Agreement, which provides for the free movement of people, goods, and services within the European Union. The league would not block all Internet traffic from non-members, just companies and organizations that aid and abet digital authoritarianism and cybercrime. Of course, the CCP is one of those bad actors, so China would be cut off. During the Cold War, Dean Acheson observed, Washington and its allies settled for creating "half a world, a free half" because the alternative was watching an authoritarian menace overwhelm the whole world.[34] The United States needs a similar approach to the current digital struggle between democracy and authoritarianism.

Achieving multinational cooperation on these initiatives will be challenging, especially with traditional European allies. Europeans and Americans have different ideas about data security and privacy, and European governments fear U.S. digital dominance almost as much as they do Chinese hegemony. The United States is home to 68 percent of the market capitalization of the world's seventy largest digital platforms, whereas Europe is home to only 3.6 percent.[35] With such a small market share, Europe has little incentive to defend a system that seems tilted heavily in America's favor. That's why the European Commission is pursuing "digital sovereignty" vis-à-vis Washington and Beijing.

There are still reasons to be optimistic: the EU-U.S. Trade and Technology Council, created in 2021, is designed to negotiate transatlantic cooperation on digital flows, export controls, investment screening, technology standards, and other issues. Democracies share a basic interest in networks that protect privacy, free speech, and open access to information, a fact that is becoming steadily more apparent with the expansion of an authoritarian alternative. All things equal, a Europe that will struggle to defend itself, by itself, from Chinese tech dominance should gradually move toward greater cooperation with Washington. But America can't take that cooperation for granted and should work hard to secure it by adopting national data privacy regulations more compatible with the EU's General Data Protection Regulation, signing on to a digital tax treaty, and encouraging greater competition in digital markets.[36] As during the Cold War, building solidarity against a greater evil requires convincing allies that America represents the lesser one.

Democracy protection also involves partnering with developing countries, which account for the vast majority of global growth in Internet users and digital revenues. China dominates the digital hardware market in many developing countries, and Chinese products often bring authoritarian methods with them. America and its allies need to offer alternatives, especially in India, which is the key "swing state" in U.S.-China network competition.[37] By 2027, India will have a quarter of the world's mobile device subscription growth, 1 billion smartphones, and the largest population on the planet.[38] If India adopts Chinese telecommunications and smart-city systems, its increasingly shaky democracy might not survive, and the balance of network power and ideological influence would swing sharply in Beijing's favor.

Fortunately, India has been getting tougher with China since the 2020 military clash in the Himalayas. It subsequently excluded Chinese vendors from its short list of potential 5G providers. India also joined the United States, Japan, and Australia in the first leaders-level summit of the Quad in March 2021, where the countries created, among other things, a working group focused on critical technologies. Leading Indian telecom firms are making bold moves in developing Open RAN.

But India's loyalty remains up for grabs. One reason is that its government is becoming more repressive. New Delhi leads the world in Internet shutdowns, which makes it an unlikely member of an Internet Freedom League. Another reason is that India imports nearly 40 percent of its telecommunications equipment and two-thirds of its data center equipment from China, mainly because Chinese products are cheap. Indian consumers, like those in many developing countries, probably won't pay considerably more for American or allied equipment. Case in point: After the Himalayan border clash in 2020, the Indian government banned more than 100 Chinese apps, but Chinese companies increased their market share and accounted for 75 percent of India's smartphone market by the end of 2020.[39] The Indian government has said it wants to reduce telecommunications dependence on China, but mainly by creating its own "sovereign" Internet and tech champions.

The United States can't rely on democratic solidarity alone to persuade India to join the fight for network freedom. Instead, America and its allies should try to buy New Delhi's cooperation by incentivizing companies to move telecommunications production from China to India. As of 2020, the United States sourced 73 percent of its cell phones and 93 percent of its laptops from China.[40] If Washington and other advanced democracies could shift even a fraction of their telecommunications supply chains, it would strengthen India's manufacturing sector, potentially enabling it to produce affordable alternatives to Chinese products that could be exported throughout the developing world. India has already announced its willingness to pay for the privilege; in 2021, its government allocated $1 billion in subsidies to entice the world's top computer manufacturers to relocate their China-based operations to India.[41]

Finally, the United States needs to defend democracies on the front lines of the conflict with China. Doing so is not simply a matter of protecting small, vulnerable nations: Successful authoritarian coercion in one place may encourage more brazen actions elsewhere. The most important battleground is Taiwan, where China is waging a vast subversive campaign. This campaign goes far beyond seeding disinformation and propaganda in Taiwanese media. It involves manipulating every element of Taiwan's information supply chain, from the people who produce content to the online platforms that deliver it to consumers.[42] It also involves the direct purchase of major Taiwanese media conglomerates; the use of hundreds of thousands of fake social media accounts; and an array of bribes to journalists, media groups, and politicians. Digitally isolating Beijing will be crucial to securing Taiwan's democracy. But even that won't be enough, because China has other means of "liberating" Taiwan.

## SAVING TAIWAN

There are many places where Chinese aggression is possible in this decade, but top of the list is Taiwan. China is determined to reabsorb the island, and the only sure way it can do that is to send an army across the Taiwan Strait. America has already taken the first step toward reinforcing deterrence over Taiwan: communicating, albeit obliquely, that it is willing to fight.[43] Some American analysts have argued that Washington should go further, giving Taiwan—which is not technically a treaty ally—a treaty-like guarantee of its security. That might reinforce Taiwan's resolve to resist, by demonstrating that it wouldn't have to stand up to a Chinese assault alone.[44] Yet even the strongest red-line declarations will amount to cheap talk if not backed by a stronger defense—something the United States and Taiwan currently lack.

Taiwanese and American policy makers are aware of the problem, but they aren't moving fast enough to fix it.[45] Even as the Pentagon puts protecting Taiwan at the center of U.S. defense strategy, American policy makers spend an inordinate amount of time arguing about whether to build a 355-ship navy that might be completed sometime in the 2040s. The Pentagon itself is shoveling R&D money into fancy new capabilities that might arrive a decade too late. Taiwan has adopted, in principle, the porcupine concept it needs to resist a Chinese invasion. But it keeps blowing more than a quarter of its annual defense budget on domestically made ships and submarines that will not be deployed for years, fighter aircraft that may not make it off the ground in a war, and tanks that cannot easily maneuver on beaches or in jungles or cities.[46]

At this rate, Taiwan and Washington might be ready for war in the 2030s—when what is needed is a strategy to deter or perhaps win a conflict in the 2020s. To close China's near-term window of opportunity, the United States and Taiwan will have to move rapidly, in multiple respects.

First, the Pentagon can dramatically raise the costs of a Chinese invasion by turning the international waters of the Taiwan Strait into a death trap for attacking forces—and it can do so simply by buying tools that are ready or nearly ready today. The most straightforward solution would be to position hordes of missile launchers, armed drones, electronic jammers, smart mines, and sensors at sea and on allied territory near the strait. Instead of waiting for a Chinese invasion to start and then surging missile-magnet aircraft carriers into the region, the Pentagon could use what is, in essence, a high-tech minefield to decimate China's invasion forces and cut their communications links as they load in mainland ports or putter across more than 100 miles of open water. These diffuse networks of loitering munitions and jammers would be difficult for China to eliminate without starting a region-wide war. They would not require large crews, logistics tails, or the procurement of fancy platforms. Instead, they could be installed on virtually anything that floats or flies, including legacy platforms and repurposed cargo ships, barges, and aircraft.[47]

This approach would capitalize on a key U.S. advantage: China's war aims are more ambitious, and harder to achieve, than America's. Whereas China needs to seize control of Taiwan and its surrounding waters to win the war, the United States just needs to deny Chinese forces that control, a mission that modern missiles, mines, drones, and jammers are well suited to perform.[48] This strategy would also enhance deterrence by denying China the possibility of a swift victory. China's leaders might be willing to start a short war over Taiwan, even one that kills millions. They will be less keen to fight a war that seems likely to spiral out of their control and drag on interminably, with no opportunity to declare victory. Such a messy, uncontrolled conflict could derail the economy while spurring domestic discontent and instability. It is this prospect of chaos, not the prospect of casualties, that has deterred China from fighting in the past.[49] It could do so again today if Beijing comes to fear the strait as a no-man's land of missiles, mines, and electromagnetic interference.

Second, America can't win the fight unless it stays in the fight, and that means rapidly dispersing and hardening America's bases, communications, and logistics networks in East Asia. China's theory of victory—the way it plans to defeat a technologically superior American adversary—depends heavily on "system destruction warfare."[50] This means destroying America's forward-deployed aircraft while they're parked on the tarmac and preventing a surge of U.S. forces from other regions by paralyzing their lines of communications and logistics.

To prevent China from making this theory work, the United States must scatter its forces across dozens of small operating sites in East Asia and reduce its reliance on non-stealthy weapons systems that require anything more than episodic communication or data flow. The few big bases that remain must be outfitted with hardened shelters, robust missile defenses, and fake targets to absorb Chinese missiles. Forces that are still dependent on centralized networks must prepare for communications blackouts by drilling regularly to conduct missions independent of central command. The United States doesn't need a completely air-gapped and bullet-proof force, but it does need a more resilient one that makes China's leaders doubt they can achieve "system destruction" at large scale.[51] It also needs to prepare to turn "system destruction warfare" against the CCP by using well-prepared cyberattacks, electronic warfare, and other means to shut down key Chinese capabilities in the early days of a conflict. And America's cyber warriors should proactively help Taiwan police its key servers and networks, so that China can't use its own offensive cyber capabilities to hobble Taiwanese resistance before the shooting even starts.

This relates to a third requirement: Washington needs to help Taiwan help itself. Taipei has smart plans to stock up on mobile missile launchers, mines, and radars; harden its communications infrastructure; and enlarge its army and ground-force reserves. It is moving, albeit slowly, toward the only winning strategy it has: one based on using cheap and plentiful capabilities ("large numbers of small things," as one U.S. official remarked in 2019) to inflict sky-high costs on an aggressor. The United States can hasten these preparations by donating ammunition and sensors, subsidizing Taiwanese procurement of missile launchers and mine layers, matching Taiwanese investments in vital military infrastructure, and expanding joint training on air and coastal defense and anti-submarine and mine warfare, contingent on Taipei aggressively pursuing an asymmetric approach. These plans can be modeled on the War Reserve Stocks for Allies program the United States maintains with Israel—another initiative meant to help a small, isolated democracy.[52] And the Pentagon can use its special operations forces' expertise in unconventional warfare to help Taiwan prepare for a lethal insurgency against Chinese occupiers, the prospect of which may help deter invasion in the first place.

In short, if Taiwan doesn't sprint to implement the right strategy, there's not much America can do to save it. If it does, the United States should provide money, hardware, and expertise to make the island a tougher target. All this, in turn, will require an even closer relationship than Washington and Taipei have today—a relationship that may not become a formal alliance, but one that nonetheless features the frequent high-level consultations, training and exercises, and deep military and diplomatic cooperation in peacetime that allows countries to fight effectively together when war breaks out.[53]

Fourth, the United States needs to reduce its geographic disadvantage—and buy time for these other measures to take effect—by boosting its military presence near, and even on, Taiwan. American warships and submarines should conduct regular patrols through the Taiwan Strait, even if this means redeploying forces from other regions, to reduce the odds that a conflict will begin when the nearest U.S. firepower is hundreds of miles away. America and Japan should establish joint fire-bases in the southernmost Ryukyu Islands, and they should do it now, rather than waiting for war to break out. The United States should also increase the special operations forces training missions it quietly conducts with Taiwan, so that more often than not, small groups of elite troops are already on the scene and ready to help.[54]

More dramatically, the United States could deploy its own surface-to-air and anti-ship missile batteries on Taiwan. This step may not be necessary; Taiwan has advanced missiles, and the U.S. military might be able to mass sufficient firepower by deploying surface ships and missile barges near the island. But being able to operate on Taiwan would allow the United States to make the most of that island's forbidding terrain—while ensuring that China knows the Pentagon will be in the fight from the start.

Fifth, America should develop the ability to disrupt China's military communication systems. The last thing any autocratic regime wants is to lose control over its forces. Because the PLA has mainly killed its own people since the invasion of Vietnam in 1979, it hasn't tested its command-and-control processes under wartime stress. CCP officials surely have doubts about how well a heavily politicized, still-corrupt PLA would perform in the fog of war.[55] By developing the ability—through cyberattacks and related means—to strain Chinese command-and-control mechanisms and inject confusion into military communications networks, the Pentagon can make Chinese officials wonder how glitchy their force will be in combat. And by subtly advertising that ability in peacetime, America can make Beijing question whether escalating to conflict is worth it.

Finally, the United States needs to make China realize that a Taiwan war could go big as well as long. The more allies and partners America can bring into the fight, the less appetizing that fight will look to Beijing. The PLA may talk big about nuking Japan if Tokyo gets in the way of a Taiwan invasion, but it can't really relish fighting a global superpower *and* its mightiest regional ally at the same time.[56] Similarly, the Indian and Australian navies could help Washington choke off Beijing's energy imports as they pass through the Strait of Malacca. Key European powers—especially the United Kingdom and France—can contribute a few submarines or surface combatants to a naval war in the western Pacific; they can lend their well-honed cyber expertise to help defend critical Taiwanese systems. They can also impose painful economic sanctions in the event of Chinese aggression.[57]

None of these countries can save Taiwan militarily. But they can help Washington turn a war over Taiwan into a confrontation between China and advanced democracies around the world. That's a strategic price that even Xi might hesitate to pay.

If deterrence fails, however, there will be no substitute for sinking China's invasion fleet—and even that might not force Beijing to back down. Great-power wars rarely end after the opening salvo, especially when one belligerent believes it is fighting over vital territory. The United States and its allies must prepare, materially and psychologically, for a grinding conflict that could drag on for months or years.

## THE LONG WAR

Ever since the Industrial Revolution and the advent of the mass army, great-power wars have more often been long than short. The Napoleonic Wars, the U.S. Civil War, and World Wars I and II were all decided by relentless attrition rather than rapid annihilation. If China tried and failed to invade Taiwan, it would have strong reasons to fight on. Xi would surely fear that conceding defeat to Taiwanese renegades and American imperialists would hobble China geopolitically, imperil the CCP's legitimacy, and lead to his overthrow. He might keep the war machine running, in hopes of snatching victory from the jaws of defeat or simply saving some face.

Halting a Chinese invasion of Taiwan could be the twenty-first century equivalent of France's stand on the river Marne in the opening weeks of World War I—a heroic, necessary defense that sets the stage for a protracted, bloody slugfest.

Winning that sort of conflict means, first, making sure that America and Taiwan don't run out of ammo. The United States can prepare by loading up on long-range missiles capable of wrecking China's most valuable ships and aircraft from afar. For Taiwan, the vital weapons are short-range missiles, mortars, mines, and rocket launchers. Beyond stockpiling these munitions, the United States and Taiwan need to develop the production capacity to crank out new weapons in wartime, the way America has done in nearly every other major conflict in its history. Taiwanese weapons plants will be obvious targets for Chinese missiles, so it will also be crucial to harness allied industrial might; for example, using Japan's shipbuilding capacity to design and produce simple missile barges rapidly, at scale.

At the same time, the United States and Taiwan may have to ride out a Chinese punishment campaign. When wars become protracted, the combatants typically search for new sources of leverage, as Germany did in World War I by resorting to unrestricted submarine warfare. Beijing would still have many ways to coerce Taiwan and the United States even if they sent China's amphibious fleet to the bottom of the strait. China could try to strangle Taiwan economically with a blockade or cripple U.S. and Taiwanese electrical grids and telecommunications networks with cyberattacks.[58] China could also try to bomb Taiwan into submission and perhaps even use, or threaten to use, nuclear weapons—a tactic that Beijing's rapid nuclear buildup is making somewhat more feasible and, potentially, more attractive.

Stopping that coercion from succeeding will require a combination of defense and offense. The United States and Taiwan need to redouble their efforts to defend critical networks from cyberattacks;

Taiwan needs to expand its system of civilian shelters; bulk up its stockpiles of food, fuel, and medical supplies; and prepare its population for prolonged, bloody sacrifice. But these defensive measures must be paired with offensive preparations that threaten China with painful retaliation.

By conducting exercises with allies and partners that demonstrate an ability to choke off Chinese maritime commerce, the United States can threaten to turn an extended war into an economic catastrophe for the CCP.[59] By developing the ability to conduct severe cyberattacks on China's critical infrastructure—and the CCP's political control mechanisms—the United States can threaten to bring the war home to Beijing. By preparing to sink Chinese naval vessels up and down the western Pacific, and to target whatever bases and other global military infrastructure Beijing has built, the United States can force the CCP to risk a generation of military modernization and expansion in any war over Taiwan.[60] And although the United States would obviously prefer to keep a war over Taiwan non-nuclear, it needs to have the limited nuclear options—the ability to use lower-yield weapons against ports, airfields, fleets, and other military targets—that would allow it to credibly respond to, and thereby deter, Chinese nuclear threats.[61] In sum, Washington should confront Beijing with a basic proposition: The longer the war continues, the more devastation America will inflict on China and its ruling regime.

Finally, the United States needs to prepare for war termination as seriously as it prepares for warfighting. A war with a nuclear-armed foe is unlikely to end in a total U.S. victory or a complete Chinese capitulation.[62] The better America fares, the more unpredictable a scared CCP may become. It will take lots of sustained coercion and destruction to make Beijing call it quits—but it may also take some face-saving diplomacy. If, for example, China was eventually willing to stop attacking

Taiwan in exchange for a pledge that the island would not seek, and Washington would not support, political independence, then America would be wise to accept such a bargain. (The flip side of this approach might be a quiet warning that America's war aims would escalate—perhaps encompassing formal independence for Taiwan—the longer the shooting continues.)

Washington would then have shown that it can preserve Taiwan as a barrier to Chinese expansion; Xi could claim, however dubiously, that he had taught Taipei a lesson. Wars are easy to start, but hard to end, so the United States will need to grind an aggressive China down while leaving it a way out.

## THE EUROPEAN CONNECTION

Breaking China's emerging economic empire, preventing the global erosion of democracy, saving Taiwan: These missions would be daunting under any circumstance, but they are all the more challenging following Russia's invasion of Ukraine. The United States doesn't face a single serious security crisis; it faces at least two, at opposite ends of the world's largest landmass, with the possibility of more to come.

China is the chief threat, given its colossal power and soaring ambitions: Americans are not in danger of finding themselves living in a Russo-centric world. Yet the United States can't simply abandon Europe, as some analysts advocate, and throw its resources into Asia.

Every time America has tried to disengage from Europe, disaster has struck. The most egregious example occurred after World War I, when American retrenchment contributed to a global conflagration. Recent history provides other cautionary tales. In 2001, President Bush looked Putin in the eye, determined that the dictator had a decent soul, and drew down U.S. forces in Europe to concentrate on wars in the

Middle East: In 2008, Russia invaded Georgia. The Obama administration then pursued a "reset" with Moscow before dissing Russia as a declining power and pivoting U.S. strategic attention to Asia: Putin made Washington pay by carving up Ukraine. The Trump and Biden administrations came to office determined to make China their priority: Russia then tried to destroy an independent Ukraine in a massive land grab that created a global security crisis. Peace on the continent that produced Napoleon, Mussolini, Hitler, Stalin, Milosevic, and Putin cannot be presumed.

Nor can events in Europe be sealed off from the balance of power in Asia. For one thing, Russia's revanchist and antidemocratic campaign works in tandem with China's. By meddling in democracies, challenging the credibility of NATO, carving out spheres of influence, and promoting the legitimacy of dictatorship, Moscow exposes cracks in the international order for Beijing to blast through. In addition, the three main power assets the United States needs to counter China—a free world economic bloc, security community, and democracy protection regime—would be crippled by a breakdown of order in Europe that consumes and divides America's allies there. China projects its influence across multiple regions and aims to achieve global primacy. Competing with Beijing requires rallying an international alliance of leading democracies, and many of the world's most powerful liberal states are European. That alliance will not stand if Europe falls into chaos.

This means America must pursue a double-containment strategy that deals with threats from China and Russia simultaneously. In Europe, task one is to beef up defenses on NATO's Eastern flank. European nations have promised to invest more heavily in defense, with Germany—long the continent's leading free rider—now promising to show the way.[63] But those efforts won't bear fruit for years, and they won't make enough of a difference without the Pentagon also committing more to the defense of a crucial theater. To keep insecurity and aggression from metastasizing, Washington will need sustained deployments of additional troops, armor, airpower, and naval assets to Europe and the surrounding waters.[64]

The United States also needs to take the lead in training and equipping Baltic and East European militaries to mobilize rapidly, destroy enemy tanks and aircraft, conduct raids on massed forces, and wage urban warfare. The goal would be to stand up local forces that could dish out punishment on a grand scale to Russian invaders, while eliminating any hope that Moscow can overwhelm its enemies quickly, in a fait accompli. And so long as Ukrainians or other targets of Russian aggression are resisting, Washington should support them with arms, intelligence, and other forms of succor, if only as a way of bogging Moscow down in one conflict so it can't move on to another.

An amped-up rivalry with Russia will be a contest in coercion and counter-coercion. So the United States and its wealthy democratic allies should also prepare to blunt Russian energy influence and cyberattacks by hardening critical networks, stocking up on energy resources and developing alternative means of supply, and showing that they will hit back hard against Russian ransomware attacks and other digital disruptions. Not least, the democracies will need to hold harsh financial and technological penalties in place as long as Russia breaches the bounds of acceptable international behavior: It should threaten Moscow with the proposition that military aggression will only ensure deeper economical decline.[65] Of course, a desperate Putin could be nearly as dangerous as a desperate Xi: Russia may lack China's comprehensive national power, but it has a world-menacing arsenal of nuclear weapons. So the democratic community will also need open lines of communication and a willingness to deescalate, if and when Moscow's behavior changes and the free world develops greater strength.

The bad news is that these efforts will require sustained multilateral cooperation. They will also be quite expensive: It won't work to pursue a Cold War–style strategy vis-à-vis China and Russia with post-Cold war levels of urgency and investment. At the outset of 2022, America's defense budget—and those of its allies—were hardly adequate for a dash through the danger zone against Beijing, let alone for waging intense competitions with two great-power rivals simultaneously.[66] The good news is that the democratic world has the resources to make this strategy work, if it can find the will.

Washington plus its allies in Europe and Asia dwarf Moscow and Beijing in overall power: The former group makes up well over half of the world's economic production, whereas China and Russia account for about 20 percent.[67] As of early 2022, the United States was spending about 3.2 percent of its GDP on defense—far less than roughly 7 percent it averaged during the Cold War, and a small fraction of what it spent during previous periods of emergency such as the early 1950s. If America spent even 5 percent of GDP on defense today, and key allies also upped their game, there is no economic reason the democratic world can't get the better of its challengers.[68]

Fortunately, times are changing. Russia's brutal invasion of Ukraine has drawn NATO members closer together than at any time since the end of the Cold War. By shocking the democracies out of their complacency, Putin has given them a historic opportunity to regroup and reload for an era of great power competition—not just with Russia, but also China—much the way the Korean War spurred the adoption of a sky-high defense budget and a stronger global containment barrier during the Cold War.

The United States must use the vivid specter of autocratic aggression to spur investments and collective action that previously seemed unthinkable, including accelerated Japanese and German rearmament, more detailed and robust operational planning for multinational military operations against China and Russia, deployments of advanced missiles previously banned by the Intermediate-Range Nuclear Forces Treaty on allied territory near Russia and China's borders, enhanced solidarity on technological and innovation issues, and the preloading of fierce economic penalties—such as sanctions and an oil blockade—to be used if China invades Taiwan. "Fear makes easy the task of diplomats," John Foster Dulles liked to say—it engendered the democratic cohesion the free world required to survive.[69] Ironically, Putin may have done the United States a favor: Autocratic aggression on one side of the world could provide the urgency America needs to get ready for trouble on the other.

## URGENT, NOT STUPID

Across multiple areas, America must quickly degrade Chinese coercive capabilities or at least blunt the CCP's ability to use them. Yet the whole idea of a danger-zone strategy is to avoid war, not provoke it, so there are limits to how far America should go.

The U.S. government could, for example, use a comprehensive tech embargo to drag down the Chinese economy. It could enact across-the-board trade sanctions meant to drive China's once-cheap goods from the vast American market. It could sanction China's central bank and boot many of its financial institutions out of global payments systems—the same economic death penalty America and its allies sought to impose on Russia in February 2022. Washington could even take a provocative page from its Cold War playbook by starting a major covert action program to stir up dissatisfied minorities and foment internal violence.

Any of these measures would take a toll on the CCP. But they might take a heavier toll on the United States by frightening the countries whose cooperation America must rally. What's more, they risk inciting the desperate moves Washington should be trying to forestall. The U.S. oil embargo in July 1941 did start squeezing the life out of the Japanese economy—and in doing so pushed Tokyo to attack Pearl Harbor in a deadly bid for survival.

The need to balance strength and caution is all the more reason for America not to drastically ratchet up the pressure everywhere at once, but to focus on issues where action is needed most. In fact, a danger-zone strategy should involve reacting calmly to or even encouraging initiatives that channel Chinese money and attention in less threatening directions. If Beijing wants to spend lavishly on white elephant infrastructure projects in some of the roughest neighborhoods in the world, such as the Federally Administered Tribal Areas of Pakistan, so be it.[70] If China invests heavily in aircraft carriers that won't really help it in the contingencies that worry the Pentagon most, so much the better. The United States will find it easier to do more in critical areas if it does less in nonvital areas.

For similar reasons, America will need an eyes-wide-open approach to diplomacy. If the United States has learned anything during the past thirty years, it is that no amount of diplomatic engagement will get the CCP to fundamentally change how it sees the world. War is less likely to happen "by accident," or due to poor communication, than it is to happen as a result of a calculated Chinese decision to strike.[71] Even the prospects for crisis management are limited. China has typically been ambivalent about confidence-building mechanisms—meaningful military-to-military exchanges, emergency "hotlines" linking top leaderships, clear codes of conduct for ships and planes operating near each other—because it doesn't want Washington to think crises can be successfully managed.[72]

Yet prudent diplomacy still has a role to play. Cooperation on the few issues where American and Chinese interests overlap, such as slowing climate change, can perhaps soften an intensifying rivalry. Regular meetings with high-level Chinese officials can help the United States convey its intentions on Taiwan and other issues without risking a public confrontation; they can also provide insight into the thinking of a notoriously opaque regime. In the event of a freak accident, such as a ship collision in the South China Sea, open channels of communication can prevent unwanted escalation.[73] And in general, it is strategically important for America not to be seen as closing the door to dialogue, because doing so will scare away important partners that don't want to get dragged into a U.S.-China throwdown.

The key, as during the early Cold War, is to keep American expectations realistic. The list of issues on which the United States and China can work together is short: The country that started and then ruthlessly exploited the most recent pandemic probably won't do much to help prevent the next one. Beijing also has a long track record of luring Washington into formal, high-level blab-fests—"strategic dialogues" on economics and security—that served mainly to anesthetize America to a rising challenge. And the worst thing for the United States to do would be to fall back into the familiar trap of allowing China to link cooperation on climate change or any other issue to American restraint in the security competition.[74] That's a formula for disaster when time is as short as it is today. Diplomacy, in the coming years, can complement an intensely competitive U.S. strategy. If it becomes a substitute for that strategy, however, America will find itself in a world of trouble.

A danger-zone strategy won't be easy: Navigating the 2020s will require vigorous, defensive hole-plugging as well as targeted, offensive coercion. The United States will have to run risks and accept higher tensions; it will have to make serious investments of time, energy, and resources. Above all, America—including some of its stodgiest bureaucracies—must summon wartime agility, speed, and purpose to preserve a fragile peace. America's near-term vulnerabilities have become sufficiently pronounced that it no longer has the luxury of delay. The choice, then, is between doing things that are hard now or doing things that are even harder once China has achieved strategic breakthroughs—or simply broken the system.

If the task seems arduous, the immediate returns will also be limited. Crossing the danger zone won't bring an end to the U.S.-China competition, any more than surviving the early Cold War brought that rivalry to a close. A stagnant or decaying power can still cause serious trouble in lots of places; a U.S.-China rivalry beyond 2030 could well be global in scope and extended in duration. But if America can make it through the next decade in good order, it can accomplish far more than just holding the line.

In retrospect, the first few years of the Cold War were so crucial not just because the free world addressed its most worrying vulnerabilities, but also because it began amassing what would ultimately prove to be decisive advantages. There's a similar opportunity in the U.S.-China rivalry.

By protecting a free Taiwan, Washington can preserve a potent ideological alternative to a repressive, slowing China and begin fortifying the geopolitical constraints that will keep Beijing in check. By forging a free-world economic bloc, America can help ensure that democracies set the pace in critical technologies for decades to come. By rallying ad hoc, issue-focused democratic cooperation now, Washington can lay the foundation for larger, more ambitious coalitions in the future. Patterns established in the early years of a competition can have lasting, transformative effects. If America gets its danger-zone strategy right, the long game may eventually be there for the taking, as well.

# 8

—

# Life on the Other Side

"There is a lot of ruin in a nation," the economist Adam Smith observed: The downslope for a declining power can be long indeed. In hindsight, we know that the Soviet Union lost its best chance to win the Cold War in that struggle's first decade. By the 1960s, the Soviet economy was starting to unravel; by the 1970s, the political and ideological death spiral had begun. Yet Soviet military power and geopolitical expansion reached their zenith in the late 1970s, concealing from all but the keenest eyes the fatal stagnation of the system. Not until the late 1980s and early 1990s did the empire finally collapse. Even after America got through a Cold War danger zone, it took decades of pressure and stamina to end that rivalry on U.S. terms. As President Kennedy remarked in 1962, Americans might say "we have been carrying this burden for 17 years, can we lay it down?" But "we can't lay it down, and I don't see how we are going to lay it down" anytime soon.[1]

There's an important lesson for U.S. officials today. Suppose that America succeeds in curbing Chinese expansion and deterring violent aggression during this decade of maximum danger. Suppose that the strength and cohesion of the democratic world grow during the 2020s, as ever-fiercer headwinds batter Beijing. The urgency of the U.S.-China competition might then diminish; the balance of power would become less precarious; the odds that the CCP might prevail would fall dramatically. But don't count on peace and harmony breaking out.

Even in the best-case scenario, the physical and virtual worlds are likely to be more splintered a decade from now—something closer to the "two worlds" reality of the Cold War than the "one world" dream of the post–Cold War era. The ideological lines will be starkly drawn; key theaters, such as East Asia, might be thoroughly militarized. The future of China itself could even be up for grabs.

In one scenario, a past-its-prime power could opt, after a decade of containment and frustration, to make painful diplomatic concessions and internal reforms: Perhaps Xi will end up being seen as Brezhnev to the Gorbachev who follows. But China could just as plausibly assume the role of a slumping spoiler, causing persistent mischief even as the threat of a hot war lessens and Beijing's ability to win a cold war fades. The United States could do everything right, Biden's Asia policy czar commented in 2021, and the China challenge would still prove "enormously difficult for this generation and the next."[2]

Indeed, competitions between great powers often have many phases: The taut, suspenseful years of the early Cold War gave way to the comparative respite of détente during the 1970s, which was followed by the resurgent tensions and climactic moments of the 1980s. A stagnating China will still be more economically formidable than the Soviet Union or Nazi Germany ever was; a China experiencing a demographic catastrophe will still have hundreds of millions of people more than the United States. All this means America probably will also have to transition from one phase of the competition to another—from a sprint through the 2020s to a strategy for the longer haul.

Getting through the danger zone may mark the end of the beginning rather than the beginning of the end. So even as the United States faces up to the challenges of a vital decade, it should start preparing for life on the other side.

## THE PERILS OF SUCCESS

America doesn't always have a plan. But when it does, the world gets remade. A U.S. danger-zone strategy will be no exception. It won't preserve the world we know today. It will fundamentally alter the structure of world politics, and not entirely for the better. The good news is that these changes are fairly predictable. The bad news is that they essentially entail a new cold war.

If America adopts a successful danger-zone strategy, China won't establish the geopolitically dominant techno-bloc that gives U.S. officials nightmares; America's digital coalition will be bigger, stronger, and well positioned to prevail in the end. But the world will still become more divided economically and technologically, with America and its allies on one side and a declining but defiant China and its motley crew of autocratic partners—including Russia—on the other.

Decoupling between the two blocs will accelerate, as America and its allies cut China out of supply chains, split the Internet, and fortify the technological defenses of the free world. The U.S.-China trade and tech wars that began in 2017 and escalated in the 2020s will rage on indefinitely. These new "forever wars" may not involve military combat, but both countries will deploy every nonmilitary weapon in their coercive arsenals—tariffs, investment restrictions, technology embargos, financial sanctions, visa restrictions, and cyber espionage— to expand their respective spheres and to weaken the rival's economy. Other countries will find it progressively harder to hedge their bets by maintaining trade and tech links with both blocs. Instead, the United

States and China will push partners to pick sides and re-route their supply chains.

As the technological world splinters, the consequences for ordinary people will be profound. When people travel from one bloc to another—assuming they can even get a visa—they'll enter a different digital world. Their phones won't work and their favorite websites, including their email server and precious social media apps, won't be available. Sending files from one bloc to another will be a nightmare. This will be a far better world than one in which Chinese techno-imperialism runs rampant, but it will still be an uglier world than many Americans can imagine today.

The same goes for the situation in maritime East Asia. One of the most economically dynamic regions will become highly militarized as country after country follows Taiwan's example and loads up on advanced missiles, mines, and drones to defend their coastlines from Chinese naval encroachments. East Asian sea lanes will be chock full of warships, including those from other regions, as the United States rallies a vast multinational coalition to protect freedom of navigation and deter Chinese aggression—and China's navy rushes out to meet them. Close encounters between allied and Chinese forces will be common, and the threat of an armed clash will be ever present. China will face a formidable containment barrier to military conquest, but maintaining that barrier will entail severe risks for all involved.

Ideological competition will also get more vicious. The United States and China aren't just promoting particular technologies or trade networks; they are espousing different ways of life. If America does things right during the 2020s, China and its cronies won't be able to debilitate the world's democracies and start a new century of autocratic ascendancy. But confrontations over governance issues—human rights violations and crimes against humanity in China, legacies of racism in the United States and other democracies—will play out in international bodies, high-profile summits, and public polemics.[3] A coup in Latin America or a democratic breakthrough in sub-Saharan Africa will become a geopolitical crisis as well as a political one. Political warfare will intensify, as the CCP meddles aggressively in the domestic affairs of America and other democracies, and Washington returns fire by trying to demonstrate the weaknesses of digital authoritarianism within China and around the world.

The United States will have a relatively strong stance in this contest, as in other areas of rivalry. Yet the outcomes of an effective danger-zone strategy only look good compared to the ramifications of failure.

## CHINA IN THE 2030s

What will happen to China as this new cold war unfolds? There's a lot we don't know about China's future, but there are three extremely important things we do know. Collectively, they imply that China will be economically sluggish, internationally hated, and politically unstable by the 2030s.

First, China's demographic crisis will be kicking into high gear. We discussed China's long-term demographic problems in chapter 2, but even in the medium term, the crunch will be severe. From 2020 to 2035, China will lose roughly 70 million working-age adults and gain 130 million senior citizens.[4] That's a France-sized population of young workers, consumers, and taxpayers gone—and a Japan-sized population of elderly pensioners gained—in just fifteen years. And then things will get really bad. From 2035 to 2050, China will lose an additional 105 million workers and gain another 64 million seniors.[5] As early as 2030, therefore, China will be careening down a demographic mountain and headed toward a cliff.

The speed and scale of China's population collapse could very well cripple its economy. On average, a country loses 1 percentage point of GDP growth for every percentage point decline in its labor force growth rate—and China's workforce won't just stop growing, it will contract nearly 7 percent from 2020 to 2035 and another 11 percent from 2035 to 2050.[6] Meanwhile, spending on pensions and health care will need to double as a share of GDP from 2020 to 2035 (and triple by 2050) to keep tens of millions of seniors from falling into abject poverty.[7] The financial and physical burdens of providing elder care on an industrial scale will stunt the savings, professional development, and consumption of China's dwindling population of able-bodied adults.

This dire situation—a population that is rapidly aging *and* shrinking—effectively rules out both investment-driven growth (China's current model) and consumption-driven growth (America's current model that China aspires to adopt). That leaves export-driven growth—a strategy that worked wonders for China during the globalizing 1990s but is poorly suited for a balkanized world of severe trade barriers and militarized sea lanes.

Xi hopes to short-circuit this problem by showering money on emerging markets now to spur future demand for Chinese exports. But those hopes will be dashed by a second inconvenient fact: Most of China's overseas loans will mature around 2030, and many won't be paid back.

In the 2010s, the Chinese government doled out roughly $1 trillion in loans and trade credits to more than 150 countries, including 80 percent of the world's developing countries.[8] Most of those loans were scheduled to be repaid within fifteen years.[9] But many won't be, because they were used to fund financially dubious projects in unstable countries. More than half of China's Belt and Road partners have credit ratings below investment grade.[10] The Chinese government itself has estimated that it will lose 80 percent of the value of its investments in South Asia, 50 percent in Southeast Asia, and 30 percent in Central Asia.[11]

When the bulk of these overseas loans comes due around 2030, Beijing either will have to write off hundreds of billions of dollars in losses—a move sure to infuriate Chinese taxpayers, who will be suffering a severe economic slowdown—or seize assets in partner countries, many of which can barely afford to feed their people. The CCP has set itself up to be despised at home and abroad.

For a glimpse of what this vitriol might look like, consider the global hysteria that erupted when China seemingly, but not really, seized a Sri Lankan port in 2017 after the country defaulted on its loans.[12] Charges of "debt-trap diplomacy" reverberated from New Delhi to Tokyo to Washington, droves of countries dropped out of BRI or demanded to renegotiate their contracts, and anti-China political parties swept into power in several partner nations.[13] Meanwhile, Chinese citizens wondered aloud why their government was investing, and losing, billions overseas when more than half of China's population still lived on less than $10 per day.

The backlash coming for China in the early 2030s will be orders of magnitude worse than the Sri Lankan debacle, because it will involve many more countries and a lot more money. Researchers have described China's recent lending spree as a "twin" of the boom that catalyzed the so-called Third-World Debt Crisis of the 1980s, when dozens of poor countries defaulted on hundreds of billions of dollars of loans and suffered a "lost decade" of zero economic growth.[14] The lenders in that case (big banks in a dozen or so rich countries) eventually had to forgive one-third of the debts they were owed. Most of the defaulting countries were forced into IMF and World Bank "structural adjustment" (aka austerity) programs, which triggered riots across the developing world.

Today, China has loaded up those same countries with similar levels of debt as a share of their economies. The only difference is that the Chinese government is far and away the main lender, so it will have to clean up the coming mess and deal with the diplomatic fallout alone. Debt collection is a nasty business. Given the extent of its reckless lending, China could find itself hemorrhaging friends and soft power.

The third thing we know about China is that it faces a looming succession crisis.[15] Xi Jinping is an obese smoker with a stressful job and will turn 80 years old in 2033. While he might rule for years hence, actuarial tables suggest otherwise. At the very least, CCP officials will be thinking about a post-Xi era and start jockeying for position in the early 2030s, if not before. Nobody knows how the power struggle will play out, not even Xi, because he demolished the CCP's few norms of succession and power-sharing when he appointed himself president of everything for life in 2018.

The makeup of China's post-danger-zone government is therefore a known unknown. It will definitely be in flux. All of the current members of China's top ruling body, the Politburo standing committee, will be past retirement age by 2027. No young leader has the cachet to fill Xi's enormous shoes, and time is fading fast for anyone to prove otherwise.

Even if Xi announces his retirement and designates a successor—moves he understandably has hesitated to make considering that 41 percent of the autocrats that abdicated during the past century ended up exiled, imprisoned, or dead within a year of leaving office—his protégé might not make it to the throne.[16] Members of Xi's coalition could splinter into factions; constituencies that were punished or marginalized under Xi could try to reclaim power. Xi's authority is formidable, but never forget that he had to purge more than a million senior CCP members to get it. As a result, there is no shortage of ambitious and aggrieved capos scheming to replace him.[17]

China's history provides little comfort to those hoping for a seamless transfer of power. The PRC has had only one completely formalized and orderly leadership succession in its history: when Xi himself took office in 2012.[18] The pre-PRC period isn't any more reassuring: Half of China's 282 emperors across 49 dynasties were murdered, overthrown, forced to abdicate, or compelled to commit suicide.[19] Less than half of them chose a successor, the majority only in the last years of their reign, and these successors were typically murdered by political rivals.[20] In short, violent chaos is common, and anything is possible.

## SPOILER ALERT

Although we don't know who will lead China after Xi or how they will come to power, we do have a sense of the structural forces that person or persons will face once in office: a sluggish economy, strategic encirclement, and, hopefully, a successful U.S. danger-zone strategy. These factors will shape the range of options available to Beijing in the 2030s and after, even if they won't necessarily determine which course China takes.

Perhaps the best-case possibility is that Xi is replaced by a Chinese Gorbachev—a reformer who eventually proves willing to liberalize at home and retrench abroad. The Soviets initially raged against the dying of the light when they realized they were falling behind the West in the early 1980s. But after mid-decade, the geopolitical pressure and domestic stagnation became unbearable, and the Soviet leadership reluctantly called off the Cold War. Gorbachev's government slashed aid and loans to allies, withdrew in defeat from Afghanistan, opened up economic sectors to Western corporations, cut defense spending, demobilized half a million troops, and accepted onerous arms-control agreements. Even hardliners signed off on this full-spectrum retreat.

As the USSR's highest-ranking military officer, Dmitry Yazov, later explained: "We simply lacked the power to oppose the USA, England, Germany, France, Italy—all the flourishing states that were united in the NATO bloc. We had to seek a dénouement. . . . We had to continually negotiate and reduce, reduce, reduce."[21]

With its superpower dreams in tatters, China, too, might seek détente by easing up in the Taiwan Strait, abiding by international law in the South China Sea, forswearing political meddling in democratic governments, and playing by the rules of an open global economy. The CCP might undertake some political and economic reforms at home, undoing the worst repression of the Xi years in an effort to rejuvenate the system and recharge the CCP's legitimacy. America and China would still be competitors, of a sort; Xi's portrait might still hang next to Mao's in Tiananmen Square. But the CCP would have moved on from his hyper-revisionist agenda.

Yet an alternative, and more likely, outcome is that Xi is replaced by a Chinese Putin, a vengeful streetfighter who oversees China's transition from aspiring superpower to prickly spoiler. The threat of China as a peer-competitor will be fading rapidly. But in its place will emerge a giant rogue state aiming to defend itself by subverting an international order it can no longer hope to dominate.

Instead of forging its own empire, China will wage guerrilla warfare on the U.S.-led order. Where China once threatened outright military conquest, it will engage in rampant "gray zone" aggression, sending paramilitaries and coast guard and fishing vessels to park themselves on small bits of contested territory, thereby creating facts on the ground without firing a shot. Where China once hoped to dominate technological innovation, it will focus on dominating technological adoption, stealing or importing advanced technology from abroad and deploying it rapidly on a massive scale. Instead of exporting its repressive governance model around the world, China will practice political warfare by proxy, hiring cyber mercenaries on the sly to disrupt U.S. and allied networks and sow chaos in liberal societies. And Beijing will continue to crack down hard on dissent at home. The Uighurs and Tibetans will be detained and sterilized out of existence, and the CCP panopticon will be upgraded and expanded continually. Rather than giving up as its prospects for hegemony dwindle, a post-Xi China would buckle down for a long battle with a superior coalition.

These two scenarios may be the most likely, but they are not the only possibilities. Maybe China will collapse into civil war. Maybe some of its technological moonshots, meant to rescue the country from decline, will pay off. Maybe something totally unexpected will happen. If the short-term threat from China is undeniable, the country's long-term status remains an open question.

## GOING LONG

One thing seems clear: Even after America exits the period of greatest risk, it probably won't enter a time of tranquility. More likely than not, the United States will still be waging a contest with plenty of ups and downs, no shortage of shocks and surprises. Washington will need to shift gears in the 2030s from a danger-zone strategy to an approach that can last as long as the competition does. In making that transition, ten principles may be helpful.

First, *decide what victory looks like*. It's easy to envision what defeat looks like a decade from now: A Chinese-dominated Taiwan that serves as a springboard for regional expansion, entire regions that are technologically handcuffed to Beijing, a world where fragile democracies are overawed by assertive autocracy. The goal of a danger-zone strategy is to prevent the worst from happening—to keep this dystopian future from quickly becoming our reality. But that's really an interim objective, a way station en route to a destination America has not identified.

Does the United States seek some form of competitive coexistence with a reformed China—a relationship in which elements of rivalry remain, but rules of the road are established and America's vital interests are protected? Can it accept a scenario in which a smaller and weaker Chinese sphere of influence sits, indefinitely, side-by-side with a larger, more vibrant American one—the type of arrangement that prevailed in Cold War Europe until the Soviet bloc collapsed? Or is the CCP an incorrigible regime with hostility to the American-led world woven into its DNA, in which case competition must continue until that regime evolves from within or its power collapses to the point it can no longer threaten the outside world?[22]

These are big, sensitive issues. In the harried 2020s, it will be tempting to simply focus on checking Chinese power in the here and now. And, of course, the question of how competition with Beijing ends is not fully America's to answer: The choices that China's people and leaders make will be the most critical factor. Yet it would still be a mistake to take a wait-and-see approach.

The United States will need to decide whether a danger-zone strategy is a bridge to a period in which it explores reconciliation or a live-and-let-live approach with a chastened rival—or a prelude to a long, grim campaign against an unredeemable regime. In devising particular policies, American officials must know whether the goal is to integrate a reformed China back into a global order that can be made whole again or simply to maintain barriers to its expansion until the regime changes or its power dramatically declines. And how the United States responds to a changing China, in the 2030s and after, will depend on where America ultimately wants the relationship to go. In the near term, there are always reasons for busy officials to put off abstract questions about how a protracted rivalry might end. In the long term, the United States won't thrive in competition with China unless it knows what it is trying to achieve.

Second, *learn to pace yourself.* In any competition, there are times when speed is more important than endurance—when a country has no choice but to run as hard as it can. There was no such thing as "too much," Acheson said during the awful winter of 1950–51, because "the danger couldn't be greater than it is."[23] Yet no country can sprint forever.

Acheson's experience proves the point. Waging the Korean War and undertaking a massive military buildup were necessary responses to a surge of Communist aggression, but they were so costly, in lives and dollars, that they led the Eisenhower administration to seek cheaper, less onerous forms of containment. During the 1960s, the United States so overtaxed itself in Vietnam that it was psychologically, strategically, and economically hobbled for years thereafter. Doing too much, for too long, will eventually make it impossible to do enough.

Looking beyond the 2020s, Washington must find a sustainable strategy. In protracted contests, *not* competing everywhere is the price of being effective anywhere. America must determine where it will do whatever it takes to stay ahead of Beijing (in the East Asian military balance and the tech rivalry, for instance) and where the energy is not worth the reward (in Central Asia and parts of Africa, for example). American officials should also think about when to surge and when to slow down—what moments might reward a furious dash to close looming vulnerabilities or leave a lagging rival permanently in the dust, and what moments might require taking a strategic breather, even if that means giving the enemy one. Once Taiwan has been turned into a strategic porcupine, the spread of digital authoritarianism has been halted, and America and its democratic partners are clearly leading the contest to produce the world's key technology and standards, for example,

Washington might find a modest respite—even within a competition that will require enduring resolve.

There's no magic formula for this: Acheson himself learned, when North Korea attacked South Korea, that unexpected challenges can demand unwanted commitments, and that the importance of some positions becomes clear only when they are attacked. But if Washington doesn't take the issue of pacing seriously, America could thrive in a short race and still stumble in a longer one.

Third, *shape the rivalry by shaping the system.* The most important thing the United States did during the Cold War was not the destruction it visited upon its enemy but the creation it achieved with its friends. By building a vibrant democratic community from the wreckage of a shattered world, America helped the non-Communist countries resist Soviet coercion even as Moscow's power grew. By creating an example of relative freedom and prosperity, it eventually forced Soviet leaders and citizens to ask what had gone wrong in their own empire, which then encouraged them to undertake the reforms that brought it crashing down. The United States didn't win the Cold War by treating that contest as a purely bilateral duel. America blocked Soviet aggression and bankrupted Soviet ideology by shaping a better world for the countries that took its side.[24]

The world is a lot less shattered today than in 1945, but the point holds. For now, throwing China back will require lots of disruption—breaking supply chains, splitting the Internet, turning maritime East Asia into an armed camp. The United States may have to temporarily downgrade institutions, such as the World Trade Organization, that govern the liberal international order, because those institutions were not designed to deal with an authoritarian predator inside the gates. Looking farther into the future, though, America's ability to constrain China—and drive home the CCP's folly—will hinge on the strength, resilience, and attractiveness of the world it builds around Beijing.

This may mean creating new international organizations to replace bodies that China has corrupted. It will require stitching together trade arrangements that promote greater integration and dynamism among countries committed to a world made safe from Chinese aggression. It could involve building out organizations such as the Quad into forums for broader cooperation across an array of issues, and gradually linking and formalizing the democratic partnerships that are already springing up in response to China's challenge.[25] A global coalition of democracies isn't feasible in the near term, but it could serve as a useful longer-term objective. In general, this approach means reviving the Cold War–era vision of a healthy international order that can benefit all like-minded nations while leaving those that threaten that vision on the outside. In the coming decades, the strongest check on Chinese power will be the bonds between the countries Beijing threatens. Which means that Washington should view the ad hoc groups it must rally today as the beginning of a process of multilateral construction extending for many years to come.

This isn't to say that Washington should go easy on China; a fourth principle is that America must *fight asymmetrically and impose costs relentlessly*. The longer the rivalry goes, the more important it is to play to one's strengths and exploit the enemy's weaknesses. Similarly, the key to bankrupting a rival is to drive up the price it must pay to defend its interests. The path to success in protracted struggle, longtime Pentagon strategist Andrew Marshall observed, is to steer that struggle into areas of relative advantage while making the enemy spend exorbitantly to stay in the game.[26]

The United States should thus cultivate assets that bring unparalleled advantages, such as the dollar's global dominance—which is critical to any long tech war—and the network of alliances that allows Washington to orchestrate global pushback against Beijing. It should

promote targeted responses to global Chinese initiatives, such as joining forces with other democracies to promote a select number of high-
quality infrastructure initiatives, rather than fighting Beijing for the
allegiance of every kleptocratic regime. It should identify areas in
which small U.S. investments—such as providing technical expertise
to countries assessing Chinese investment and financing—can frustrate larger, expensive CCP endeavors.[27] And it should pursue strategies that allow it to impose asymmetric costs—such as turning the
western Pacific into a "no-man's sea" or using tech cutoffs to break firms
and industries that Beijing has built at a steep price.[28]

The United States can also impose costs by taking advantage of
the mistakes that high-handed, prickly autocrats are prone to make.
Beijing has a habit of blowing up at the slightest criticism, thereby
reminding other countries how unpleasant Chinese hegemony will be.
That tendency is rooted in Xi's regime, which seems to have trouble
distinguishing between behavior that works for a dictator at home and
behavior that wins allies abroad. And it opens up a world of possibilities for the United States to engage in subtle, strategic needling—such
as working, as it did with the Europeans and other countries in 2021,
to slap multilateral sanctions on repressive Chinese officials—and then
to profit from the diplomatic self-harm that follows.

Indeed, any strategy should make the CCP pay for its greatest
vulnerability: the brutal, corrupt, and increasingly totalitarian nature
of its rule. The United States doesn't need to pursue regime change
to make Beijing work harder and spend more to defend its domestic authority. Such a policy could involve spoofing the government's
digital control mechanisms, speaking out on behalf of those abused by
the CCP regime, coordinating multilateral sanctions against repressive
officials, and finding ways of introducing unbiased news into the Chinese information ecosystem, as the West did to the Soviet bloc during

the Cold War. Washington might also consistently highlight the most awful characteristics of the regime in global forums, to create trade-offs between the domestic control the CCP requires and the international prestige it craves. If this triggers Chinese outbursts that hurt Beijing's own cause, so much the better. China's hypersensitivity to domestic challenges and international condemnation is itself a weakness that America can exploit.

Fifth, *continually invest in your key sources of strength.* During the 2020s, Washington will be grabbing whatever tools it can find to break China's momentum. Capabilities that take years to develop won't do much good; advice along the lines of "First, get your house in order" is really just a counsel of paralysis. That advice does, however, become more relevant as a struggle drags on.

At the Cold War's end, America was cashing in on investments it had made over decades: the alliances it had built, the cutting-edge military capabilities it had developed, even the institutions it had created, such as the U.S. Information Agency, with the superpower rivalry in mind. The advanced weapons featured in the Reagan buildup were often the fruits of government-funded research and development in the 1950s and 1960s. The United States could mobilize its allies for a climactic offensive because it had long poured its energies into those relationships. America had competitive capital to spend at a crucial moment because it had assiduously amassed that capital over many years.

The United States will only stay ahead of China if it repeats this feat: rebuilding government capabilities in areas, such as information warfare and economic statecraft, that will be central in a new age of rivalry; recapitalizing the innovation ecosystem that underpins U.S. economic and military excellence; and continually tending to its alliances so that they are strong enough to handle the demands placed upon them. This last point is crucial: America's China strategy requires lots of help from friends that will have to take risks and absorb costs of their own in contending with Beijing. That places a premium on diligently doing the day-to-day labor of alliance management, of showing that the United States remains committed to those allies' security, and of pursuing—when it comes to tech, trade, or any other issue—an approach that promotes America's own interests by also promoting the interests of its friends. The United States can go it alone, as President Trump seemed to envision, or it can beat China. It cannot do both things at once.

What about addressing America's domestic dysfunction? This brings us to a sixth principle: *Use a new era of global tension to ignite a new era of self-improvement.*

America's internal problems are real, and the United States won't profit from China's decline if the domestic foundations of its own power also collapse. A list of repairs would include revamping immigration policy to ensure a growing population with plenty of high-skilled workers, reinvesting in education and basic research, revitalizing the country's physical and digital infrastructure, combating corruption, and mitigating polarization that has effects ranging from political gridlock to political violence.[29] The great strength of America's democracy is resilience, and the country has come through worse periods before—during the 1930s, when the future of capitalism and democracy were in doubt, or even the late 1960s, when domestic upheaval and violence were rampant. Yet domestic rejuvenation will be essential to prosecuting Sino-American rivalry.

The latter, fortunately, can help with the former. The China threat won't magically create national unity, and the precedent of McCarthyism reminds us that fear can turbocharge the self-destructive impulses of even the strongest democracies. But the United States has previously used foreign challenges as an impetus to internal renewal, whether by creating a world-class university system during World War II and the Cold War or attacking state-sponsored segregation as a means of winning the ideological fight with Moscow.[30] The China threat is, in a limited way, starting to revive this tradition: It is already spurring greater investment in semiconductors, scientific research and development, and other areas the United States ought to be emphasizing even if the CCP didn't exist.[31]

Reforms that seem impossible in times of peace can become possible amid the harsh demands of rivalry. The United States can once again win a twilight struggle if it makes the most of the domestic opportunities that foreign crises create.

Seventh, *make negotiation a part of competition*. The principles we've offered so far are meant to ensure that America can keep its edge over a declining but formidable power. Washington will need to work hard and play tough to make that happen. It will also need to talk to the other side.

To be sure, U.S. officials should have a healthy skepticism about the odds of diplomatic breakthroughs in the next few years. Moreover, negotiations with a secretive adversary are always fraught: There is an extensive record of authoritarian regimes, including China's, signing and then cheating outrageously on solemn international accords.[32] Countries that leap too enthusiastically into negotiations usually end up paying a price. Yet whatever strategic objective America chooses, careful negotiations can still serve important ends.

On several issues, from limiting climate change to regulating the military uses of emerging technologies, some cooperation may prove fruitful because the absence thereof could prove disastrous. If the United States shows, over the next decade, that China cannot get its way in the Taiwan Strait or other hot spots—and that nonstop coercion simply blows back on the CCP—there could emerge opportunities to selectively tamp down tensions. But perhaps the best reason to pursue negotiation as part of competition is that the former can be a means of winning the latter.

Negotiations can be a way of probing a rival's intentions and finding out whether it is still committed to objectives inimical to our own. Judicious diplomacy can dial down the intensity of the contest at moments when Washington might otherwise struggle to keep up: During the 1970s, for instance, U.S.-Soviet talks capped the nuclear arms race while America was winded after Vietnam.[33] Not least, periodically exploring whether cooperation is possible can help convince America's citizens and allies that competition remains necessary by showing that it is not Washington that is preventing peace. Truly transformative diplomacy—the type that ends a rivalry—typically follows, rather than precedes, a strategy of sustained, cutthroat competition. But prudent negotiations can make a long rivalry a bit safer and less burdensome for America, and thereby make it more likely that the country will stick with that rivalry long enough to win it.

An eighth point involves a counterintuitive approach to the unholy entente between Russia and China: *Pushing your rivals together may be a prelude to pulling them apart.* So long as Russia and China are on their current trajectories, with their current leadership, there probably isn't much the United States can do to induce a breakup. Trying to pull a "reverse Kissinger"—using clever diplomacy to peel Putin away from Xi, in imitation of the U.S. opening to China during the 1970s—wouldn't work. Sino-Russian relations aren't nearly combustible enough to produce the sort of blowup that happened in the late 1960s, and any bid to buy Moscow's cooperation through geopolitical concessions would just destabilize Europe at a crucial time. A related approach, one of dramatically reducing the U.S. commitment to NATO to focus exclusively on Asia, would blow a gaping hole in America's global posture and alienate many of the European democracies Washington needs on its side against Beijing.

There are times, as during World War II, when the United States doesn't have a good alternative to containing two dangerous rivals simultaneously. That's the situation in which Washington finds itself today.

In the near-term, unfortunately, a policy of dual containment may encourage closer Sino-Russian cooperation. Yet here a different legacy of the Cold War becomes relevant. During the 1950s, Dwight Eisenhower calculated that a policy of maximum pressure was more likely to rupture the Sino-Soviet relationship than one of eager engagement, because pressure would force the lesser ally—Beijing—into a reliance on the stronger—Moscow—that would eventually make both parties queasy. Eisenhower wagered, correctly, that Washington would only find its chance to exploit tensions between two ambivalent allies after it had demonstrated that their relationship would produce more pain than profit.[34]

Today as before, it is hard to imagine that two continent-sized, globally ambitious, geopolitical jackals can remain close friends forever. And today as before, the best way of highlighting Sino-Russian differences may be encouraging a closer embrace.

If the United States and its allies wish to promote an eventual strategic rethink in Moscow, they must first prove that Russia's policy of geopolitical revisionism and alignment with Beijing will not pay—and that the alternative to tolerable relations with the West is ever-increasing dependence on a China whose abrasiveness and ambition know few bounds. In the same vein, distancing Beijing from Moscow may require showing, repeatedly, that Russian adventures will make life harder for China by stimulating greater fears of autocratic aggression and rallying democracies everywhere to strengthen the order Xi aims to overturn.

This is, admittedly, a strategy for the long run. Protracted rivalry sometimes requires making bets that may not pay off for many years.

This relates to a ninth point: *Be ready to extend the olive branch.* America won't succeed over a short or a long competition without exerting a lot of pressure. The United States must repeatedly frustrate Beijing's attempts at expansion; it must make China pay dearly for attempts to upend the status quo. But the goal of competition is not to remain in a state of tension forever; it is to achieve a better status quo. Doing so, in the context of rivalry with a nuclear-armed great power, may eventually require holding a hard line with a soft touch.

One reason the Cold War ended quietly and triumphantly is that America knew when to take yes for an answer: Once the Soviet Union started retrenching and reforming in the late 1980s, the Reagan and Bush administrations used a mix of carrots and sticks—continued geopolitical pressure, high-level summitry, lavish public praise, and promises of better diplomatic and economic ties—to keep them coming. It also pays to consider, in advance, the possibilities for breaking through entrenched hostility: Richard Nixon was primed to conduct the opening to China in the early 1970s because he had been thinking about such an opportunity for years.[35]

At some point, a China that has been successfully contained and strained may once again start changing in ways that make it less threatening to the United States. That won't be the time to let America's guard down. It will, however, be the moment to encourage constructive moves.

The United States will have to convince a future China—whether it is run by Xi's disciples, a reformer within the CCP, or an altogether different regime—that moderation will help rather than harm its national security. It will have to demonstrate that as China becomes less aggressive and repressive, it will enjoy a better relationship with the world. If Washington makes the right moves in this decade and after, it can win the competition. But that will require sustaining enough coercion to convince Beijing that fundamental changes are necessary, as well as offering—when the time is right—enough conciliation to convince it that those changes are desirable.

Finally, *be patient*. Getting through the danger zone requires an ethos of urgency and action: "Signs and signals call for speed," said Franklin Roosevelt in 1940, another moment when the world hung in the balance—"full speed ahead."[36] The period after that, however, will reward the incremental accumulation of advantage in a contest that may not end anytime soon.

The long haul can be very long indeed. Kennan preached patience in the late 1940s because he thought the Cold War might last ten to fifteen years.[37] It took more than forty instead. During that period, the level of danger waxed and waned, but the necessity of bearing uncomfortable burdens and navigating the murky area between war and peace was a constant. Containment delivered a remarkable payoff, but that victory took decades to achieve.

America's task, in this decade, is to prevent a peaking China from imposing its will on the world. Yet strategic urgency must be followed by strategic patience: Washington's reward for getting through the danger zone could be a ticket to a longer struggle in which America's advantages prove decisive only over a generation or more. That may seem like a meager prize for a country that likes quick, decisive solutions. But it is surely worth winning, in view of the perils that America and the world confront today.

# Epilogue

When we were writing this book, we chose to open it with a fictional, yet plausible, description of a Taiwan crisis in January 2025. When the book was actually released, in August 2022, there was a very real Taiwan crisis underway. China had just conducted its largest show of force in the western Pacific in a quarter century; the world was given a preview of how a war over Taiwan might unfold. It would be an understatement to say that the episode left official Washington a bit freaked out.

The trigger was a visit by an eighty-two-year-old woman—not the kind of thing that usually strikes fear into a brutal dictator's heart. Yet in this case, the woman was then-Speaker of the House Nancy Pelosi, the first speaker to travel to Taiwan since the late 1990s. Beijing, ever sensitive to Taiwan's international status and relations with Washington, responded with controlled fury.

Xi's PLA fired ballistic missiles directly over Taiwan and into the sea lanes around it. (For good measure, the PLA splashed one missile into Japan's exclusive economic zone, a not-so-subtle warning to Tokyo.) Chinese jets probed the island's air defenses and obliterated the median line of the Taiwan Strait; drones violated the airspace of Taiwan's outlying islands. Chinese naval vessels prowled the waters all around Taiwan, as they would need to if ordered to blockade the island or protect an invasion force. Cyberattacks and information operations simulated the sort of interference one might expect in a military conflict. All told, Chinese forces practiced many of the operations they would need to strangle Taiwan economically, bludgeon it into submission, or clear the path for an amphibious assault.

The concern in Washington was palpable. National security officials canceled vacations and tried to de-escalate the crisis. The United States and its close allies issued statements calling on Beijing to exercise restraint. Countries in Asia and around the world began to wonder if a catastrophic war between America and China, the two largest economies on earth, was really possible and what it might mean for them.

The immediate crisis wound down once Xi decided he had made his point. In November, after Xi had secured a third term as General Secretary of the Chinese Communist Party, he and Biden had their first in-person summit in Bali, at which they pledged to try to avoid a new cold war, let alone a hot war.[1] Yet even as tensions temporarily subsided, China's behavior had dramatized some of the key themes of this book.

One theme was confidence. The military Xi showed off in August 2022 was not your father's PLA. This PLA was an increasingly sophisticated, high-tech military that was rehearsing just the sort of joint operations it would need to take on Taiwan while holding the island's potential allies at bay. The crisis was a warning to Taipei, Tokyo, and Washington—among others—that Xi has formidable coercive tools at his disposal.

A second theme, though, was anxiety. The crisis occurred as China's economy was being weighed down not just by deep structural problems, but also by persistent "zero-COVID" restrictions. And it came at a time when Beijing was finding it harder to conceal its fear that Taiwan was, politically and diplomatically, slipping away.

In meetings with their American counterparts during the year prior, Chinese officials had vented their displeasure at expanding U.S. arms sales and diplomatic contacts with Taiwan. In October 2021, Foreign Minister Wang Yi slammed America's support for the "Taiwan independence forces"—in other words, the current government of Taiwan—and demanded a "real one-China policy, instead of a fake one."[2] The crisis thus reflected the same mixture of strength and weakness that informs so much of Chinese statecraft—and it convinced many in the democratic world that things could soon get even worse.

Following the August crisis, U.S. officials privately told us that they worried America and China might be headed for war in the next three to five years. This wasn't anything different from what they were saying in public. Secretary of State Antony Blinken warned that Xi was accelerating his timeline for unification. The head of the Central Intelligence Agency urged audiences to take the threat of an invasion very seriously. America's top naval officer said that the fleet needed to be ready for war at any time. When one of us traveled to Japan and Australia in late 2022—after Xi Jinping had stacked the Communist Party with his acolytes and turned the Central Military Commission into something that looked vaguely like a war council—the message was much the same. In early 2023, the head of U.S. Air Mobility Command—citing a scenario remarkably similar to that outlined in the opening pages of this book—informed subordinates, "My gut tells me that we will fight in 2025."[3]

At the time Biden took office, in January 2021, it was still a fringe position to argue that war in the western Pacific was a near-term or even a medium-term possibility. Two years later, the idea that America and China were entering a period of sharp tension and high danger no longer seemed so outlandish. The question is whether Washington will be ready.

Since our book was first published in August 2022, the United States and its allies have made notable progress in two areas: laying down a military barrier to Chinese expansion in East Asia, and staying ahead of Beijing in critical technologies. In both cases, smart strategies, long touted by experts, have finally begun to take shape—yet in both cases, much remains to be done.

After years of delay, a more dispersed and resilient military posture is emerging in East Asia—one that can't easily be wiped out by a surprise Chinese missile attack but can threaten to send China's navy and any invasion fleet to the bottom of the sea. The United States is accelerating arms transfers to Taiwan and stockpiling munitions in the region. Determined to avoid becoming "the Ukraine of Asia," Taipei has extended mandatory military service for male citizens from four months to a full year, raised military spending by 10 percent, and agreed in principle to adopt the sort of asymmetric defense that provides the best chance of fending off a Chinese invasion.

Meanwhile, Japan is shedding decades of pacifism to partner with the United States as a regional protector. Tokyo plans to nearly double defense spending within five years and equip its so-called self-defense force with hundreds of offensive missiles that can hit the Chinese mainland. Japan is also massing shooters and sensors on its southern Ryukyu Islands, which stretch to within 100 miles of Taiwan. By 2025, those units will be joined by a U.S. Marine Littoral Regiment armed with anti-ship missiles. Together, these forces can potentially use the shore to control the sea, targeting Chinese air and naval forces as they putter through the East China Sea and Taiwan Strait. If a newly proposed U.S.-Japanese joint headquarters becomes operational, the two countries will field an interoperable force with three times China's number of aircraft carriers, destroyers, and cruisers.

The U.S.-Philippines alliance also seems to be coming back to life after six years of decay during the presidency of Rodrigo Duterte. His successor, Ferdinand "Bongbong" Marcos Jr., has expanded an agreement to provide U.S. forces with periodic access to nine bases, some of which are on the northern island of Luzon, near Taiwan. If these plans are implemented, then a few years from now, China could face U.S. forces operating from locations up and down the western Pacific. It would then have to hit far more targets, and attack more sovereign nations, to knock the U.S. military out of the fight.

In the race for technological primacy, the United States, Japan, and the Netherlands have launched a major offensive by colluding to cut China off from advanced computer chips and the machines to make them. If sustained, these export controls could set back China's microchip industry by decades and destroy the CCP's dreams of becoming an AI superpower. The United States is also making progress on speeding up innovation in democracies. The CHIPS and Science Act has given the U.S. semiconductor industry a shot in the arm, while joint research & development projects among democracies are popping up across a range of critical technologies. Recent developments in U.S.-India relations are especially notable. With a vibrant tech community and the world's largest population, India is the crucial "swing state" in U.S.-Chinese tech competition in the Global South. To prevent China from swallowing market share there, the United States and India have launched an Initiative on Critical and Emerging Technology that aims to expand cooperation on AI, telecommunications, and militarily-relevant technologies, such as jet engines.

These and other developments—Australia stocking up on sea mines and expanding bases for U.S. bombers, major companies announcing plans to relocate operations from China to Southeast Asia or Mexico, and the reinvigoration of Western unity in the wake of Russia's invasion of Ukraine—are promising. Yet many of these initiatives remain more aspirational than operational and they could be ultimately overwhelmed by negative trends.

In the United States, for example, members of Congress on the far right and left are aiming to slash the defense budget. The U.S. navy is still shrinking rapidly relative to China's, and only a third of the fleet is mission-capable at any given time. Roughly $19 billion in arms to Taiwan remain undelivered and stuck in regulatory purgatory, while two-thirds of Taiwan's young adults oppose Taipei's recent decision to extend military conscription. Japan's military budget is increasing, but even after it doubles in five years, it will still be less than a third the size of China's current military budget. While the war in Ukraine has jolted the United States and its allies into action, it also has depleted U.S. weapons stockpiles, and recent wargames suggest U.S. forces might run out of advanced missiles in a few weeks or even days in a major clash over Taiwan.

On the economic front, the situation looks similarly precarious. The U.S. government lacks political will to negotiate new multilateral trade deals, making it extremely difficult to nudge Asian and European nations away from dangerous economic dependence on Beijing. Far from decoupling, most countries, including the United States, are increasing their total trade with China. The CCP may ultimately fail to attain technological primacy in many industries, but it is well on its way to dominating "choke points" in global supply chains, including testing and packaging computer chips, production of basic pharmaceutical ingredients, and hoarding of lithium needed to produce electric vehicles. Across the Global South—from Latin America to Africa to Southeast, Central, and South Asia—China remains broadly popular, at least among the elites that do lucrative and often corrupt business with Beijing. Initiatives designed to break China's emerging monopoly—Build Back Better World, the EU's Global Gateway—look paltry in comparison with China's moneybags.

Most troubling, Xi Jinping has cemented his position as dictator for life, effectively guaranteeing that the coming era of peak China will coincide with that of maximum Xi. By all accounts, he looks determined to power through what he calls "stormy seas" ahead. "History has repeatedly proven that using struggle to seek security leads to the survival of security, while using compromise to seek security leads to the death of security," he declared in late 2022.[4] The United States and its allies have started to make real progress in checking China's revanchist ambitions, but Beijing won't stand still, and herein lies the great challenge of navigating the danger zone. To avoid catastrophe, the United States and its allies have to slam shut the window of opportunity for Chinese revisionism. Leaving it ajar or closing it slowly might only encourage China to rush through.

# Acknowledgments

This book is a product of the extraordinary institutions whose support allowed us to write it; namely, the Johns Hopkins School of Advanced International Studies, Tufts University, and the American Enterprise Institute, where we first hatched the idea for the project in one of the Foreign and Defense Policy team's regular seminars. It is also a product of exchanges with numerous individuals who helped shape our views, even if they might violently disagree with those views. An incomplete list would include James Baker, Sasha Baker, Jude Blanchette, Jason Blessing, Dan Blumenthal, Tarun Chhabra, Zack Cooper, Mackenzie Eaglen, Nicholas Eberstadt, Charles Edel, Francis Gavin, Michael Green, Adri Guha, Toby Harshaw, Jonathan Hillman, Robert Kagan, Colin Kahl, Klon Kitchen, Rebecca Lissner, Oriana Skylar Mastro, Andrew May, Evan Montgomery, Danielle Pletka, Mira Rapp-Hooper, Ely Ratner, Mary Sarotte, Kori Schake, Andrew Shearer, Derek Scissors, David Shipley, James Stavridis, James Steinberg, Jake Sullivan, and Thomas Wright. Dan Kurtz-Phelan at *Foreign Affairs*, Cameron Abadi at *Foreign Policy*, and Prashant Rao at *The Atlantic* published articles in which we began developing some of the ideas featured in this book. At Norton, John Glusman and Helen Thomaides were a delight to work with, as was our agent, Rafe Saga-lyn. John Bolton (not *that* John Bolton), Zach Wheeler, and Emily Carr provided valuable research assistance. Our greatest thanks go, of course, to our families, who continued—during this as during previ-ous projects—to show us far more strategic patience than we deserve.

# Notes

## Introduction

1. David Crenshaw and Alicia Chen, "'Heads Bashed Bloody': China's Xi Marks Communist Party Centenary with Strong Words for Adversaries," *Washington Post*, July 1, 2021.

2. Kristin Huang, "Mainland Chinese Magazine Outlines How Surprise Attack on Taiwan Could Occur," *South China Morning Post*, July 2, 2021.

3. See the video linked in tweet by Jennifer Zeng, July 13, 2021, https://twitter .com/jenniferatntd/status/1414971285160005634?s=11.

4. Sarah Sorcher and Karoun Demirjian, "Top U.S. General Calls China's Hypersonic Weapon Test Very Close to a Sputnik Moment," *Washington Post*, October 27, 2021.

5. "Rise of China Now Top News Story of the 21st Century," Global Language Monitor, December 30, 2019, https://languagemonitor.com/top-words-of-21st -century/global-language-monitor-announces-that-truth-is-the-top-word-in -the-english-language-for-the-21st-century/.

6. Yan Xuetong, "Becoming Strong: The New Chinese Foreign Policy," *Foreign Affairs*, July/August 2021; Clyde Prestowitz, *The World Turned Upside Down: America, China, and the Struggle for Global Leadership* (New Haven, CT: Yale University Press, 2021); Oystein Tunsjo, *The Return of Bipolarity in World Politics* (New York: Columbia University Press, 2018); Graham Allison, *Destined for War: Can America and China Escape Thucydides's Trap?* (Boston: Houghton Mifflin Harcourt, 2017); Kai-Fu Lee, *AI Superpowers: China, Silicon Valley, and the New World Order* (Boston: Mariner Books, 2018); Gideon Rachman, *Eastern-*

*ization: Asia's Rise and America's Decline from Obama to Trump and Beyond* (New York: Other Press, 2017); Ian Bremmer, "China Won: How China's Economy Is Poised to Win the Future," *Time*, November 2, 2017.

7.  "Biden Warns China Will 'Eat Our Lunch' on Infrastructure Spending," BBC. com, February 12, 2021, https://www.bbc.com/news/business-56036245.

8.  Kishore Mahbubani, *Has China Won? The Chinese Challenge to American Primacy* (New York: Public Affairs, 2020).

9.  For examples, see Rush Doshi, *The Long Game: China's Grand Strategy to Displace the American Order* (Oxford: Oxford University Press, 2021); Pavneet Singh, Eric Chewning, and Michael Brown, "Preparing the United States for the Superpower Marathon with China," Brookings Institution, April 2020, https://www.brookings.edu/research/preparing-the-united-states-for-the-superpowermarathon-with-china/; Michael Pillsbury, *The Hundred-Year Marathon: China's Secret Strategy to Replace America as the Global Superpower* (New York: St. Martin's, 2016).

10. Xi Jinping, "Uphold and Develop Socialism with Chinese Characteristics," *Palladium Magazine*, January 5, 2013, https://palladiummag.com/2019/05/31/xi -jinping-in-translation-chinas-guiding-ideology/.

11. Sebastian Horn, Carmen M. Reinhart, and Christoph Trebesch, "China's Overseas Lending," *Journal of International Economics*, 133 (November 2021): 1–32.

12. We first published versions of this argument in Michael Beckley and Hal Brands, "Competition with China Could Be Short and Sharp: The Risk of War Is Greatest in the Next Decade," *Foreign Affairs*, December 17, 2020; Michael Beckley and Hal Brands, "Into the Danger Zone: The Coming Crisis in U.S.-China Relations," American Enterprise Institute, January 2021; and Hal Brands and Michael Beckley, "China Is a Declining Power—and That's the Problem," *Foreign Policy*, September 24, 2021. A few other analysts have described similar themes, but the conventional wisdom about China's trajectory remains mostly intact. For insightful challenges, see Dan Blumenthal, *The China Nightmare: The Grand Ambitions of a Decaying State* (Washington, DC: AEI Press, 2020); Jude Blanchette, "Xi's Gamble: The Race to Consolidate Power and Stave Off Disaster," *Foreign Affairs*, July/August 2021.

13. See Robert Strassler, ed., *The Landmark Thucydides: A Comprehensive Guide to the Peloponnesian War* (New York: Simon & Schuster, 2008); and Allison, *Destined for War*; A.F.K. Organski, *World Politics* (New York: Knopf, 1968).

14. Ed Imperato, *General MacArthur: Speeches and Reports 1908–1964* (Paducah, KY: Turner, 2000), 122.

15. Bill Gertz, "U.S. Pacific Intel Chief: Coming Chinese Attack on Taiwan Could Target Other Nations," *Washington Times*, July 8, 2021.

# 1. The Chinese Dream

1. Xi Jinping, "Secure a Decisive Victory in Building a Moderately Prosperous Society in All Respects and Strive for the Great Success of Socialism with Chinese Characteristics for a New Era," Xinhua, October 18, 2017, http://www.xinhuanet.com/english/download/Xi_Jinping's_report_at_19th_CPC_National_Congress.pdf.
2. Xi Jinping, "Uphold and Develop Socialism with Chinese Characteristics," *Palladium Magazine*, January 5, 2013, https://palladiummag.com/2019/05/31/xi-jinping-in-translation-chinas-guiding-ideology/.
3. Avery Goldstein, *Rising to the Challenge: China's Grand Strategy and International Security* (Stanford: Stanford University Press, 2005); Andrew Nathan and Andrew Scobell, *China's Search for Security* (New York: Columbia University Press, 2014).
4. PPS-39, "To Review and Define United States Policy Toward China," September 7, 1948, *Foreign Relations of the United States, 1948*, Vol. II: Document No. 122 (Washington, DC: U.S. Department of State, Office of the Historian). Hereafter cited as *FRUS*, followed by year, volume, and document number.
5. "GDP (Constant 2010 US$)—China," World Bank, https://data.worldbank.org/indicator/NY.GDP.MKTP.KD?locations=CN, accessed April 29, 2021.
6. Alyssa Leng and Roland Rajah, "Chart of the Week: Global Trade Through a U.S.-China Lens," Lowy Institute, *The Interpreter*, December 18, 2019.
7. John Garnaut, "Engineers of the Soul: Ideology in Xi Jinping's China," *Sinocism*, January 16, 2019, https://sinocism.com/p/engineers-of-the-soul-ideology-in.
8. Susan Shirk, *China: Fragile Superpower* (New York: Oxford University Press, 2008), 8.
9. "The 'One Simple Message' in Xi Jinping's Five Years of Epic Speeches," *South China Morning Post*, November 2, 2017; Elizabeth Economy, *The Third Revolution: Xi Jinping and the New Chinese State* (New York: Oxford University Press, 2018).
10. "China's Xi Says Political Solution for Taiwan Can't Wait Forever," Reuters, October 6, 2013.
11. "China Won't Give Up 'One Inch' of Territory Says President Xi to Mattis," BBC News, June 28, 2018.
12. Jennifer Lind, "Life in China's Asia: What Regional Hegemony Would Look Like," *Foreign Affairs*, March/April 2018; Zbigniew Brzezinski, *The Grand Chessboard: American Primacy and Its Geostrategic Imperatives* (New York: Basic Books, 1997), 60.

13. Xi Jinping, "New Asian Security Concept for New Progress in Security Co-operation," May 21, 2014, https://www.fmprc.gov.cn/mfa_eng/zxxx_662805/t1159951.shtml.

14. Tom Mitchell, "China Struggles to Win Friends over South China Sea," *Financial Times*, July 13, 2016. See also Aaron Friedberg, "Competing with China," *Survival*, June/July 2018, 22.

15. Fu Ying, "The U.S. World Order Is a Suit That No Longer Fits," *Financial Times*, January 6, 2016.

16. Daniel Tobin, "How Xi Jinping's 'New Era' Should Have Ended U.S. Debate on Beijing's Ambitions," Center for Strategic and International Studies, May 2020.

17. "Commentary: Milestone Congress Points to New Era for China, the World," Xinhua, October 24, 2017, http://www.xinhuanet.com/english/2017-10/24/c_136702090.htm.

18. Hu Xijin, "What Drives China-U.S. Game: Washington Believes Being Poor Is Chinese People's Fate," *Global Times*, September 6, 2021.

19. For instance, "Full Text: China's National Defense in the New Era," Xinhuanet, July 24, 2019, http://www.xinhuanet.com/english/2019-07/24/c_138253389.htm.

20. See Doshi, *The Long Game: China's Grand Strategy to Displace the American Order* (Oxford: Oxford University Press, 2021); Michael Pillsbury, *The Hundred-Year Marathon: China's Secret Strategy to Replace America as the Global Superpower* (New York: St. Martin's, 2016).

21. Nadège Rolland, *China's Vision for a New World Order*, National Bureau of Asian Research, January 2020, 6.

22. Liza Tobin, "Xi's Vision for Transforming Global Governance," *Texas National Security Review*, November 2018; Timothy Heath, Derek Grossman, and Asha Clark, *China's Quest for Global Primacy* (Washington, DC: RAND Corporation, 2021).

23. Andrew Nathan, "China's Challenge," in *Authoritarianism Goes Global: The Challenge to Democracy*, ed. Marc Plattner and Christopher Walker (Baltimore: Johns Hopkins University Press, 2016), 30–31.

24. Henry Kissinger, *Diplomacy* (New York: Simon & Schuster, 1994), 21.

25. Jeffrey Goldberg, "The Obama Doctrine," *The Atlantic*, April 2016.

26. Fareed Zakaria, "The New China Scare," *Foreign Affairs*, January/February 2020.

27. Stockholm International Peace Research Institute, Military Expenditure Database, https://www.sipri.org/databases/milex, accessed August 2021.

28. Department of Defense, *Military and Security Developments Involving the People's Republic of China, 2020*, https://media.defense.gov/2020/Sep/01/2002488689/-1/-1/1/2020-DOD-CHINA-MILITARY-POWER-REPORT-FINAL.PDF.

29. Nick Childs and Tom Waldwyn, "China's Naval Shipbuilding: Delivering on Its Ambition in a Big Way," IISS Military Balance Blog, May 1, 2018; Geoffrey Gresh, *To Rule Eurasia's Waves: The New Great Power Competition at Sea* (New Haven, CT: Yale University Press, 2020); "Navy Official: China Training for 'Short Sharp War' with Japan," USNI News, February 18, 2014.

30. Anthony Esguerra, "U.S. Expert Tells China to 'Stop Shitting' in Contested Waters. Literally," *Vice*, July 13, 2021.

31. Felipe Villamor, "Duterte Says Xi Warned Philippines of War Over South China Sea," *New York Times*, May 19, 2017; Ely Ratner, "Course Correction: How to Stop China's Maritime Advance," *Foreign Affairs*, July/August 2017.

32. Paul Shinkman, "China Issues New Threats to Taiwan: 'The Island's Military Won't Stand a Chance,'" *U.S. News & World Report*, April 9, 2021.

33. Liu Xin and Yang Sheng, "Initiative 'Project of the Century': President Xi," *Global Times*, May 5, 2017.

34. Peter Ferdinand, "Westward Ho—the China Dream and 'One Belt, One Road': Chinese Foreign Policy under Xi Jinping," *International Affairs*, 92, no. 4 (July 2016): 941–957.

35. Daniel Markey, *China's Western Horizon: Beijing and the New Geopolitics of Eurasia* (New York: Oxford University Press, 2020), 168.

36. Sheena Greitens, "Dealing with Demand for China's Global Surveillance Exports," Brookings Institution, April 2020, 2.

37. Jacob Helberg, *The Wires of War: Technology and the Global Struggle for Power* (New York: Simon & Schuster, 2021).

38. Elsa Kania, "'AI Weapons' in China's Military Innovation," Brookings Institution, April 2020; Julian Gewirtz, "China's Long March to Technological Supremacy," *Foreign Affairs*, August 27, 2019.

39. "Xi Urges Breaking New Ground in Major Country Diplomacy with Chinese Characteristics," Xinhua, June 24, 2018; Daniel Kliman, Kristine Lee, and Ashley Feng, *How China Is Reshaping International Organizations from the Inside Out* (Washington, DC: Center for a New American Security, 2019).

40. Hal Brands, "Democracy vs. Authoritarianism: How Ideology Shapes Great-Power Conflict," *Survival*, October/November 2018, 61–114.

41. Xi Jinping, "Uphold and Develop Socialism with Chinese Characteristics," January 5, 2013, https://palladiummag.com/2019/05/31/xi-jinping-in-translation-chinas-guiding-ideology/.

42. Jojje Olsson, "China Tries to Put Sweden on Ice," *The Diplomat*, December 30, 2019.

43. Anne-Marie Brady, "Magic Weapons: China's Political Influence Activities under Xi Jinping," Woodrow Wilson International Center for Scholars, Septem-

ber 2017, https://www.wilsoncenter.org/article/magic-weapons-chinas-political-influence-activities-under-xi-jinping.

44. "China Is Becoming More Assertive in International Legal Disputes," *The Economist*, September 11, 2021.

45. Toshi Yoshihara and James Holmes, *Red Star over the Pacific: China's Rise and the Challenge to U.S. Maritime Strategy* (Annapolis, MD: U.S. Naval Institute Press, 2018).

46. Jay Solomon, "Clinton Presses, Courts Beijing," *Wall Street Journal*, October 29, 2010.

47. Andrew Nathan and Andrew Scobell, "How China Sees America: The Sum of Beijing's Fears," *Foreign Affairs*, September/October 2012.

48. Jude Blanchette, *China's New Red Guards: The Return of Radicalism and the Rebirth of Mao Zedong* (New York: Oxford University Press, 2019), 127.

49. James Mann, *About Face: A History of America's Curious Relationship with China from Nixon to Clinton* (New York: Vintage Books, 2000), 358.

50. Fu Ying, "After the Pandemic, Then What?," China-US Focus, June 28, 2020, https://www.chinausfocus.com/foreign-policy/ after-the-pandemic-then-what.

51. See Barbara Demick, "The Times, Bloomberg News, and the Richest Man in China," *New Yorker*, May 5, 2015.

52. Wang Jisi and Kenneth Lieberthal, *Addressing U.S.-China Strategic Distrust*, Brookings Institution, March 2012, 11.

53. Blanchette, *China's New Red Guards*, 128.

54. Li Ziguo quoted in Evan Osnos, "Making China Great Again," *New Yorker*, January 1, 2018.

55. Wang and Lieberthal, *Addressing U.S.-China Strategic Distrust*, 10–11; Evan Osnos, "The Future of America's Contest with China," *New Yorker*, January 13, 2020.

56. Samuel Kim, "Human Rights in China's International Relations," in *What if China Doesn't Democratize? Implications for War and Peace*, ed. Edward Friedman and Barrett McCormick (New York: M.E. Sharpe, 2000), 130–131.

57. Graham Allison, *Destined for War: Can America and China Escape Thucydides's Trap?* (Boston: Houghton Mifflin Harcourt, 2017), 151.

58. Zhou Xin, "Xi Jinping Calls for 'New Long March' in Dramatic Sign that China Is Preparing for Protracted Trade War," *South China Morning Post*, May 21, 2019.

59. Marshall to Donald Rumsfeld, May 2, 2002, Department of Defense Freedom of Information Act Electronic Reading Room; Michael Green, *By More than Providence: Grand Strategy and American Power in the Asia-Pacific Since 1783* (New York: Columbia University Press, 2016).

60. Nicholas Spykman, *America's Strategy in World Politics: The United States and the Balance of Power* (New York: Harcourt and Brace, 1942), 20–22.

61. Allison, *Destined for War*, 108.

62. Michael Schuman, *Superpower Interrupted: The Chinese History of the World* (New York: Public Affairs, 2020), 4.

63. Schuman, *Superpower Interrupted*, 311.

64. Minxin Pei, "Assertive Pragmatism: China's Economic Rise and Its Impact on Chinese Foreign Policy," IFRI Security Studies Department, Fall 2006, https://www.ifri.org/sites/ default/files/atoms/files/Prolif_Paper_Minxin_Pei.pdf.

65. Joshua Kurlantzick, *State Capitalism: How the Return of Statism Is Transforming the World* (New York: Oxford University Press, 2016), 83.

66. See Timothy Heath, "What Does China Want? Discerning the PRC's National Strategy," Asian Security, Spring 2012, 54–72; Nathan and Scobell, *China's Search for Security*; Brands, "Democracy vs. Authoritarianism."

67. John Garver, *China's Quest: The History of the Foreign Relations of the People's Republic of China* (New York: Oxford University Press, 2016), 499.

68. Doshi, *Long Game*; Zhang Liang, *The Tiananmen Papers: The Chinese Leadership's Decision to Use Force Against Their Own People—In Their Own Words*, ed. Andrew Nathan and Perry Link (New York: Public Affairs, 2001), 457.

69. Joshua Kurlantzick, "China's Charm Offensive in Southeast Asia," *Current History*, September 2006.

70. Yan Xuetong, "From Keeping a Low Profile to Striving for Achievement," *Chinese Journal of International Politics*, April 2014, 155–156.

71. Jeffrey Bader, *Obama and China's Rise: An Insider's Account of America's Asia Strategy* (Washington, DC: Brookings Institution Press, 2012), 80.

72. Yan, "From Keeping a Low Profile to Striving for Achievement"; Doshi, *Long Game*.

73. Osnos, "Future of America's Contest"; Rush Doshi, "Beijing Believes Trump Is Accelerating American Decline," *Foreign Policy*, October 12, 2020.

74. Kurt Campbell and Mira Rapp-Hooper, "China Is Done Biding Its Time: The End of Beijing's Foreign Policy Restraint?" *Foreign Affairs*, July 15, 2020.

75. "China Says U.S. Cannot Speak from 'A Position of Strength,'" BBC News, March 19, 2021.

76. Office of the Director of National Intelligence, *Annual Threat Assessment of the U.S. Intelligence Community*, April 9, 2021, https://www.dni.gov/files/ODNI/documents/assessments/ATA-2021-Unclassified-Report.pdf.

77. Chris Buckley, "'The East is Rising': Xi Maps Out China's Post-Covid Ascent," *New York Times*, March 3, 2021.

78. Yuen Yuen Ang, "Chinese Leaders Boast about China's Rising Power. The Real Story Is Different," *Washington Post*, April 13, 2021.

79. Buckley, "'East is Rising'"; William Zheng, "Xi Jinping Says China Is 'Invincible,' Regardless of Challenges Ahead," *South China Morning Post*, May 6, 2021.

## 2. Peak China

1. On these issues, see Chao Deng and Liyan Qi, "China Stresses Family Values as More Women Put Off Marriage, Childbirth," *Wall Street Journal*, April 19, 2021; Grady McGregor, "Is China's Population Growing or Shrinking? It's a Touchy Topic for Beijing," *Fortune*, April 30, 2021; "China Set to Report First Population Decline in Five Decades," *Financial Times*, April 27, 2021; Alicia Chen, Lyric Li, and Lily Kuo, "In Need of a Baby Boom, China Clamps Down on Vasectomies," *Washington Post*, December 9, 2021.

2. "Report by Four Chinese Marshals," July 11, 1969, Digital Archive, Cold War International History Project, https://digitalarchive.wilsoncenter.org/document/117146.pdf?v=81762c8101f0d237b21dca691c5824e4.

3. See Margaret MacMillan, *Nixon and China: The Week That Changed the World* (New York: Penguin, 2007).

4. Andrew J. Nathan and Andrew Scobell, *China's Search for Security* (New York: Columbia University Press, 2012).

5. Gordan H. Chang, *Friends and Enemies: The United States, China, and the Soviet Union, 1948–1972* (Redwood City, CA.: Stanford University Press, 1990).

6. Henry Kissinger, *Years of Upheaval* (Boston: Little, Brown, 1982), 233.

7. Zbigniew Brzezinski, *Power and Principle: Memoirs of the National Security Adviser, 1977–1981* (New York: Farrar, Straus and Giroux, 1983), 412.

8. Jinglian Wu, *Understanding and Interpreting Chinese Economic Reform*, 2nd ed. (Singapore: Gale Asia, 2014).

9. Barry J. Naughton, *The Chinese Economy*, 2nd ed. (Cambridge, MA: MIT Press, 2018), 179.

10. Arvind Subramanian and Martin Kessler, "The Hyperglobalization of Trade and Its Future," Working Paper 13–6 (Washington, DC: Peterson Institute for International Economics, 2013).

11. World Bank, *World Development Indicators* (Washington, DC: World Bank, 2021).

12. For a good comparative account, see Francis Fukuyama, *Political Order and Political Decay: From the Industrial Revolution to the Globalization of Democracy* (New York: Farrar, Straus and Giroux, 2014); David Lampton, *Following the Leader: Ruling China, from Deng Xiaoping to Xi Jinping* (Berkeley: University of California Press, 2014).

13. Ruchir Sharma, "The Demographics of Stagnation: Why People Matter for Economic Growth," *Foreign Affairs*, March/April 2016.

14. United Nations, Department of Economic and Social Affairs, Population Division, *World Population Prospects: The 2019 Revision*, Online ed., rev. 1 (New York: United Nations, 2019).

15. United Nations, Department of Economic and Social Affairs, Population Division, *World Population Prospects: The 2019 Revision*.

16. Fang Cai and Dewen Wang, "Demographic Transition: Implications for Growth," in *The China Boom and Its Discontents*, ed. Ross Garnaut and Ligang Song (Canberra: Asia-Pacific Press, 2005), 34–52; Wang Feng and Andrew Mason, "Demographic Dividend and Prospects for Economic Development in China," paper presented at UN Expert Group Meeting on Social and Economic Implications of Changing Population Age Structures, Mexico City, August 31–September 2, 2005; David E. Bloom, David Canning, and Jaypee Sevilla, *The Demographic Dividend: A New Perspective on the Economic Consequences of Population Change* (Santa Monica, CA: RAND, 2003).

17. Alan Fernihough and Kevin Hjortshøj O'Rourke, "Coal and the European Industrial Revolution," *Economic Journal*, 131, no. 635 (April 2021): 1135–1149.

18. Gavin Wright, "The Origins of American Industrial Success, 1879–1940," *American Economic Review*, 80, no. 4 (September 1990): 651–668.

19. Gordon C. McCord and Jeffrey D. Sachs, "Development, Structure, and Transformation: Some Evidence on Comparative Economic Growth." NBER Working Paper 19512 (Cambridge, MA: National Bureau of Economic Research, 2013).

20. United Nations, Department of Economic and Social Affairs, Population Division, *World Population Prospects: The 2019 Revision*, Online ed., rev. 1 (New York: United Nations, 2019).

21. Stein Emil, Emily Goren, Chun-Wei Yuan, et al., "Fertility, Mortality, Migration, and Population Scenarios for 195 Countries and Territories from 2017 to 2100: A Forecasting Analysis for the Global Burden of Disease Study," *The Lancet*, 396, no. 10258 (October 2020): 1285–1306; Stephen Chen, "China's Population Could Halve Within the Next 45 Years, New Study Warns," *South China Morning Post*, September 30, 2021.

22. Yong Cai, Wang Feng, and Ke Shen, "Fiscal Implications of Population Aging and Social Sector Expenditure in China," *Population and Development Review*, 44, no. 4 (December 2018): 811–831.

23. Nicholas Eberstadt and Ashton Verdery, "China's Shrinking Families: The Demographic Trend That Could Curtail Beijing's Ambitions," *Foreign Affairs*, April 7, 2021.

24. Guangzong Mu, "Birth Rate Falling Below 1 Percent an Early Warning," *China Daily*, December 29, 2021.

25. Amanda Lee, "China Population: Concerns Grow as Number of Registered Births in 2020 Plummet," *South China Morning Post*, February 9, 2021; Mu, "Birth Rate Falling Below 1 Percent an Early Warning."

26. Mary Hanbury, "Adult Diaper Sales in China Could Exceed Infant Diaper Sales by 2025, Research Suggests," *Business Insider*, November 29, 2021.

27. See, for instance, "Is China's Population Shrinking?" *The Economist*, April 29, 2021; Eric Zhu and Tom Orlik, "When Will China Rule the World? Maybe Never," Bloomberg, July 5, 2021.

28. Mu, "Birth Rate Falling Below 1 Percent an Early Warning."

29. Cheryl Heng, "China Census: Millions of 'Bare Branch' Men Locked Out of Marriage Face Cost of One-Child Policy," *South China Morning Post*, May 17, 2021.

30. Chao Deng and Liyan Qi, "China Stresses Family Values as More Women Put Off Marriage, Childbirth," *Wall Street Journal*, April 19, 2021.

31. Valerie Hudson and Andrea den Boer, *Bare Branches: The Security Implications of Asia's Surplus Male Population* (Cambridge, MA: MIT Press, 2004).

32. Nathan Chow, "Understanding China," DBS Bank, April 9, 2018.

33. Penn World Table, Version 10.0, https://www.rug.nl/ggdc/productivity/pwt/?lang=en.

34. Chris Buckley and Vanessa Piao, "Rural Water, Not City Smog, May Be China's Pollution Nightmare," *New York Times*, April 11, 2016.

35. China Power Team, "How Does Water Security Affect China's Development?" *China Power*, August 26, 2020, https://chinapower.csis.org/china-water-security/; Jing Li, "80 Percent of Groundwater in China's Major River Basins Is Unsafe for Humans, Study Reveals." *South China Morning Post*, April 11, 2018; David Stanway and Kathy Chen, "Most of Northern China's Water is Unfit for Human Touch," *World Economic Forum*, June 28, 2017.

36. Charles Parton, "China's Acute Water Shortage Imperils Economic Future," *Financial Times*, February 27, 2018; China Power Team, "How Does Water Security Affect China's Development?" Center for Strategic and International Studies, https://chinapower.csis.org/china-water-security/.

37. "China Needs Nearly $150 Billion to Treat Severe River Pollution," Reuters, July 25, 2018; "China Starts 8,000 Water Clean-Up Projects Worth US $100 Billion in First Half of Year," *South China Morning Post*, August 24, 2017.

38. Tsukasa Hadano, "Degraded Farmland Diminishes China's Food Sufficiency," *Nikkei Asia*, April 4, 2021.

39. "China's Inefficient Agricultural System," *The Economist*, May 21, 2015.

40. Dominique Patton, "More Than 40 Percent of China's Arable Land Degraded: Xinhua," Reuters, November 4, 2014.

41. Edward Wong, "Pollution Rising, Chinese Fear for Soil and Food," *New York Times*, December 30, 2013.

42. "Halting Desertification in China," World Bank, Results Brief, July 26, 2021; Jariel Arvin, "Worst Sandstorm in a Decade Chokes Beijing," *Vox*, March 16, 2021; Daniel Rechtschaffen, "How China's Growing Deserts Are Choking the Country," *Forbes*, September 18, 2017; Josh Haner, Edward Wong, Derek Watkins, and Jeremy White, "Living in China's Expanding Deserts," *New York Times*, October 24, 2016.

43. Jasmine Ng, "China's Latest Crackdown Targets Binge Eating and Wasting Food," Bloomberg News, November 1, 2021.

44. Jude Clemente, "China Is the World's Largest Oil and Gas Importer," *Forbes*, October 17, 2019.

45. International Energy Agency, *World Energy Outlook* (Paris: International Energy Agency, 2016).

46. Daron Acemoglu and James Robinson, *Why Nations Fail: The Origins of Power, Prosperity, and Poverty* (New York: Crown, 2012).

47. Fukuyama, *Political Order and Political Decay*.

48. Andrew J. Nathan, "What Is Xi Jinping Afraid Of?" *Foreign Affairs*, December 8, 2017; N.S. Lyons, "The Triumph and Terror of Wang Huning," *Palladium Magazine*, October 11, 2021.

49. Tom Mitchell, Xinning Liu, and Gabriel Wildau, "China's Private Sector Struggles for Funding as Growth Slows," *Financial Times*, January 21, 2019. See also Nicholas Lardy, *The State Strikes Back: The End of Economic Reform in China* (Washington, DC: Peterson Institute for International Economics, 2019).

50. Jean C. Oi, *Rural China Takes Off: Institutional Foundations of Economic Reform* (Berkeley: University of California Press, 1999).

51. James Areddy, "Former Chinese Party Insider Calls U.S. Hopes of Engagement 'Naïve,'" *Wall Street Journal*, June 29, 2021; Elizabeth C. Economy, *The Third Revolution: Xi Jinping and the New Chinese State* (New York: Oxford University Press, 2018).

52. "China Is Conducting Fewer Local Policy Experiments under Xi Jinping," *The Economist*, August 18, 2018.

53. "What Tech Does China Want?" *The Economist*, August 14, 2021.

54. Daniel H. Rosen, "China's Economic Reckoning: The Price of Failed Reforms," *Foreign Affairs*, July/August 2021.

55. David. H. Autor, David Dorn, and Gordon H. Hanson, "The China Shock: Learning from Labor-Market Adjustment to Large Changes in Trade," *Annual Review of Economics*, 8 (October 2016): 205–240.

56. Daniel C. Lynch, *China's Futures: PRC Elites Debate Economics, Politics, and Foreign Policy* (Stanford: Stanford University, Press, 2015), chap. 2.

57. Jeremy Diamond, "Trump: 'We Can't Continue to Allow China to Rape Our Country,'" CNN, May 2, 2016; Tania Branigan, "Mitt Romney Renews Promise to Label China a Currency Manipulator," *The Guardian*, October 23, 2012.

58. Global Trade Alert, https://www.globaltradealert.org.

59. Global Trade Alert, https://www.globaltradealert.org/country/all/affected -jurisdictions_42/period-from_20090101/period-to_20210509.

60. Sidney Lung, "China's GDP Growth Could Be Half of Reported Number, Says US Economist at Prominent Chinese University," *South China Morning Post*, March 10, 2019; Yingyao Hu and Jiaxiong Yao, "Illuminating Economic Growth." IMF Working Paper No. 19/77 (Washington, DC: International Monetary Fund, 2019); Wei Chen, Xilu Chen, Chang-Tai Hsieh, and Zheng Song, "A Forensic Examination of China's National Accounts." NBER Working Paper No. w25754 (Cambridge, MA: National Bureau of Economic Research, 2019); Luis R. Martinez, "How Much Should We Trust the Dictator's GDP Estimates?" University of Chicago Working Paper (Chicago: University of Chicago, August 9, 2019).

61. Salvatore Babones, "How Weak Is China? The Real Story Behind the Economic Indicators," *Foreign Affairs*, January 31, 2016.

62. The Conference Board, "Total Economy Database," https://www.conference -board.org/data/economydatabase, accessed May 2021.

63. Guanghua Chi, Yu Liu, Zhengwei Wu, and Haishan Wu, "Ghost Cities Analysis Based on Positioning Data in China," Baidu Big Data Lab, 2015; Wade Shepard, *Ghost Cities of China* (London: Zed Books, 2015).

64. "A Fifth of China's Homes Are Empty. That's 50 Million Apartments," Bloomberg News, November 8, 2018. See also James Kynge and Sun Yi, "Evergrande and the End of China's 'Build, Build, Build' Model," *Financial Times*, September 21, 2021.

65. Nathaniel Taplin, "Chinese Overcapacity Returns to Haunt Global Industry," *Wall Street Journal*, January 10, 2019; *Overcapacity in China: An Impediment to the Party's Reform Agenda* (Beijing: European Chamber of Commerce in China, 2016).

66. Koh Qing, "China Wasted $6.9 Trillion on Bad Investment post-2009," Reuters, November 20, 2014.

67. "The Lives of the Parties: China's Economy Is More Soviet Than You Think," *The Economist*, December 15, 2018.

68. A point made well in Barry Naughton, *The Rise of China's Industrial Policy, 1978 to 2020* (Boulder: Lynne Rienner, 2021).

69. Global Debt Monitor, Institute of International Finance, July 16, 2020.

70. Logan Wright and Daniel Rosen, *Credit and Credibility: Risks to China's Economic Resilience* (Washington, DC: Center for Strategic and International Studies, October 2018), 1.

71. "The Coming Debt Bust," *The Economist*, May 7, 2016.

72. Kan Huo and Hongyuran Wu, "Banks Raise Dams, Fend Off Toxic Debt Crisis," *Caixin*, December 1, 2015; Frank Tang, "China Estimates Shadow Banking Worth US$12.9 Trillion As It Moves to Clean Up High-risk Sector," *South China Morning Post*, December 7, 2020.

73. Kellee S. Tsai, *Back-Alley Banking: Private Entrepreneurs in China* (Ithaca, NY: Cornell University Press, 2004); Frank Tang, "China's P2P Purge Leaves Millions of Victims Out in the Cold, with Losses in the Billions, As Concerns of Social Unrest Swirl," *South China Morning Post*, December 29, 2020.

74. "Total Credit to the Non-Financial Sector," Bank for International Settlements, https://stats.bis.org/statx/srs/table/f1.2, accessed August 9, 2021.

75. Daniel H. Rosen, "China's Economic Reckoning: The Price of Failed Reforms," *Foreign Affairs*, July/August 2021.

76. For an extended discussion and sources on the points in this paragraph, see Michael Beckley, *Unrivaled: Why America Will Remain the World's Sole Superpower* (Ithaca, NY: Cornell University Press, 2018), 48–52.

77. National Science Board. *Science and Engineering Indicators 2020* (Arlington, VA: National Science Foundation, 2020).

78. Andrew Imbrie, Elsa B. Kania, and Lorand Laskai, "Comparative Advantage in Artificial Intelligence: Enduring Strengths and Emerging Challenges for the United States," CSET Policy Brief, January 2020; Will Hunt, Saif M. Khan, and Dahlia Peterson, "China's Progress in Semiconductor Manufacturing Equipment: Accelerants and Policy Implications," CSET Policy Brief, March 2021.

79. Saif M. Khan and Carrick Flynn, "Maintaining China's Dependence on Democracies for Advanced Computer Chips," Brookings Institution, Global China, April 2020.

80. Xiaojun Yan and Jie Huang, "Navigating Unknown Waters: The Chinese Communist Party's New Presence in the Private Sector," *China Review*, 17, no. 2 (June 2017): 38.

81. Daniel Lynch, *China's Futures: PRC Elites Debate Economics, Politics, and Foreign Policy* (Stanford: Stanford University Press, 2015).

82. Tom Holland, "Wen and Now: China's Economy Is Still 'Unsustainable,'" *South China Morning Post*, April 10, 2017.

83. Jane Cai, "Chinese Premier Li Keqiang Warns of Challenges over Jobs, Private Sector, Red Tape," *South China Morning Post*, May 2021.

84. Chris Buckley, "2019 Is a Sensitive Year for China. Xi Is Nervous," *New York Times*, February 25, 2019; Chris Buckley, "Vows of Change in China Belie Private Warning," *New York Times*, February 14, 2013.

85. Sui-Lee Wee and Li Yuan, "China Sensors Bad Economic News Amid Signs of Slower Growth," *New York Times*, September 28, 2018.

86. Lingling Wei, "Beijing Reins in China's Central Bank," *Wall Street Journal*, December 8, 2021.

87. Data come from Shanghai's Hurun Research Institute. For reporting on these data, see David Shambaugh, "China's Coming Crack Up," *Wall Street Journal*, March 6, 2015; Robert Frank, "More than a Third of Chinese Millionaires Want to Leave China," CNBC, July 6, 2018; Robert Frank, "Half of China's Rich Plan to Move Overseas," CNBC, July 17, 2017.

88. Christian Henrik Nesheim, "2 of 3 Investor Immigrants Worldwide Are Chinese, Reveals Statistical Analysis," *Investment Migration Insider*, February 25, 2018.

89. Data available from China Labour Bulletin, https://clb.org.hk. For reporting, see Javier C. Hernandez, "Workers' Activism Rises as China's Economy Slows. Xi Aims to Rein Them In," *New York Times*, February 6, 2019; "Masses of Incidents: Why Protests Are So Common in China," *The Economist*, October 4, 2018.

90. Chen Tianyong quoted in Li Yuan, "China's Entrepreneurs Are Wary of Its Future," *New York Times*, February 23, 2019.

91. Adrian Zenz, "China's Domestic Security Spending: An Analysis of Available Data," *China Brief*, 18, no. 4 (March 12, 2018).

92. Sheena Chestnut Greitens, "Domestic Security in China under Xi Jinping," *China Leadership Monitor*, March 1, 2019.

93. Simina Mistreanu, "Life Inside China's Social Credit Laboratory," *Foreign Policy*, April 3, 2018.

94. Richard McGregor, *Xi Jinping: The Backlash* (London: Penguin Ebooks, 2019), chap. 2.

## 3. The Closing Ring

1. Jeff Smith, "The Simmering Boundary: A 'New Normal' at the India-China Border? Part 1," Observer Research Foundation, June 13, 2020; Robert Barnett, "China Is Building Entire Villages in Another Country's Territory," *Foreign Policy*, May 7, 2021.

2. On the background and the encounter, see Jeffrey Gettleman, Hari Kumar, and Sameer Yasir, "Worst Clash in Decades on Disputed India-China Border Kills

20 Indian Troops," *New York Times*, June 16, 2020; Charlie Campbell, "China and India Try to Cool Nationalist Anger After Deadly Border Clash," *Time*, June 20, 2020; Michael Safi and Hannah Ellis-Petersen, "India Says 20 Soldiers Killed on Disputed Himalayan Border with China," *The Guardian*, June 16, 2020; H.B. discussion with Indian official, July 2021.

3. Andrew Chubb, "China Warily Watches Indian Nationalism," *China Story*, December 22, 2020.

4. "Defence Ministry Approves Purchase of 33 New Fighter Jets Including 21 MiG-29s from Russia," *Hindustan Times*, July 2, 2020; "Huawei and ZTE Left Out of India's 5G Trials," BBC News, May 5, 2021; Joe Biden, Narendra Modi, Scott Morrison, and Yoshide Suga, "Our Four Nations Are Committed to a Free, Open, Secure, and Prosperous Indo-Pacific Region," *Washington Post*, March 13, 2021; Michele Kelemen, "Quad Leaders Announce Effort to Get 1 Billion COVID-19 Vaccines to Asia," NPR, March 12, 2021.

5. Sudhi Ranjan Sen, "India Shifts 50,000 Troops to Chinese Border in Historic Move," Bloomberg, June 27, 2001; H.B. discussion with Indian official, July 2021.

6. Ken Moriyasu, "India and Vietnam Will Define the Future of Asia: Kurt Campbell," *Nikkei Asia*, November 20, 2021.

7. Gettleman, Kumar, and Yasir, "Worst Clash in Decades."

8. C. Vann Woodward, "The Age of Reinterpretation," *American Historical Review*, 66, no. 1 (October 1960): 1–16.

9. Kori Schake, *Safe Passage: The Transition from British to American Hegemony* (Cambridge, MA: Harvard University Press, 2017).

10. Richard Javad Heydarian, *The Indo-Pacific: Trump, China, and the New Struggle for Global Mastery* (New York: Palgave Macmillan, 2020), 160.

11. G. John Ikenberry, *Liberal Leviathan: The Origins, Crisis, and Transformation of the American World Order* (Princeton, NJ: Princeton University Press, 2011).

12. Toshi Yoshihara and Jack Bianchi, *Seizing on Weakness: Allied Strategy for Competing with China's Globalizing Military* (Washington, DC: Center for Strategic and Budgetary Assessments, 2021), 44; Andrew J. Nathan and Andrew Scobell, *China's Search for Security* (New York: Columbia University Press, 2012).

13. Yoshihara and Bianchi, *Seizing on Weakness*, esp. 44; Robert Ross, "China's Naval Nationalism: Sources, Prospects, and the U.S. Response," *International Security*, 34, no. 2 (Fall 2009): 46–81.

14. Thomas Christensen, *The China Challenge: Shaping the Choices of a Rising Power* (New York: Norton, 2015), xv.

15. Christensen, *China Challenge*, xiv.

16. "Bush Lays Out Foreign Policy Vision," CNN, November 19, 1999; David

Lampton, *Same Bed, Different Dreams: Managing U.S.-China Relations, 1989–2000* (Berkeley: University of California Press, 2001).

17. Robert B. Zoellick, "Whither China: From Membership to Responsibility?" U.S. Department of State, September 21, 2005.

18. Art Pine, "U.S. Faces Choices on Sending Ships to Taiwan," *Los Angeles Times,* March 20, 1996.

19. Thomas Lippman, "Bush Makes Clinton's China Policy an Issue," *Washington Post,* August 20, 1999.

20. H.B. conversation with U.S. intelligence official, May 2016; Aaron Friedberg, *Beyond Air-Sea Battle: The Debate over U.S. Military Strategy in Asia* (New York: Routledge, 2014).

21. James Mann, *About Face: A History of America's Curious Relationship with China from Nixon to Clinton* (New York: Vintage Books, 2000), 293–296; Dan Kliman and Zack Cooper, "Washington Has a Bad Case of China ADHD," *Foreign Policy,* October 27, 2017.

22. Richard Bernstein and Ross Munro, *The Coming Conflict with China* (New York: Vintage, 1998); Aaron L. Friedberg, *A Contest for Supremacy: China, America, and the Struggle for Mastery in Asia* (New York: Norton, 2011).

23. Prashanth Parameswaran, "U.S. Blasts China's 'Great Wall of Sand' in the South China Sea," *Diplomat,* April 1, 2015.

24. Eric Heginbotham, Michael Nixon, Forrest E. Morgan, et al., *The U.S.-China Military Scorecard: Forces, Geography, and the Evolving Balance of Power* (Santa Monica, CA: RAND Corporation, 2015).

25. "China Challenging U.S. Military Technological Edge: Pentagon Official," Reuters, January 28, 2014.

26. Brian Wang, "Google's Eric Schmidt Says U.S. Could Lose Lead in AI and Basic Science Research to China," *Next Big Future,* November 1, 2017.

27. Giuseppe Macri, "Ex-NSA Head: Chinese Hacking Is 'The Greatest Transfer of Wealth in History,'" *Inside Sources,* November 4, 2015.

28. Michael Pillsbury, *The Hundred-Year Marathon: China's Secret Strategy to Replace America as the Global Superpower* (New York: Griffin, 2015); Kurt Campbell and Ely Ratner, "The China Reckoning: How Beijing Defied American Expectations," *Foreign Affairs,* March/April 2018.

29. David Larter, "White House Tells the Pentagon to Quit Talking About 'Competition' with China," *Navy Times,* September 26, 2016.

30. *National Security Strategy of the United States of America,* December 2017, https://trumpwhitehouse.archives.gov/wp-content/uploads/2017/12/NSS-Final-12-18-2017-0905.pdf; *Summary of the 2018 National Defense Strategy of the United States of America,* https://dod.defense.gov/Portals/1/Documents/pubs/2018

-National-Defense-Strategy-Summary.pdf; "U.S. Strategic Framework for the Indo-Pacific," February 2018, https://trumpwhitehouse.archives.gov/wp -content/uploads/2021/01/IPS-Final-Declass.pdf.

31. U.S. Department of State, Policy Planning Staff, *The Elements of the China Challenge*, November 2020; Iain Marlow, "U.S. Security Bloc to Keep China in 'Proper Place,' Pompeo Says," Bloomberg News, October 23, 2019.

32. Christopher Wray, Remarks at Hudson Institute, July 7, 2020, https://www .fbi.gov/news/speeches/the-threat-posed-by-the-chinese-government-and-the -chinese-communist-party-to-the-economic-and-national-security-of-the -united-states.

33. Haspel Remarks at University of Louisville, September 26, 2018, https://www .cia.gov/stories/story/remarks-for-central-intelligence-agency-director-gina -haspel-mcconnell-center-at-the-university-of-louisville/.

34. Josh Rogin, *Chaos Under Heaven: Trump, Xi, and the Battle for the 21st Century* (Boston: Houghton Mifflin, 2021); Bethany Allen-Ebrahimian, "Special Report: Trump's U.S.-China Transformation," Axios, January 19, 2021.

35. John Bolton, "The Scandal of Trump's China Policy," *Wall Street Journal*, June 17, 2020.

36. "Internal Chinese Report Warns Beijing Faces Tiananmen-Like Global Backlash over Virus," Reuters, May 4, 2020; Laura Silver, Kat Devlin, and Christine Huang, "Unfavorable Views of China Reach Historic Highs in Many Countries," Pew Research Center, October 6, 2020.

37. Demetri Sevastopulo, "Biden Warns China Will Face 'Extreme Competition' from U.S.," *Financial Times*, February 7, 2021.

38. Jim Garamone, "Biden Announces DOD China Task Force," *Defense News*, February 10, 2021; Alex Leary and Paul Ziobro, "Biden Calls for $50 Billion to Boost U.S. Chip Industry," *Wall Street Journal*, March 31, 2021.

39. Biden's Remarks at Munich Security Conference, February 19, 2021, https:// www.whitehouse.gov/briefing-room/speeches-remarks/2021/02/19/remarks -by-president-biden-at-the-2021-virtual-munich-security-conference/.

40. Steven Lee Myers and Chris Buckley, "Biden's China Strategy Meets Resistance at the Negotiating Table," *New York Times*, July 26, 2021.

41. Dai Xu, "14 Misjudgments: China's '4 Unexpected' and '10 New Understandings' About the U.S.," May 26, 2020, https://demclubathr.files.wordpress .com/2020/06/what-china-doesnt-realize-us-china-relations-in-2020-dai-xu -weibo-may-26–2020.pdf.

42. Election Study Center, National Chengchi University, "Taiwanese/Chinese Identification Trend Distribution," January 25, 2021, https://esc.nccu.edu.tw/ PageDoc/Detail?fid=7800&id=6961.

43. "Taiwan to Boost Defense Budget 10% in Face of China Pressure," *Nikkei Asia*, August 13, 2020; Gabriel Dominguez, "Taiwan Developing New Asymmetric Warfare Concepts to Counter China's Growing Military Capabilities, Says Pentagon," *Janes Defence News*, September 2, 2020; Drew Thompson, "Hope on the Horizon: Taiwan's Radical New Defense Concept," *War on the Rocks*, October 2, 2018.

44. "Taiwan Says It Will Fight to the End if Attacked as China Sends More Jets," *The Guardian*, April 7, 2021; Yimou Lee, "Taiwan's Special Defence Budget to Go Mostly on Anti-Ship Capabilities," Reuters, October 5, 2021.

45. Michael Crowley, "Biden Backs Taiwan, but Some Call for Clearer Warning to China," *New York Times*, April 8, 2021.

46. Felix Chang, "The Ryukyu Defense Line: Japan's Response to China's Naval Push into the Pacific Ocean," Foreign Policy Research Institute, February 8, 2021; Ken Moriyasu, "U.S. Eyes Using Japan's Submarines to 'Choke' Chinese Navy," *Nikkei Asia*, May 5, 2021; Makiko Inoue and Ben Dooley, "Japan Approves Major Hike in Military Spending, with Taiwan in Mind," *New York Times*, December 23, 2021.

47. Mark Episkopos, "Japan Is Investing Big in Its F-35 Stealth Fighter Fleet," *National Interest*, May 6, 2021.

48. Dzirhan Mahadzir, "U.S. Marine F-35Bs to Embark on Japan's Largest Warship," USNI News, September 30, 2021.

49. "Japan, U.S. Defence Chiefs Affirm Cooperation on Taiwan: Kyodo," Reuters, March 21, 2021; "Japan Deputy PM Comment on Defending Taiwan if Invaded Angers China," Reuters, July 6, 2021; "U.S. and Japan Draw Up Joint Military Plan in Case of Taiwan Emergency," Reuters, December 24, 2021.

50. Birch T. Tan, "Understanding Vietnam's Military Modernization Efforts," *The Diplomat*, November 25, 2020.

51. Michael Beckley, "The Emerging Military Balance in East Asia: How China's Neighbors Can Check Chinese Naval Expansion," *International Security*, 42, no. 2 (Fall 2017): 78–119.

52. H.B. discussion with senior U.S. naval official, January 2018.

53. Jon Grevatt, "Indonesia Announces Strong Increase in 2021 Defence Budget," *Janes*, August 18, 2020.

54. Koya Jibiki, "Indonesia Looks to Triple Submarine Fleet After Chinese Incursions," *Nikkei Asia*, May 30, 2021.

55. Joel Gehrke, "Philippines's Duterte Rebukes Top Diplomat for Profanity-Laced Message to China: 'Only the President Can Curse,'" *Washington Examiner*, May 4, 2021.

56. "Philippines Beefs Up Military Muscle in Wake of Alleged Chinese Aggression in South China Sea," ABC News, April 21, 2021.

57. Bill Hayton, "Pompeo Draws a Line Against Beijing in the South China Sea," *Foreign Policy*, July 15, 2020.

58. Keith Johnson, "Australia Draws a Line on China," *Foreign Policy*, May 4, 2021.

59. "'Inconceivable' Australia Would Not Join U.S. to Defend Taiwan," Reuters, November 13, 2011.

60. William Mauldin, "India's Narendra Modi Emphasizes Security Ties in Address to Congress," *Wall Street Journal*, June 8, 2016.

61. Abishek Bhalla, "Indian Navy Ends Jam-Packed Year with Vietnamese Navy in South China Sea," *India Today*, December 27, 2020; "Anti-Ship Version of Supersonic Cruise Missile Testfired from Andaman Nicobar Islands," *New Indian Express*, December 1, 2020; Tanvi Madan, "Not Your Mother's Cold War: India's Options in U.S.-China Competition," *Washington Quarterly*, Winter 2021.

62. Giannis Seferiadis, "EU Hopes for Tech Alliance with Biden After Trump Huawei 5G Ban," *Nikkei Asia*, January 12, 2021.

63. Abhijnan Rej, "France-led Multination Naval Exercise Commences in Eastern Indian Ocean," *The Diplomat*, April 5, 2021; Antoine Bondaz and Bruno Tertrais, "Europe Can Play a Role in a Conflict Over Taiwan. Will It?" *World Politics Review*, March 23, 2021; Josh Rogin, "China Is Testing the West. We Shouldn't Back Down," *Washington Post*, December 23, 2021.

64. Li Jingkun, "Xi Jinping's U.K. Visit Rings in a Golden Age of Bilateral Ties," *China Today*, November 10, 2015; Lionel Barber, "Boris Johnson's 'Global Britain Tilts toward Asia,'" *Nikkei Asia*, March 23, 2021.

65. Dalibor Rohac, "The Czechs are Giving Europe a Lesson on How to Deal with China," *Washington Post*, September 3, 2020.

66. "Canada Launches 58-Nation Initiative to Stop Arbitrary Detentions," Reuters, February 15, 2021.

67. Luke Patey, *How China Loses: The Pushback Against Chinese Global Ambitions* (Oxford: Oxford University Press, 2021); Vincent Ni, "EU Efforts to Ratify China Investment Deal 'Suspended' after Sanctions," *The Guardian*, May 4, 2021.

68. William Pesek, "Singapore's Trade-War Worries Bad for Everyone," *Asia Times*, October 4, 2019.

69. For instance, Mitsuru Obe, "Decoupling Denied: Japan Inc Lays Its Bets on China," *Financial Times*, February 16, 2021.

70. Andrea Kendall-Taylor and David Shullman, "China and Russia's Dangerous Convergence: How to Counter an Emerging Partnership," *Foreign Affairs*, May 3, 2021; Hal Brands and Evan Braden Montgomery, "One War Is Not Enough: Strategy and Force Planning for Great-Power Competition," *Texas National Security Review*, 3, no. 2 (Spring 2020): 80–92.

71. This paragraph, and the "no limits" quote in the previous paragraph, draws on Hal

Brands, "The Eurasian Nightmare: Chinese-Russian Convergence and the Future of American Order," *Foreign Affairs*, February 25, 2022.

72. We are indebted to Peter Feaver for this insight.

73. Reid Standish, "China in Eurasia Briefing: How Far Will Beijing Go in Backing Putin?" *Radio Free Europe/Radio Liberty*, March 2, 2022.

74. On these ideas, see Jared Cohen and Richard Fontaine, "Uniting the Techno-Democracies: How to Build Digital Cooperation," *Foreign Affairs*, November/December 2020; Hal Brands and Zack Cooper, "The Great Game with China is 3D Chess," *Foreign Policy*, December 30, 2020; Steve Holland and Guy Faulconbridge, "G7 Rivals China with Grand Infrastructure Plan," Reuters, June 13, 2021.

75. "GDP Per Capita (current US$)," World Bank, https://data.worldbank.org/indicator/NY.GDP.PCAP.CD, accessed May 2021.

76. Michael Beckley, *Unrivaled: Why America Will Remain the World's Sole Superpower* (Ithaca, NY: Cornell University Press, 2018), 34.

77. "Top China Generals Urge More Spending for U.S. Conflict 'Trap,'" Bloomberg News, March 9, 2021.

78. "Has the Wind Changed? PLA Hawks General Dai Xu and General Qiao Liang Release Odd Articles," GNews, July 11, 2020, https://gnews.org/257994/; for slightly different translations, see "Xi's Intellectual Warriors Are Outgunning 'Realists' of Deng Xiaoping Era," *Business Standard*, August 19, 2020; Dai Xu, "14 Misjudgments."

79. Minnie Chan, "'Too Costly': Chinese Military Strategist Warns Now Is Not the Time to Take Back Taiwan by Force," *South China Morning Post*, May 4, 2020.

80. Katsuji Nakazawa, "Analysis: China's 'Wolf Warriors' Take Aim at G-7," *Nikkei Asia*, May 13, 2021.

81. Steven Lee Myers and Amy Qin, "Why Biden Seems Worse to China than Trump," *New York Times*, July 20, 2021.

82. Amanda Kerrigan, "Views from the People's Republic of China on U.S.-China Relations Since the Beginning of the Biden Administration," Center for Naval Analyses, September 2021.

83. Richard McGregor, "Beijing Hard-Liners Kick Against Xi Jinping's Wolf Warrior Diplomacy," Lowy Institute, July 28, 2020.

## 4. Danger: Falling Powers

1. Paul Kennedy, *The Rise and Fall of the Great Powers: Economic Change and Military Conflict from 1500 to 2000* (New York: Random House, 1987), 209.

2. A.J.P. Taylor, *The Struggle for Mastery in Europe, 1848–1918* (New York: Oxford University Press, 1954), xxxii.

3.  Marc Trachtenberg, "A Wasting Asset: American Strategy and the Shifting Nuclear Balance, 1949–1954," *International Security*, 13, no. 3 (Winter 1988–89): 41.

4.  Annika Mombauer, *Helmuth von Moltke and the Origins of the First World War* (New York: Cambridge University Press, 2001), 172.

5.  Robert Strassler, ed., *The Landmark Thucydides: A Comprehensive Guide to the Peloponnesian War* (New York: Simon & Schuster, 2008), 65.

6.  Jack S. Levy, "Declining Power and the Preventive Motivation for War," *World Politics*, 40, no. 1 (October 1987), 83; A.F.K. Organski, *World Politics* (New York: Knopf, 1968).

7.  Graham Allison, *Destined for War: Can America and China Escape Thucydides's Trap?* (Boston: Houghton Mifflin Harcourt, 2017); Robert Strassler, ed., *Landmark Thucydides*, 16.

8.  Gideon Rachman, "Year in a Word: Thucydides' Trap," *Financial Times*, December 19, 2018.

9.  Donald Kagan, *On the Origins of War and the Preservation of Peace* (New York: Anchor, 1996), 44; Donald Kagan, *The Outbreak of the Peloponnesian War* (Ithaca, NY: Cornell University Press, 1969).

10. For the data underlying this section as well as a longer description of selection criteria and specific cases, see Michael Beckley, "When Fast-Growing Great Powers Slow Down: Historical Evidence and Implications for China," National Bureau of Asian Research, January 2021.

11. There is a parallel to the famous J-curve theory of revolution, which holds that revolts tend to occur not after decades of misery, but when an economic slowdown follows a sustained expansion. James C. Davies, "Toward a Theory of Revolution," *American Sociological Review*, 27, no. 1 (February 1962): 5–19.

12. John Chipman, *French Power in Africa* (Oxford: Blackwell, 1989); Pierre Lellouche and Dominique Moisi, "French Policy in Africa: A Lonely Battle Against Destabilization," *International Security*, 3, no. 4 (Spring 1979): 108–133; Andrew Hansen, "The French Military in Africa," Council on Foreign Relations, February 8, 2008.

13. Walter LaFeber, *The Clash: U.S.-Japanese Relations Throughout History* (New York: Norton, 1997), 366; Jennifer Lind, "Pacifism or Passing the Buck? Testing Theories of Japanese Security Policy," *International Security*, 29, no. 1 (Summer 2004): 92–121.

14. David O. Whitten, "The Depression of 1893," EH.net, https://eh.net/encyclopedia/the-depression-of-1893/; Charles Hoffman, "The Depression of the Nineties," *Journal of Economic History* (June 1956): 137–164.

15. David Healy, *U.S. Expansionism: The Imperialist Urge in the 1890s* (Madison: University of Wisconsin Press, 1970), 27.

16. Marc-William Palen, "The Imperialism of Economic Nationalism, 1890–1913," *Diplomatic History*, 39, no. 1 (January 2015): 157–185.

17. Benjamin O. Fordham, "Protectionist Empire: Trade, Tariffs, and United States Foreign Policy, 1890–1914," *Studies in American Political Development*, 31, no. 2 (October 2017): 170–192.

18. Healy, *U.S. Expansionism*, 176; Walter LaFeber, *The New Empire: An Interpretation of American Expansion, 1860–1898* (Ithaca, NY: Cornell University Press, 1963); Kevin Narizny, *The Political Economy of Grand Strategy* (Ithaca, NY: Cornell University Press, 2007), chaps. 2–4.

19. See Patrick McDonald, *The Invisible Hand of Peace: Capitalism, the War Machine, and International Relations Theory* (New York: Cambridge University Press, 2009); Kent E. Calder, *Crisis and Compensation: Public Policy and Political Stability in Japan* (Princeton, NJ: Princeton University Press, 1988).

20. Dietrich Geyer, *Russian Imperialism: The Interaction of Domestic and Foreign Policy, 1860–1914* (New Haven, CT: Yale University Press, 2009), 205.

21. Peter Gatrell, *Government, Industry and Rearmament in Russia, 1900–1914* (New York: Cambridge University Press, 1994), 21, 24.

22. Dale Copeland, *Economic Interdependence and War* (Princeton, NJ: Princeton University Press, 2015), 108; Brian Taylor, *Politics and the Russian Army: Civil-Military Relations, 1689–2000* (Cambridge, UK: Cambridge University Press, 2003), 69; Stephen Anthony Smith, *Russia in Revolution: An Empire in Crisis, 1890 to 1928* (New York: Oxford University Press, 2017), 18.

23. The following paragraphs draw on Beckley, "When Fast-Growing Great Powers Slow Down."

24. Valerie Bunce and Aida Hozic, "Diffusion-Proofing and the Russian Invasion of Ukraine," *Demokratizatsiya* 24, no. 4 (Fall 2016): 435–446.

25. Anders Aslund, *Russia's Crony Capitalism: The Path from Market Economy to Kleptocracy* (New Haven, CT: Yale University Press, 2019), 240; Kathryn Stoner, *Russia Resurrected: Its Power and Purpose in a New Global Order* (New York: Oxford University Press, 2021).

26. E. Wayne Merry, "The Origins of Russia's War in Ukraine: The Clash of Russian and European Civilization Choices for Ukraine," in Elizabeth A. Wood, William E. Pomeranz, E. Wayne Merry, and Maxim Trudolyubov, eds., *Roots of Russia's War in Ukraine* (New York: Columbia University Press, 2015), ch. 1.

27. Elias Gotz, "It's Geopolitics, Stupid: Explaining Russia's Ukraine Policy," *Global Affairs*, 1, no. 1 (2015): 3–10.

28. Samuel Charap and Timothy J. Colton, *Everyon Loss: The Ukraine Crisis and the Ruinous Contest for Post-Soviet Eurasia* (New York: Routledge, 2017).

29. Christopher Miller, *Putinomics: Power and Money in Resurgent Russia* (Chapel Hill: University of North Carolina Press, 2018): 140–145; Daniel Treisman, "Why Putin Took Crimea: The Gambler in the Kremlin," *Foreign Affairs*, May/June 2016; Gotz, "It's the Geopolitics, Stupid."

30. Copeland, *Economic Interdependence and War*, chaps. 4–5; Adam Tooze, *The Wages of Destruction: The Making and Breaking of the Nazi Economy* (New York: Penguin, 2008).

31. Bernard Wasserstein, *Barbarism and Civilization: A History of Europe in Our Time* (New York: Oxford University Press, 2007), 13–14; Paul Kennedy, *The Rise of the Anglo-German Antagonism, 1860–1914* (London: Allen & Unwin, 1980), 464; Taylor, *Struggle for Mastery*, xxvii; Angus Maddison, *The World Economy: Historical Statistics* (Paris: OECD, 2003), table 1b, 48–49.

32. David Calleo, *The German Problem Reconsidered: Germany and the World Order, 1870 to the Present* (New York: Cambridge University Press, 1980).

33. This was why Bismarck considered the annexation of Alsace and Lorraine in 1871 to have been a mistake—it ensured lasting French enmity.

34. Charles Kupchan, *The Vulnerability of Empire* (Ithaca, NY: Cornell University Press, 1994), 370.

35. Taylor, *Struggle for Mastery*, 372–402; Fritz Fischer, *Germany's Aims in the First World War* (New York: Norton, 1967); "Bernhard von Bulow on Germany's 'Place in the Sun,'" 1897, https://ghdi.ghi-dc.org/sub_document.cfm?document_id=783.

36. Eyre Crowe, "Memorandum on the Present State of British Relations with France and Germany," January 1, 1907, https://en.wikisource.org/wiki/Memorandum_on_the_Present_State_of_British_Relations_with_France_and_Germany.

37. Kennedy, *Rise of the Anglo-German Antagonism*, 420.

38. Immanuel Geiss, *German Foreign Policy 1871–1914*, Vol. IX (London: Routledge, 1976), 121.

39. Kennedy, *Rise of the Anglo-German Antagonism*, 55.

40. Copeland, *Economic Interdependence*, 125.

41. Annika Mombauer, *The Origins of the First World War: Diplomatic and Military Documents* (Manchester, UK: Manchester University Press, 2013), 33; Taylor, *Struggle for Mastery*, 403–482.

42. Kennedy, *Rise and Fall*, 213–214.

43. Mombauer, *Helmuth von Moltke;* Jack Snyder, "Civil-Military Relations and the Cult of the Offensive, 1914 and 1984," *International Security*, 9, no. 1 (Summer 1984): 108–146.

44. Dale Copeland, *The Origins of Major War* (Ithaca, NY: Cornell University Press,

2001), 70; Allison, *Destined for War*, 80–81; Hew Strachan, *The First World War: Volume I: To Arms* (New York: Oxford University Press, 1993).

45. Stephen Van Evera, "The Cult of the Offensive and the Origins of the First World War," *International Security*, 9, no. 1 (Summer 1984): 81.

46. Martin Gilbert, *The First World War: A Complete History* (New York: Henry Holt, 1994), 5–14.

47. Copeland, *Economic Interdependence*, esp. 126–131; Max Hastings, *Catastrophe 1914: Europe Goes to War* (New York: Vintage, 2013), 12.

48. Volker Berghahn, *Imperial Germany: Economy, Society, Culture, and Politics* (New York: Berghahn, 2005), 266.

49. Van Evera, "Cult of the Offensive," 69, 66, 68; Fischer, *Germany's Aims*.

50. See Annika Mombauer, *Origins of the First World War: Controversies and Consensus* (New York: Routledge, 2013), 16.

51. Konrad H. Jarausch, "The Illusion of Limited War: Chancellor Bethmann Hollweg's Calculated Risk, July 1914," *Central European History*, 2, no. 1 (March 1969): 58.

52. Mombauer, *Origins of the First World War: Diplomatic and Military Documents*, 459; Copeland, *Origins of Major War*, 79–117; Immanuel Geiss, "The Outbreak of the First World War and German War Aims," *Journal of Contemporary History*, 1, no. 3 (July 1966): 75–91.

53. Hastings, *Catastrophe 1914*, 81.

54. Jarausch, "Illusion of Limited War," 48.

55. Jack Snyder, "Better Now than Later: The Paradox of 1914 as Everyone's Favored Year for War," *International Security*, 39, no. 1 (Summer 2014): 71.

56. G.C. Allen, *A Short Economic History of Modern Japan, 1867–1937* (New York: Palgrave Macmillan, 1981), 91.

57. Kenneth Pyle, *Japan Rising: The Resurgence of Japanese Power and Purpose* (New York: PublicAffairs, 2007), 163.

58. LaFeber, *The Clash*, 148; Akira Iriye, *The Origins of the Second World War in Asia and the Pacific* (New York: Routledge, 1987).

59. Masato Shizume, "The Japanese Economy During the Interwar Period: Instability in the Financial System and the Impact of the World Depression," *Bank of Japan Review*, May 2009, chart 1.

60. Iriye, *The Origins of the Second World War*, 6.

61. Nobuya Bamba, *Japanese Diplomacy in a Dilemma: New Light on Japan's China Policy, 1924–1929* (Ontario: UBC Press, 2002), 56, 62.

62. Herbert Bix, *Hirohito and the Making of Modern Japan* (New York: Harper, 2001), 227.

63. Akira Iriye, "The Failure of Economic Expansion: 1918–1931," in *Japan in Crisis: Essays on Taisho Democracy*, ed. Bernard Silberman and H.D. Harootunian (Princeton, NJ: Princeton University Press, 1974), 265.

64. S.C.M. Paine, *The Japanese Empire: Grand Strategy from the Meiji Restoration to the Pacific War* (New York: Cambridge University Press, 2017), 110–113.

65. Christopher Thorne, *The Limits of Foreign Policy: The West, the League, and the Far Eastern Crisis of 1931–1933* (London: Macmillan, 1972), 32; Michael Green, *By More than Providence: Grand Strategy and American Power in the Asia-Pacific Since 1783* (New York: Columbia University Press, 2016), 152.

66. James Crowley, *Japan's Quest for Autonomy: National Security and Foreign Policy, 1930–1938* (Princeton, NJ: Princeton University Press, 1966), 208; Michael Barnhart, *Japan Prepares for Total War: The Search for Economic Security, 1919–1941* (Ithaca, NY: Cornell University Press, 1987).

67. Kenneth Colegrove, "The New Order in East Asia," *Far Eastern Quarterly*, 1, no. 1 (November 1941): 6.

68. Green, *By More than Providence*, 156.

69. See esp. Bix, *Hirohito*, 308; Crowley, *Japan's Quest for Autonomy*, 286–290; J.W. Dower, *Empire and Aftermath: Yoshida Shigeru and the Japanese Experience, 1878–1954* (Cambridge, MA: Harvard University Press, 1988), 139.

70. Pyle, *Japan Rising*, 176.

71. Bix, *Hirohito*, 374; Eri Hotta, *Japan 1941: Countdown to Infamy* (New York: Vintage, 2013), esp. 23–57.

72. S.C.M. Paine, *The Wars for Asia, 1911–1949* (New York: Cambridge University Press, 2012), 185.

73. Waldo Heinrichs, *Threshold of War: Franklin D. Roosevelt and American Entry into World War II* (New York: Oxford University Press, 1988), 7; Barnhart, *Japan Prepares*, 91–114.

74. Pyle, *Japan Rising*, 192.

75. See esp. Iriye, *Origins of the Second World War*; also Robert Dallek, *Franklin Roosevelt and American Foreign Policy, 1932–1945* (New York: Oxford University Press, 1995); Rana Mitter, *Forgotten Ally: China's World War II, 1937–1945* (Boston: Houghton Mifflin, 2013).

76. Jonathan Utley, *Going to War with Japan, 1937–1941* (New York: Fordham University Press, 2005), 16.

77. Dallek, *Franklin Roosevelt*, passim; Heinrichs, *Threshold of War*, 10; Gerhard Weinberg, *A World at Arms: A Global History of World War II* (New York: Cambridge University Press, 2020), 260.

78. Paine, *Japanese Empire*, 153; Barnhart, *Japan Prepares*, 162–262.

79. Jeffrey Record, *Japan's Decision for War in 1941: Some Enduring Lessons* (Carlisle Barracks, PA: Strategic Studies Institute, 2009), 25.

80. Ernst Presseisen, *Germany and Japan: A Study in Totalitarian Diplomacy, 1933–1941* (The Hague: Springer, 1958), 241–243.

81. Heinrichs, *Threshold of War*, 183.

82. Heinrichs, *Threshold of War*, 182; Scott Sagan, "The Origins of the Pacific War," *Journal of Interdisciplinary History*, 18, no. 4 (Spring 1988): 903–908.

83. Paine, *Japanese Empire*, 148–149; Bix, *Hirohito*, 400, 406–407; LaFeber, *The Clash*, 197–200; Hosoya Chihiro, "Britain and the United States in Japan's View of the International System, 1937–1941," in *Anglo-Japanese Alienation, 1919–1952*, ed. Ian Nish (New York: Cambridge University Press, 1982).

84. Sagan, "Origins," 912.

85. Ikuhiko Hata, "Admiral Yamamoto's Surprise Attack and the Japanese Navy's War Strategy," in *From Pearl Harbor to Hiroshima: The Second World War in Asia and the Pacific, 1941–45*, ed. Saki Dockrill (New York: St. Martin's, 1994), 65.

86. Hotta, *Japan 1941*, 201.

87. Sagan, "Origins," 893.

88. Adam Tooze, *The Deluge: The Great War, America, and the Remaking of the Global Order, 1916–1931* (New York: Penguin, 2014), 3.

## 5. The Gathering Storm

1. John Feng, "China's Xi Jinping Says Soon No Enemy Will Be Able to Defeat the Country," *Newsweek*, May 6, 2021.

2. Sheena Chestnut Greitens, "Internal Security & Grand Strategy: China's Approach to National Security Under Xi Jinping," Statement before the U.S.-China Economic & Security Review Commission, January 2021.

3. Xi Jinping, "National Security Matter of Prime Importance," Xinhua, April 15, 2014, http://www.xinhuanet.com//politics/2014-04/15/c_1110253910.htm.

4. Xi Jinping, "Safeguard National Security and Social Stability," *Qiushi*, April 25, 2014, http://en.qstheory.cn/2020-12/07/c_607612.htm.

5. Xi, "Safeguard National Security and Social Stability."

6. Alastair Iain Johnston, "China's Contribution to the U.S.-China Security Dilemma," in *After Engagement: Dilemmas in U.S.-China Security Relations*, ed. Jacques Delisle and Avery Goldstein (Washington, DC: Brookings Institution, 2021), 92–97.

7. "The CCP Central Committee-Formulated Proposal for the 14th Five-Year National Economic and Social Development Plan, and 2035 Long-Term Goals," Xinhua, http://www.xinhuanet.com/2020-10/29/c_1126674147.htm.

8. Jude Blanchette, "Ideological Security as National Security," CSIS, December 2, 2020.

9. Sheena Chestnut Greitens, *Preventive Repression: Internal Security & Grand Strategy in China Under Xi Jinping*, unpublished manuscript, 2021.

10. Sheena Chestnut Greitens, "Counterterrorism and Preventive Repression: China's Changing Strategy in Xinjiang," *International Security*, 44, no. 3 (Winter 2019–20): 9–47.

11. This paragraph and the phrase "Lenin trap" draw from Walter Russell Mead, "Imperialism Will Be Dangerous for China," *Wall Street Journal*, September 17, 2018.

12. Vladimir Ilich Lenin, *Imperialism as the Highest Stage of Capitalism* (Brattleboro, VT: Echo Point Books, 2020).

13. Sebastian Horn, Carmen M. Reinhart, and Christoph Trebesch, "China's Overseas Lending," NBER Working Paper 26050 (Cambridge, MA: National Bureau of Economic Research, 2019).

14. Daniel H. Rosen, "China's Economic Reckoning: The Price of Failed Reforms," *Foreign Affairs*, July/August 2021.

15. See Luke Patey, *How China Loses: The Pushback Against Chinese Global Ambitions* (Oxford: Oxford University Press, 2021).

16. James Crabtree, "China's Radical New Vision of Globalization," *NOEMA*, December 10, 2020; "China's "Dual-Circulation" Strategy Means Relying Less on Foreigners," *The Economist*, November 7, 2020.

17. Andrew Rennemo, "How China Joined the Sanctions Game," *The Diplomat*, February 8, 2021.

18. Matt Pottinger, Testimony Before the United States–China Economic and Security Review Commission, April 15, 2021, https://www.uscc.gov/sites/default/files/2021-04/Matt_Pottinger_Testimony.pdf.

19. "Time Holds the Key to 6G," *NewElectronics*, December 14, 2020, https://www.newelectronics.co.uk/electronics-technology/time-holds-the-key-to-6g/232997/.

20. Michael Brown, Eric Chewning, and Pavneet Singh, "Preparing the United States for the Superpower Marathon with China," Brookings Institution, April 2020.

21. Chris Miller, "America Is Going to Decapitate Huawei," *New York Times*, September 15, 2020.

22. Richard Aboulafia, "China's Potemkin Aviation Can't Survive Without Washington's Help," *Foreign Policy*, February 16, 2021.

23. Julian Gewirtz, "The Chinese Reassessment of Interdependence," *China Leadership Monitor*, June 1, 2020.

24. Nina Xiang, "Foreign Dependence the Achilles' Heel in China's Giant Tech Sector," *Nikkei Asia*, January 31, 2021.

25. Gewirtz, "Chinese Reassessment."

26. Paul Mozur and Steven Lee Meyers, "Xi's Gambit: China Plans for a World Without American Technology," *New York Times*, March 20, 2021.

27. Mozur and Meyers, "Xi's Gambit."

28. Lingling Wei, "China's New Power Play: More Control of Tech Companies' Troves of Data," *Wall Street Journal*, June 12, 2021; Emily Weinstein, "Don't Underestimate China's Military-Civil Fusion Efforts," *Foreign Policy*, February 5, 2021.

29. Matt Pottinger and David Feith, "The Most Powerful Data Broker in the World Is Winning the War Against the U.S.," *New York Times*, November 30, 2021; also Jonathan Hillman, "China Is Watching You," *The Atlantic*, October 18, 2021.

30. Catherine Clifford, "Google CEO: A.I. Is More Important than Fire or Electricity," CNBC.com, February 1, 2018.

31. Hal Brands, "China's Lead in the AI War Won't Last Forever," Bloomberg Opinion, November 12, 2019; "Artificial Intelligence," Accenture, https://www.accenture.com/us-en/insights/artificial-intelligence-summary-index; Jim Garamone, "Esper Says Artificial Intelligence Will Change the Battlefield," DOD News, September 9, 2020.

32. Gregory Allen, "Understanding China's AI Strategy: Clues to Chinese Strategic Thinking on Artificial Intelligence and National Security," Center for a New American Security, February 2019.

33. Jonathan Hillman, *The Digital Silk Road: China's Quest to Wire the World and Win the Future* (New York: Harper Business, 2021).

34. Henry Ridgwell, "U.S. Warns Information-Sharing at Risk as Britain Approves Huawei 5G Rollout," Voice of America, January 29, 2020.

35. Hillman, *Digital Silk Road*, esp. 2–3; also Abigail Opiah, "China Mobile International Launches First European Data Centre," *Capacity*, December 20, 2019; Max Bearak, "In Strategic Djibouti, a Microcosm of China's Growing Foothold in Africa," *Washington Post*, December 30, 2019; Jonathan Hillman and Maesea McCalpin, "Huawei's Global Cloud Strategy," *Reconnecting Asia*, May 17, 2021.

36. Hillman, *Digital Silk Road*, 2–3.

37. Valentina Pop, Sha Hua, and Daniel Michaels, "From Lightbulbs to 5G, China Battles West for Control of Vital Technology Standards," *Wall Street Journal*, February 8, 2021.

38. Quoted in Pop, Hua, and Michaels, "From Lightbulbs to 5G."

39. Will Hunt, Saif M. Khan, and Dahlia Peterson, "China's Progress in Semiconductor Manufacturing Equipment: Accelerants and Policy Implications," CSET Policy Brief, March 2021.

40. Derek Scissors, Dan Blumenthal, and Linda Zhang, "The U.S.-China Global Vaccine Competition," American Enterprise Institute, February 2021.

41. See Tim Culpan, "China Isn't the AI Juggernaut the West Fears," Bloomberg Opinion, October 11, 2021.

42. Varieties of Democracy Project, 2019, version 9, https://doi.org/10.23696/vdemcy19.

43. John Garver, *China's Quest: The History of the Foreign Relations of the People's Republic of China* (New York: Oxford University Press, 2016), 479.

44. World Bank, "World Development Indicators," GDP Per Capita Growth Rate, https://databank.worldbank.org/source/world-development-indicators, accessed August 10, 2021.

45. Quoted in George J. Church, "China: Old Wounds Deng Xiaoping," *Time*, January 6, 1986.

46. Samuel Huntington, *The Third Wave: Democratization in the Late Twentieth Century* (Norman: University of Oklahoma Press, 1993). For data, see the Mass Mobilization Project, https://massmobilization.github.io.

47. M.E. Sarotte, "China's Fear of Contagion: Tiananmen Square and the Power of the European Example," *International Security*, 37, no. 2 (Fall 2012): 156–182; Karrie J. Koesel and Valerie J. Bunce, "Diffusion-Proofing: Russian and Chinese Responses to Waves of Popular Mobilizations Against Authoritarian Rulers," *Perspectives on Politics*, 11, no. 3 (September 2013): 753–768.

48. Christopher Walker and Jessica Ludwig, "The Long Arm of the Strongman: How China and Russia Use Sharp Power to Threaten Democracies," *Foreign Affairs*, May 12, 2021.

49. Elizabeth C. Economy, "Exporting the China Model," Testimony Before the U.S.-China Economic and Security Review Commission Hearing on The "China Model," March 13, 2020.

50. Sarah Repucci and Amy Slipowitz, *Freedom in the World 2021: Democracy Under Seige* (Washington, DC: Freedom House, 2021).

51. Robert Kagan, "The Strongmen Strike Back," *Washington Post*, March 14, 2019.

52. See Yaroslav Trofimov, Drew Henshaw, and Kate O'Keeffe, "How China Is Taking over International Organizations, One Vote at a Time," *Wall Street Journal*, September 29, 2020.

53. Hal Brands, "How Far Will China's Surveillance State Stretch?" Bloomberg Opinion, August 12, 2020; Jonathan Kearsley, Eryk Bagshaw, and Anthony Galloway, "'If You Make China the Enemy, China Will Be the Enemy': Beijing's Fresh Threat to Australia," *Sydney Morning Herald*, November 18, 2020.

54. See the articles in the January 2019 issue of the *Journal of Democracy* collectively titled "The Road to Digital Unfreedom"; Richard Fontaine and Kara Frederick, "The Autocrat's New Toolkit," *Wall Street Journal*, March 15, 2019.

55. Tiberiu Dragu and Yonatan Lupu, "Digital Authoritarianism and the Future

of Human Rights," *International Organization*, 75, no. 4 (February 2021): 991–1017.

56. Sheena Chestnut Greitens, "Dealing with Demand for China's Global Surveillance Exports," Global China, Brookings Institution, April 2020.

57. Alina Polyakova and Chris Meserole, "Exporting Digital Authoritarianism: The Russian and Chinese Models," Brookings Institution Policy Brief, August 2019.

58. Andrea Kendall-Taylor, Erica Frantz, and Joseph Wright, "The Digital Dictators: How Technology Strengthens Autocracy," *Foreign Affairs*, March/April 2020.

59. Ross Andersen, "The Panopticon Is Already Here," *The Atlantic*, September 2020.

60. Jessica Chen Weiss, "A World Safe for Autocracy? China's Rise and the Future of Global Politics," *Foreign Affairs*, July/August 2019.

61. "Democracy Under Siege," Freedom House, 2021, https://freedomhouse.org/report/freedom-world/2021/democracy-under-siege.

62. Michael J. Mazarr, Abigail Casey, Alyssa Demus, et al., *Hostile Social Manipulation* (Santa Monica, CA: RAND Corporation, 2019); Jeff Kao, "How China Built a Twitter Propaganda Machine Then Let It Loose on Coronavirus," ProPublica, March 26, 2020.

63. Robert Kagan, *The Return of History and the End of Dreams* (New York: Knopf, 2008).

64. As Franklin Roosevelt warned in his 1940 State of the Union Address.

65. Zheng Bijian, "China's Peaceful Rise to Great Power Status," *Foreign Affairs*, September/October 2005.

66. For two of many examples, see Thomas J. Christensen, "Windows and War: Trend Analysis and Beijing's Use of Force," in *New Directions in the Study of China's Foreign Policy*, ed. Robert S. Ross and Alastair Iain Johnston (Stanford: Stanford University Press, 2006), chap. 3; M. Taylor Fravel, "Power Shifts and Escalation: Explaining China's Use of Force in Territorial Disputes," *International Security*, 32, no. 3 (Winter 2007–2008): 44–83.

67. Michael Peck, "Slaughter in the East China Sea," *Foreign Policy*, August 7, 2020.

68. Helene Cooper, "Patrolling Disputed Waters, U.S. and China Jockey for Dominance," *New York Times*, March 30, 2016.

69. Paul V. Kane, "To Save Our Economy, Ditch Taiwan," *New York Times*, November 10, 2011.

70. Michael O'Hanlon, "Why China Cannot Conquer Taiwan," *International Security*, 25, no. 2 (Fall 2000): 51–86.

71. Thomas Shugart, *First Strike: China's Missile Threat to U.S. Bases in Asia* (Washington, DC: Center for A New American Security, 2017).

72. Michael Beckley, "China Keeps Inching Closer to Taiwan," *Foreign Policy*, October 19, 2020.

73. Samson Ellis and Cindy Wang, "Taiwan Warns China Could 'Paralyze' Island's Defenses in Conflict," Bloomberg, September 1, 2021.

74. Thomas H. Shugart III, "Trends, Timelines, and Uncertainty: An Assessment of the State of Cross-Strait Deterrence," Testimony Before the U.S.-China Economic and Security Review Commission, February 18, 2021.

75. Mackenzie Eaglen and Hallie Coyne, "The 2020s Tri-Service Modernization Crunch," American Enterprise Institute, March 2021.

76. Sydney Freedberg, "U.S. 'Gets Its Ass Handed to It' in Wargames: Here's a $24 Billion Fix," *Breaking Defense*, March 7, 2019.

77. Oriana Mastro, "The Taiwan Temptation: Why Beijing Might Resort to Force," *Foreign Affairs*, July/August 2021, 61.

78. Mastro, "The Taiwan Temptation."

79. Xi Jinping, "Secure a Decisive Victory in Building a Moderately Prosperous Society in All Respects and Strive for the Great Success of Socialism with Chinese Characteristics for a New Era," Delivered at the 19th National Congress of the Communist Party of China, October 18, 2017.

80. Gabriel Collins and Andrew S. Erickson, *U.S.-China Competition Enters the Decade of Maximum Danger: Policy Ideas to Avoid Losing the 2020s* (Houston: Baker Institute for Public Policy, Rice University, 2021), 35.

81. "A Conversation with US Indo-Pacific Command's Adm. Philip Davidson," American Enterprise Institute, March 4, 2021, https://www.aei.org/events/a-conversation-with-us-indo-pacific-commands-adm-philip-davidson/.

82. Alison Kaufman and Daniel Hartnett, "Managing Conflict: Examining Recent PLA Writings on Escalation Control," CNA China Studies, February 2016, 68. For an example, see Guangqian Peng and Youzhi Yao, eds., *The Science of Military Strategy* (Beijing: Military Science Publishing House, 2005), 327.

83. Tara Copp, "'It Failed Miserably': After Wargaming Loss, Joint Chiefs Are Overhauling How the U.S. Military Will Fight," *Defense One*, July 26, 2021.

84. Hal Brands and Evan Braden Montgomery, "One War Is Not Enough: Strategy and Force Planning for Great-Power Competition," *Texas National Security Review*, 3, no. 2 (Spring 2020): 80–92.

85. *Providing for the Common Defense: The Assessment and Recommendations of the National Defense Strategy Commission*, U.S. Institute for Peace, November 2018, 14. The members of this commission included several high-level appointees in the Biden administration. One of the authors of this book (Brands) was the lead author of the report.

86.  The phrase is adapted from Eaglen and Coyne, "2020s Tri-Service Moderniza-tion Crunch."

## 6. What One Cold War Can Teach Us About Another

1.  Benn Steil, *Marshall Plan: Dawn of the Cold War* (New York: Simon & Schuster, 2018), 15.
2.  Editorial Note, in *Foreign Relations of the United States, 1947*, Vol. III: Document No. 133 (Washington, DC: U.S. Department of State, Office of the Historian). Hereafter cited as *FRUS*, followed by year, volume, and document number.
3.  PPS-1, "Policy with Respect to American Aid to Western Europe," May 23, 1947, Box 7, Charles Bohlen Papers, Record Group 59, National Archives and Records Administration (NARA), College Park, MD; also John Lewis Gaddis, *George F. Kennan: An American Life* (New York: Penguin, 2011), 264–270.
4.  Robert Jervis, *Perception and Misperception in International Politics* (Princeton, NJ: Princeton University Press, 2017), 239.
5.  For this reason, the Soviet Union doesn't technically qualify for inclusion in the set of cases presented in chapter 4. But as this chapter shows, there are still strong parallels between the problems the Soviet Union presented for America in the early Cold War and the strategic dilemmas a bellicose, insecure China creates today.
6.  Office of Strategic Services, "Problems and Objectives of United States Policy," April 12, 1945, *Declassified Documents Reference System* (DDRS).
7.  Kennan to Secretary of State, February 22, 1946, *FRUS, 1946*, Vol. I: Document No. 475.
8.  X (Kennan), "The Sources of Soviet Conduct," *Foreign Affairs*, July 1947, 566–582.
9.  Harry S. Truman's Statement, February 6, 1946, American Presidency Project (APP), University of California–Santa Barbara.
10. Robert Pollard, *Economic Security and the Origins of the Cold War, 1945–1950* (New York: Columbia University Press, 1985), 151; Melvyn Leffler, *A Preponderance of Power: National Security, the Truman Administration, and the Cold War* (Stanford: Stanford University Press, 1992), 7.
11. Hal Brands, *The Twilight Struggle: What the Cold War Teaches Us About Great-Power Rivalry Today* (New Haven, CT: Yale University Press, 2022), 16; Marc Trachtenberg, *A Constructed Peace: The Making of the European Settlement, 1945–1963* (Princeton, NJ: Princeton University Press, 1999), 87–90, 96–99.
12. PPS 33, "Factors Affecting the Nature of the U.S. Defense Arrangements in the Light of Soviet Policies," June 23, 1948, *State Department Policy Planning Staff Papers*, Vol. 2 (New York: Garland, 1983), 289.

13. Samuel F. Wells, *Fearing the Worst: How Korea Transformed the Cold War* (New York: Columbia University Press, 2020), 251.

14. Memorandum for the Record, January 24, 1951, in *FRUS, 1951*, Vol. I: Document No. 7; Marc Trachtenberg, "A Wasting Asset: American Strategy and the Shifting Nuclear Balance, 1949–1954," *International Security*, 13, no. 3 (Winter 1988–89): 5–49.

15. Harry S. Truman, Farewell Address, January 15, 1953, APP.

16. "President Harry S. Truman's Address Before a Joint Session of Congress," March 12, 1947, Avalon Project, Yale Law School, https://avalon.law.yale .edu/20th_century/trudoc.asp.

17. Harry S. Truman, *Years of Trial and Hope* (Garden City, NY: Doubleday, 1956), 124–128.

18. Harry S. Truman, Address, September 2, 1947, APP.

19. Harry S. Truman's News Conference, January 29, 1948, APP; John Lewis Gaddis, *Strategies of Containment: A Critical Appraisal of American National Security Policy during the Cold War* (New York: Oxford University Press, 2005), chaps. 2–3.

20. PPS-13, "Resumé of World Situation," November 6, 1947, *FRUS, 1947*, Vol. I: Document No. 393.

21. G. John Ikenberry, *Liberal Leviathan: The Origins, Crisis, and Transformation of the American World Order* (Princeton, NJ: Princeton University Press, 2011), 199.

22. Gaddis, *Strategies of Containment*, 112.

23. See Forrest Pogue, *George C. Marshall: Statesmen, 1945–1959* (New York: Penguin, 1989), 334.

24. Hal Brands, *What Good Is Grand Strategy? Power and Purpose in American Statecraft from Harry S. Truman to George W. Bush* (Ithaca, NY: Cornell University Press, 2014), 37–41; Shu Guang Zhang, *Deterrence and Strategic Culture: Chinese-American Confrontations, 1949–1958* (Ithaca, NY: Cornell University Press, 1992), 40–42.

25. Michael Schaller, "Securing the Great Crescent: Occupied Japan and the Origins of Containment in Southeast Asia," *Journal of American History*, 69, no. 2 (September 1982): 392–414.

26. Bruce to State, June 26, 1950, *FRUS, 1950*, Vol. II: Document No. 99; William Stueck, *The Korean War: An International History* (Princeton, NJ: Princeton University Press, 1995), passim, esp. 30–36.

27. Irwin Wall, *The United States and the Making of Postwar France, 1945–1954* (New York: Cambridge University Press, 1991), 195.

28. Memorandum of Conversation, January 8, 1952, Box 99, President's Secretary's File, Harry S. Truman Presidential Library; Leffler, *Preponderance of Power*, 406–418.

29. Marshall in James Forrestal Diary, November 7, 1947, Box 147, James Forrestal Papers, Seeley Mudd Manuscript Library (SMML), Princeton University.

30. George Kennan, "Planning of Foreign Policy," June 18, 1947, Box 298, Kennan Papers, SMML.

31. Gaddis, *George F. Kennan*, 254–255; Joseph Jones, *The Fifteen Weeks, February 21–June 5, 1947* (New York: Harcourt, Brace & World, 1964); Dean Acheson, *Present at the Creation: My Years in the State Department* (New York: Norton, 1969), 212–225.

32. Dunn to Secretary, February 7, 1948, *FRUS, 1948*, Vol. III: Document No. 511; Dunn to Secretary, June 16, 1948, *FRUS, 1948*, Vol. III: Document No. 543; Kaeten Mistry, *The United States, Italy and the Origins of Cold War: Waging Political Warfare, 1945–1950* (New York: Cambridge University Press, 2014).

33. Because the U.S. Constitution gives Congress the power to declare war, no treaty can commit the United States to use force automatically. The North Atlantic Treaty did the next best thing. The operative text states: "The Parties agree that an armed attack against one or more of them in Europe or North America shall be considered an attack against them all" and that each country will respond with "such action as it deems necessary, including the use of armed force."

34. "Meeting of the Secretary of Defense and the Service Chiefs with the Secretary of State 1045 Hours," October 10, 1948, Box 147, Forrestal Papers, SMML.

35. Michael Lind, *The American Way of Strategy: U.S. Foreign Policy and the American Way of Life* (New York: Oxford University Press, 2006), 107.

36. Leffler, *Preponderance of Power*; Robert Beisner, *Dean Acheson: A Life in the Cold War* (New York: Oxford University Press, 2006).

37. CIA, "Threats to the Security of the United States," September 28, 1948, CIA Freedom of Information Act Electronic Reading Room (CIA FOIA).

38. "The World Position and Problems of the United States," August 30, 1949, Box 299, Kennan Papers, SMML.

39. Office of the Secretary of Defense, Historical Office, "Almost Successful Recipe: The United States and East European Unrest Prior to the 1956 Hungarian Revolution," February 2012, Electronic Briefing Book 581, National Security Archive; Gregory Mitrovich, *Undermining the Kremlin: America's Strategy to Subvert the Soviet Bloc, 1947–1956* (Ithaca, NY: Cornell University Press, 2000).

40. NSC-68, "United States Objectives and Programs for National Security," April 12, 1950, President's Secretary's Files (PSF), HSTL; "Statement by the President on the Situation in Korea," June 27, 1950, APP.

41. Trachtenberg, "Wasting Asset," 21.

42. "Estimated U.S. and Soviet/Russian Nuclear Stockpiles, 1945–94," *Bulletin of*

*the Atomic Scientists*, December 1994, 59; Allan Millett, Peter Maslowski, and William Feis, *For the Common Defense: A Military History of the United States* (New York: Free Press, 2012), 467–491.

43. Memorandum for the President, August 25, 1950, Box 187, National Security Council Files, Truman Library.

44. Quoted in Julian Zelizer, *Arsenal of Democracy: The Politics of National Security—From World War II to the War on Terrorism* (New York: Basic Books, 2010), 102.

45. Report on "Soviet Intentions" Prepared by Joint Intelligence Committee, April 1, 1948, *FRUS, 1948*, Vol. I, Part 2: Document No. 14.

46. NIE-17, "Probable Soviet Reactions to a Remilitarization of Western Germany," December 27, 1950, CIA FOIA.

47. Radio Report to the American People, April 11, 1951, APP; also Douglas to Lovett, April 17, 1948, *FRUS, 1948*, Vol. III: Document No. 73.

48. Stueck, *Korean War*, 205–206.

49. Beisner, *Dean Acheson*, 156; Dean Acheson, "Soviet Reaction to Free World's Growing Strength," *Department of State Bulletin*, October 20, 1952, 597.

50. Ambassador in France (Caffery) to Secretary of State, July 3, 1947, *FRUS, 1947*, Vol. III: Document No. 182.

51. Eisenhower to Harriman, December 14, 1951, Box 278, Averill Harriman Papers, Library of Congress; Trachtenberg, *Constructed Peace*, chap. 4.

52. NSC 135/3, "Reappraisal of United States Objectives and Strategy for National Security," September 25, 1952, Box 169, National Security Council File, Truman Library.

53. Table 3.1, "Outlays by Superfunction and Function: 1940–2024," in Office of Management and Budget, Historical Tables, 50–51, https://www.whitehouse.gov/wp-content/uploads/2019/03/hist-fy2020.pdf; Robert Bowie and Richard Immerman, *Waging Peace: How Eisenhower Shaped an Enduring Cold War Strategy* (New York: Oxford University Press, 1998).

54. NSC Meeting, December 21, 1954, *FRUS, 1952–1954*, Vol. II, Part 1: Document No. 143; Mira Rapp-Hooper, *Shields of the Republic: The Triumph and Peril of America's Alliances* (Cambridge, MA: Harvard University Press, 2020).

55. Giovanni Arrighi, "The World Economy and the Cold War, 1970–1990," in *The Cambridge History of the Cold War*, Vol. III, ed. Melvyn Leffler and Odd Arne Westad (New York: Cambridge University Press, 2010), 28.

56. Table 3.1, "Outlays by Superfunction and Function," 51–52; Aaron Friedberg, *In the Shadow of the Garrison State: America's Anti-Statism and Its Cold War Grand Strategy* (Princeton, NJ: Princeton University Press, 2000). This was true even during the Reagan buildup of the 1980s, when defense spending hovered around 6 percent of GNP.

57. See John Lewis Gaddis, *The Long Peace: Inquiries into the History of the Cold War* (New York: Oxford University Press, 1986).

58. Herbert Meyer to William Casey, "What Should We Do About the Russians?" June 28, 1984, CIA FOIA.

59. On the 1970s and 1980s, see Hal Brands, *Making the Unipolar Moment: U.S. Foreign Policy and the Rise of the Post-Cold War Order* (Ithaca, NY: Cornell University Press, 2016).

60. Robert Kagan, *The Jungle Grows Back: America and Our Imperiled World* (New York: Knopf, 2018), 68–69.

## 7. Into the Danger Zone

1. H.B. discussion with U.S. official, May 2021.

2. David Lynch, "Biden Orders Sweeping Review of U.S. Supply Chain Weak Spots," *Washington Post*, February 24, 2021; Carla Babb, "Pentagon Launches Effort to Better Address China Challenge," Voice of America, June 9, 2021.

3. Uri Friedman, "The New Concept Everyone in Washington is Talking About," *The Atlantic*, August 6, 2019.

4. "Remarks by President Biden in Press Conference," March 25, 2021, https://www.whitehouse.gov/briefing-room/speeches-remarks/2021/03/25/remarks-by-president-biden-in-press-conference/.

5. See Michael Beckley and Hal Brands, "America Needs to Rediscover Strategic MacGyverism," *National Interest*, March 27, 2021.

6. Bruce A. Bimber and Steven W. Popper, *What Is a Critical Technology?* (Santa Monica, CA: RAND, 1994).

7. George Modelski and William R. Thompson, *Leading Sectors and World Powers* (Columbia: University of South Carolina Press, 1996).

8. Stephen G. Brooks and William C. Wohlforth, "Power, Globalization, and the End of the Cold War: Reevaluating a Landmark Case for Ideas," *International Security*, 25, no. 3 (Winter 2000–2001): 35.

9. For example, the United States applies a 25 percent tariff to American chips that are assembled, tested, and packaged (ATP) in China and exported back to the United States. These tariffs harm U.S. chipmakers such as Intel, even though low-value-added ATP activities in China pose little risk of technology transfer. Meanwhile, Chinese chipmakers export few chips to the United States, so they are less affected by these tariffs.

10. See Hal Brands, Peter Feaver, and William Inboden, "Maybe It Won't Be So Bad: A Modestly Optimistic Take on COVID and World Order," in *COVID-19 and World Order: The Future of Conflict, Competition, and Cooperation*, ed. Hal

Brands and Francis J. Gavin (Baltimore: Johns Hopkins University Press, 2020), chap. 16.

11. Melissa Flagg, "Global R&D and a New Era of Alliances," Center for Security and Emerging Technology, June 2020, https://cset.georgetown.edu/research/global-rd-and-a-new-era-of-alliances/.

12. A point also made by Aaron Friedberg, "An Answer to Aggression: How to Push Back Against Beijing," *Foreign Affairs*, September/October 2020.

13. Daniel Kliman, Ben Fitzgerald, Kristine Lee, and Joshua Fitt, "Forging an Alliance Innovation Base," Center for a New American Security, March 29, 2020.

14. On this point, see Derek Scissors, "The Most Important Number for China Policy," *AEIdeas*, January 3, 2022.

15. For a list of critical technologies, see Emma Rafaelof, "Unfinished Business: Export Control and Foreign Investment Reforms," U.S.-China Economic and Security Review Commission, Issue Brief, June 1, 2021.

16. Rob Schmitz, "U.S. Pressures Europe to Find Alternatives to Huawei," NPR.org, February 15, 2020.

17. Stu Woo and Alexandra Wexler, "U.S.-China Tech Fight Opens New Front in Ethiopia," *Wall Street Journal*, May 22, 2021.

18. Brarini Chakraborty, "China Hints at Denying America Life-saving Coronavirus Drugs," Fox News, March 13, 2020.

19. Ivan Krastev and Mark Leonard, *The Crisis of American Power: How Europeans See Biden's America* (Berlin: European Council on Foreign Relations, 2021).

20. "Mapping the Future of U.S. China Policy," Center for Strategic and International Studies, https://chinasurvey.csis.org, accessed August 2021.

21. James A. Lewis, Testimony Before the Senate Committee on Commerce, Science and Transportation, "5G Supply Chain Security: Threats and Solutions," March 4, 2020.

22. The statistics in this paragraph come from Michael Beckley, *Unrivaled: Why America Will Remain the World's Sole Superpower* (Ithaca, NY: Cornell University Press, 2018), chap. 3.

23. Chris Miller, "Weaponizing Advanced Technology: The Lithography Industry and America's Assault on Huawei," paper prepared for the America in the World Consortium, June 2021.

24. Miller, "Weaponizing Advanced Technology."

25. Derek Scissors, "Partial Decoupling from China: A Brief Guide," American Enterprise Institute, July 2020.

26. Federal Bureau of Investigation, "China: The Risk to Academia," July 2019.

27. U.S. Cyber Command, for instance, has adopted this approach in protecting

American networks. See Erica Borghard, "Operationalizing Defend Forward: How the Concept Works to Change Adversary Behavior," *Lawfare*, March 12, 2020.

28. See Thomas Wright, "Joe Biden Worries that China Might Win," *The Atlantic*, June 9, 2021; Jacob Helberg, *The Wires of War: Technology and the Global Struggle for Power* (New York: Simon & Schuster, 2021).

29. This paragraph draws on Hal Brands and Charles Edel, "A Grand Strategy of Democratic Solidarity," *Washington Quarterly*, March 2021.

30. Tim Hwang, "Shaping the Terrain of AI Competition," Center for Security and Emerging Technology, June 2020.

31. See, on the latter point, Derek Scissors, "Limits Are Overdue in the U.S.-China Technology Relationship," Statement to Senate Committee on the Judiciary, Subcommittee on Crime and Terrorism, March 4, 2020.

32. Daphne Psaledakis and Simon Lewis, "U.S. Will Not Leave Australia Alone to Face China Coercion—Blinken," Reuters, May 13, 2021.

33. Richard A. Clarke and Rob Knake, "The Internet Freedom League: How to Push Back Against the Authoritarian Assault on the Web," *Foreign Affairs*, August 12, 2019.

34. Dean Acheson, *Present at the Creation: My Years in the State Department* (New York: Norton, 1969), xvii.

35. United Nations Conference on Trade and Development, *Digital Economy Report 2019: Value Creation and Capture: Implications for Developing Countries* (New York: United Nations Publishing, 2019), 2.

36. Tom Wheeler, *Time for a U.S.—EU Digital Alliance* (Washington, DC: Brookings Institution, 2021).

37. Jonathan Hillman, *The Digital Silk Road: China's Quest to Wire the World and Win the Future* (New York: Harper Business, 2021), 226–233. On the concept of "swing states," see Richard Fontaine and Daniel Kliman, "International Order and Global Swing States," *Washington Quarterly*, Winter 2013.

38. Hillman, *Digital Silk Road*, 228.

39. "Chinese Smartphone Brands Expanded India Market Share in 2020," Reuters, January 27, 2021.

40. James Rogers, Andrew Foxall, Matthew Henderson, and Sam Armstrong, *Breaking the China Supply Chain: How the "Five Eyes" Can Decouple from Strategic Dependency* (London: The Henry Jackson Society, 2020), 26.

41. Rajesh Roy, "India Offers $1 Billion in Perks to Entice Computer Makers from China," *Wall Street Journal*, February 24, 2021.

42. Rush Doshi, "Taiwan's Election Is a Test Run for Beijing's Worldwide Propaganda Strategy," *Foreign Affairs*, January 9, 2020.

43. Michael Crowley, "Biden Backs Taiwan, but Some Call for a Clearer Warning to China," *New York Times*, April 8, 2021.

44. Michael Mazza, "Shoot It Straight on Taiwan," *War on the Rocks*, August 3, 2021.

45. See, for instance, Eric Sayers and Abe Denmark, "Countering China's Military Challenge, Today," *Defense One*, April 20, 2021.

46. Michael A. Hunzeker, "Taiwan's Defense Plans Are Going Off the Rails," *War on the Rocks*, November 18, 2021.

47. Captain R. Robinson Harris, U.S. Navy (Ret.), Andrew Kerr, Kenneth Adams, et al., "Converting Merchant Ships to Missile Ships for the Win," *Proceedings* (U.S. Naval Institute), January 2019.

48. On the basic asymmetry, see Elbridge Colby, *The Strategy of Denial: American Defense in an Age of Great-Power Conflict* (New Haven, CT: Yale University Press, 2021).

49. Sulmann Wasif Khan, *Haunted by Chaos: China's Grand Strategy from Mao Zedong to Xi Jinping* (Cambridge, MA: Harvard University Press, 2018); Burgess Laird, "War Control: Chinese Writings on the Control of Escalation in Crisis and Conflict," Center for a New American Security, 2017; Alison Kaufman and Daniel Hartnett, "Managing Conflict: Examining Recent PLA Writings on Escalation Control," Center for Naval Analysis, 2016.

50. Jeffrey Engstrom, *Systems Confrontation and System Destruction Warfare: How the Chinese People's Liberation Army Seeks to Wage Modern Warfare* (Santa Monica, CA: RAND Corporation, 2018).

51. Chris Dougherty, *More than Half the Battle: Information and Command in a New American Way of War*, Center for a New American Security, May 2021.

52. Lee His-min and Eric Lee, "The Threat of China Invading Taiwan Is Growing Every Day. What the U.S. Can Do to Stop It," NBC News, July 9, 2021; James Timbie, "Large Numbers of Small Things: A Porcupine Strategy to Use Technology to Make Taiwan a Harder Target Against Invasion," Hoover Institution, September 2021.

53. See Dan Blumenthal, "The U.S.-Taiwan Relationship Needs Alliance Management," *National Interest*, December 18, 2021.

54. Abhijnan Rej, "Marine Raiders Arrive in Taiwan to Train Taiwanese Marines," *The Diplomat*, November 11, 2020.

55. See Michael Chase, Jeffrey Engstrom, Tai Ming Cheung, et al., *China's Incomplete Military Transformation: Assessing the Weaknesses of the People's Liberation Army (PLA)* (Santa Monica, CA: RAND Corporation, 2015).

56. "China Threatens to Nuke Japan over Possible Taiwan Intervention," *Times of India*, July 20, 2021.

57. For a longer discussion of this point, see Hal Brands, "Europe Needs to Embrace China's Threat to the World," Bloomberg Opinion, April 29, 2021;

Franz-Stefan Gady, "How Europe Can Help Defend Taiwan," *Nikkei Asia*, December 17, 2021.

58. See, for instance, Lonnie Henley, "PLA Operational Concepts and Centers of Gravity in a Taiwan Conflict," Testimony Before the U.S.-China Economic and Security Review Commission, February 2021.

59. For a balanced assessment of this option, see Sean Mirski, "Stranglehold: The Context, Conduct, and Consequences of an American Naval Blockade of China," *Journal of Strategic Studies*, 36, no. 3 (July 2013): 385–421.

60. See Michele Flournoy, "How to Prevent a War in Asia," *Foreign Affairs*, June 18, 2020.

61. Elbridge Colby, "If You Want Peace, Prepare for Nuclear War: A Strategy for the New Great-Power Rivalry," *Foreign Affairs*, November/December 2018.

62. Joshua Rovner, "A Long War in the East: Doctrine, Diplomacy, and the Prospects for a Protracted Sino-American Conflict," *Diplomacy & Statecraft*, 29, no. 1 (January 2018): 129–142.

63. Maria Sheahan and Sarah Marsh, "Germany to Increase Defence Spending in Response to 'Putin's War'—Sholz," Reuters, February 27, 2022.

64. David Shlapak and Michael Johnson, *Reinforcing Deterrence on NATO's Eastern Flank: Wargaming the Defense of the Baltics* (Santa Monica: RAND Corporation, 2016).

65. See Edward Fishman and Chris Miller, "The New Russian Sanctions Playbook: Deterrence Is Out, and Economic Attrition Is In," *Foreign Affairs*, February 28, 2022.

66. Hal Brands and Evan Braden Montgomery, "One War Is Not Enough: Strategy and Force Planning for Great-Power Competition," *Texas National Security Review*, 3, no. 2 (Spring 2020): 80–92.

67. As Biden administration officials pointed out: See White House, "Press Briefing by Press Secretary Jen Psaki and National Security Advisor Jake Sullivan, February 11, 2022."

68. Kori Schake, "Lost at Sea: The Dangerous Decline of American Naval Power," *Foreign Affairs*, March/April 2022; John Lewis Gaddis, *Strategies of Containment: A Critical Appraisal of American National Security Policy during the Cold War* (New York: Oxford University Press, 2005), 393–394.

69. Quoted in Hal Brands, *The Twilight Struggle: What the Cold War Teaches Us About Great-Power Rivalry Today* (New Haven: Yale University Press, 2022), 43.

70. See, for example, "Chinese Engineers Killed in Pakistan Bus Blast," BBC.com, July 14, 2021.

71. On the rarity of "accidental war," see Marc Trachtenberg, "The 'Accidental War' Question," paper presented at Center for International Security and Coopera-

tion, March 2000, http://www.sscnet.ucla.edu/polisci/faculty/trachtenberg/cv/inadvertent.pdf.

72. Jacob Stokes and Zack Cooper, "Thinking Strategically About Sino-American Crisis Management Mechanisms," *War on the Rocks*, September 30, 2020.

73. Kevin Rudd, "Short of War: How to Keep U.S.-Chinese Confrontation from Ending in Calamity," *Foreign Affairs*, March/April 2021.

74. As the Obama administration was sometimes accused of doing, and as former Obama administration officials sometimes advocate even today. See Alex Ward, "Ben Rhodes is Worried About Joe Biden's Climate Change and China Policies," *Vox*, April 23, 2021.

## 8. Life on the Other Side

1. John F. Kennedy, Television and Radio Interview, December 17, 1962, American Presidency Project (APP).

2. David Brunnstrom and Humeyra Pamuk, "China, U.S. Can Coexist in Peace but Challenge is Enormous—White House," Reuters, July 6, 2021.

3. As happened at the Anchorage meeting between U.S. and Chinese officials in March 2021.

4. United Nations, Department of Economic and Social Affairs, Population Division, *World Population Prospects: The 2019 Revision*, Online ed., rev. 1 (New York: United Nations, 2019).

5. United Nations, Department of Economic and Social Affairs, Population Division, *World Population Prospects: The 2019 Revision*.

6. United Nations, Department of Economic and Social Affairs, Population Division, *World Population Prospects: The 2019 Revision*; Ruchir Sharma, "The Demographics of Stagnation: Why People Matter for Economic Growth," *Foreign Affairs*, March/April 2016, 18–24.

7. Yong Cai, Wang Feng, and Ke Shen, "Fiscal Implications of Population Aging and Social Sector Expenditure in China," *Population and Development Review*, 44, no. 4 (December 2018): 811–831.

8. Sebastian Horn, Carmen M. Reinhart, and Christoph Trebesch, "China's Overseas Lending." NBER Working Paper 26050 (Cambridge, MA: National Bureau of Economic Research, 2021).

9. Horn, Reinhart, and Trebesch, "China's Overseas Lending."

10. Christopher Miller, "One Belt, One Road, One Bluff," *American Interest*, May 23, 2017.

11. "The Belt-and-Road Express," *The Economist*, May 4, 2017.

12. Lee Jones and Shahar Hameiri, "Debunking the Myth of 'Debt-trap Diplomacy':

How Recipient Countries Shape China's Belt and Road Initiative," Chatham House Research Paper, August 19, 2020.

13. Tanner Greer, "The Belt and Road Strategy Has Backfired on Xi," *Palladium Magazine*, October 24, 2020.

14. Horn, Reinhart, and Trebesch, "China's Overseas Lending," 33–34.

15. For an excellent analysis of possible outcomes, see Richard McGregor and Jude Blanchette, "After Xi: Future Scenarios for Leadership Succession in Post-Xi Jinping Era," a Joint Report of the CSIS Freeman Chair in China Studies and the Lowy Institute, April 22, 2021.

16. Alexandre Debs and H.E. Goemans, "Regime Type, the Fate of Leaders, and War," *American Political Science Review*, 104, no. 3 (August 2010), table 2.

17. Richard McGregor, *Xi Jinping: The Backlash* (Melbourne: Penguin, 2019).

18. The transition from Deng Xiaoping to Jiang Zemin in the 1990s was not completely formal. Deng continued to rule behind the scenes for years after he "retired" in 1989, despite the fact that his only official position was chairman of the Chinese Bridge Playing Association. The transition from Jiang to Hu Jintao in the early 2000s was not completely orderly. Jiang handed over the CCP general secretaryship and presidency to Hu Jintao in 2002 but retained his role as chairman of the Central Military Commission (China's equivalent of commander in chief) until 2004. This would be as if George H.W. Bush had remained commander in chief of the U.S. military until two years into Bill Clinton's presidency.

19. Yuhua Wang, "Can the Chinese Communist Party Learn from Chinese Emperors?" in *The China Questions: Critical Insights into a Rising Power*, ed. Jennifer Rudolph and Michael Szonyi (Cambridge, MA: Harvard University Press, 2018), chap. 7, table 1.

20. Wang, "Can the Chinese Communist Party Learn from Chinese Emperors?"

21. Quoted in Stephen G. Brooks and William C. Wohlforth, "Power, Globalization, and the End of the Cold War: Reevaluating a Landmark Case for Ideas," *International Security*, 25, no. 3 (Winter 2000–2001): 46.

22. This paragraph draws on analysis in Hal Brands and Zack Cooper, "America Will Only Beat China When Its Regime Fails," *Foreign Policy*, March 11, 2021, a piece that is more nuanced than the title suggests. In addition, some of the principles discussed in this section draw on Hal Brands, *The Twilight Struggle: What the Cold War Teaches Us About Great-Power Rivalry Today* (New Haven, CT: Yale University Press, 2022).

23. Memorandum for the President, December 15, 1950, Box 136, Paul Nitze Papers, Library of Congress.

24. Robert Kagan, *The Jungle Grows Back: America and Our Imperiled World* (New York: Knopf, 2018).

25. Hal Brands and Charles Edel, "A Grand Strategy of Democratic Solidarity," *Washington Quarterly*, March 2021.

26. Andrew Marshall, "Long-Term Competition with the Soviets: A Framework for Strategic Analysis," RAND Corporation, April 1972.

27. Rush Doshi, *The Long Game: China's Grand Strategy to Displace the American Order* (Oxford: Oxford University Press, 2021).

28. The phrase is referenced in Eugene Gholz, Benjamin Friedman, and Enea Gjoza, "Defensive Defense: A Better Way to Protect U.S. Allies in Asia," *Washington Quarterly*, Winter 2020.

29. For a sobering analysis, see Suzanne Mettler and Robert Lieberman, "The Fragile Republic," *Foreign Affairs*, September/October 2020.

30. Thomas Borstelmann, *The Cold War and the Color Line: American Race Relations in the Global Arena* (Cambridge, MA: Harvard University Press, 2003).

31. "Congress Is Set to Make a Down-Payment on Innovation in America," *The Economist*, June 5, 2021.

32. See Eric Croddy, "China's Role in the Chemical and Biological Disarmament Regimes," *Nonproliferation Review*, 9, no. 1 (Spring 2002): 16–47. More recently, China violated its commitment not to change Hong Kong's political system for fifty years after it reabsorbed that territory.

33. John Maurer, "The Forgotten Side of Arms Control: Enhancing U.S. Advantage, Offsetting Enemy Strengths," *War on the Rocks*, June 27, 2018.

34. See John Lewis Gaddis, *The Long Peace: Inquiries into the History of the Cold War* (New York: Oxford University Press, 1986).

35. See Richard Nixon, "Asia After Vietnam," *Foreign Affairs*, October 1967.

36. Franklin Roosevelt, Address at Charlottesville, Virginia, June 10, 1940, https://www.mtholyoke.edu/acad/intrel/WorldWar2/fdr19.htm.

37. X (Kennan), "The Sources of Soviet Conduct," *Foreign Affairs*, July 1947, 566–582.

## Epilogue

1. Nandita Bose and Stanely Widianto, "Biden and Xi Clash over Taiwan in Bali but Cold War Fears Cool," Reuters, November 14, 2022.

2. "Chinese FM Urges U.S. to Change its Wrong China Policy," Xinhua, November 1, 2021.

3. See, variously, Iain Marlow, "Blinken Says China Wants to Seize Taiwan on 'Much Faster Timeline,'" Bloomberg, October 17, 2022; Olivia Gazis, "CIA Director William Burns: 'I Wouldn't Underestimate' Xi's Ambitions for Taiwan," CBS News, October 3, 2023; Mallory Shelbourne, "China's Accelerated

Timeline to take Taiwan Pushing Navy in the Pacific, Says CNO Gilday," USNI News, October 19, 2022; "Read for Yourself: The Full Memo from AMC Gen. Mike Minihan," *Air and Space Forces*, January 30, 2023; Hal Brands, "Why Japan Is Gearing Up for Possible War with China," Bloomberg, November 6, 2022; Hal Brands, "Why Australia Is Gearing Up for Possible War with China," Bloomberg, November 11, 2022.

4.    Quoted in Neil Thomas, "Xi Jinping's Power Grab Is Paying Off," *Foreign Policy*, February 5, 2023.

# Index